CELTIC
Minded 4

ESSAYS ON CELTIC FOOTBALL
CULTURE AND IDENTITIES

editor
JOSEPH M. BRADLEY

ARGYLL✠PUBLISHING

This edition first published in 2019

Previous editions in the Celtic Minded series published in 2004, reprinted 2005; 2006, 2009

Argyll Publishing
an imprint of Thirsty Books
thirstybooks.com

British Library Cataloguing-in-Publication Data.

A catalogue record for this book is available from the British Library.

ISBN 978 0 9932828 6 7

Printing: Bell & Bain Ltd, Glasgow

ACKNOWLEDGEMENTS

The author would like to thank colleagues and friends who have provided comments on drafts. Chief thanks to the contributors to this volume of essays who have assisted greatly in making this series possible.
I hope that your analysis and commentary provides knowledge and understanding and in a small way helps make Scotland a better place for all.

Dedicated to Patrick Reilly 1932-2018 RIP.
Valued contributor to Celtic Minded 1,2 and 3.
First Catholic to become Professor of English Literature at the
University of Glasgow since the 16th century Scottish Reformation.
Loving and very loved, husband, father and grandfather.

Celtic supporters demonstrate solidarity with the cause
of an independent Palestinian homeland

Artur Boruc Celtic 2005-2010

John Paul Taylor [see p57ff] pictured with his dad in 1980 in the Bernabeu to play Real Madrid in the European Cup. Many of his pals from school and the Provan CSC gave him scarves to wear at the game so they could say it had been in Madrid.

The roots, resistance and identities of part of Celtic's core support

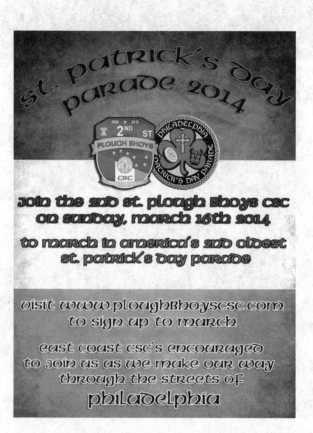

Contents

Introduction

Joseph M Bradley

The first 'Celtic Minded' book happened by chance. Published in 2004 it came about because over a number of years I had been researching supporters of numerous clubs in Scottish football as well as those of Scotland's international team. It became obvious through interviews and surveys of fans' opinions and views that there was much more to be said, than was apparent, about what motivates supporters to be attracted to, get behind, sometimes to be very much part of, a football club. Supporters had deep-seated and multi-layered ideas about all manner of things that touched on their passion for the game – history, culture, nationalism, ethnicity, the administration of football and political influences inside and outwith football and the wider society. What many fans were referring to of course were the things that take the game beyond a straightforward sports event on the field of play and can give professional football more substantial meaning.

Celtic supporters were a particular case in point. They shared similar emotions, thoughts and feelings as fans of other clubs, but the evidence demonstrated that Celtic clearly elicited a greater range of socio-cultural resonances than others. Celtic supporters also indicated that there was a lack of appropriate language, avenues or spaces to describe, speak and be listened to, and indeed, to self-represent. Sometimes, these supporters were even apprehensive about expressing relevant experiences, thoughts and identities at all. From an academic perspective, these otherwise marginalised voices and attitudes were worth exploring.

Arising from such questions a survey of available literature and an informed glance soon demonstrated that for many years the relevant material available on Celtic and its massive following had been generally fairly straightforward: bits and pieces of history, reports on games, pictures created of wonderful footballers, stories from the annuls of supporting the club. However, apart from some hints and references, most was little out of the ordinary: interesting to followers of Celtic maybe, but not much more. As far as the mainstream media was concerned, it was frequently characterized by stories and reports that lacked depth, context and informed reflection: also by sensationalism, inaccuracy and too often in Scotland, bias and prejudice.

On the basis of what was available, it was difficult to recognize, and indeed understand, what it was about following Celtic that gave it the meaningfulness that numerous supporters talked about: 'presumed' even. If Celtic and the community it was born from, and that had traditionally provided the vast majority of its support, was as distinctive in Scotland/Britain as some people suggested, if people would metaphorically have 'walked a million miles', if so many got so much from watching and winning and participating as part of Celtic's life, there was undeniably much missing in the available literature. With some honourable exceptions, it would have for example been quite difficult to work out from a great deal of what had been published what Celtic great Tommy Burns meant when he said: 'When you pull on that jersey you're not just playing for a football club, you're playing for a people and a cause.'

For much of the past, apart from a few mentions, some indicators, often superficial, ill-informed, haphazard and stereotypical, of the ethnic Irish and Catholic religious origins and roots and contemporary identities of the club and support, there was little more of substance to indicate distinctive and unique repute. These parts of the club and its support were largely missing from a majority of available accounts, occasionally only viewed as part of an historical artefact providing a sentimental memory, even commercial advantage with some smart marketing,

Although the argument for being unique was often stated by such as Tommy Burns or indirectly implied by others, it was still sometimes difficult to see what was that 'different' from Manchester United, Liverpool, Barcelona, Bayern Munich or Aberdeen. The colour of a football strip, a long history, a great atmosphere at big games, even winning trophies, is hardly sufficient to make a club 'special' in the ways that Celtic fans referred to, and revered, their club. After all, most clubs are special to their supporters. The obvious question was, what comprises Celtic's special, rather unique, significance?

In addition, was there something about being in Scotland that made the Celtic experience 'different' – indeed, was this itself an element of the club and support's uniqueness? Why had the club and some of its supporters often conspired, mostly unconsciously, to render the fundamentals of the club marginal, almost out of reach? Why did the contemporary Scottish media, and others, misrepresent, mock and abuse even, much of what in reality made Celtic and its support distinctive?

Considerably related to any story of substance regarding Celtic's origins, history and experience, although people of Irish descent constitute Scotland's largest multi-generational ethnic community, there also remains a dearth of published works that considers and recognises various aspects and achievements of the country's Irish diaspora. A traditional and long established absence in school educational materials and within the popular mainstream media means that there is much illiteracy in terms of knowledge and understanding of the experiences of the Irish in Scotland. This also means that Handley's (1964), Gallagher's (1987), Devine's (edited) work (1991) stand out as some of the few academic contributions of the late twentieth century, despite by the time of their publications, a significant Irish presence already having been in Scotland for more than 100 years.

Thus, Celtic Minded came out in 2004. It wasn't thought of as the start of a series. But after the collection of papers and essays and accounts of supporters had to be quickly reprinted, it was realised that a seam of interest that was telling had been touched upon. It was evident to the historian Professor Tom Devine when asked to write a foreword: 'Celtic Minded is a football book with a difference,' he wrote:

'The book's true value. . . [lies in] addressing the subject of football as an important social and cultural force in modern Scottish society. [It is] a highly readable account of the Catholic Irish immigrant community which gave birth to the club. The reader will find impressive accounts of the relationship between Celtic FC and such varied and controversial topics as national identities, modern Scottish culture, Irish diaspora, racism, bigotry and sectarianism.'

Interest was such that a series was born and Celtic Minded 2 (2006) and Celtic Minded 3 (2009) followed, the latter dedicated to the memory of Tommy Burns, magnificent servant to the club (and his community) and local boy of Glasgow's east end who had passed away in 2008, and a precious contributor to that very volume.

Other contributors to the series also wrote in a way that few had been able or willing to in the past. They challenged many of the stereotypes and prejudices embedded in Scottish football and society. Thus, the Celtic Minded series has become a football community speaking and representing itself in print: a collection of memories, otherwise hidden stories, declarations and assertions for those that have frequently been voiceless. The series therefore has not only been liberating, but represents a critical contribution towards an enhanced understanding of not only Celtic FC but also the history of the Irish in Scotland. It shows all too clearly that soccer has played an important role in the internal and external narratives intrinsic to this community's experiences. It allows for scholarly exploration and reflection on Celtic's social, cultural, economic, ethnic and religious exceptionality, while facilitating understanding the club and its supporters' identities. Taken together the contributions to this series demonstrate Celtic fans' historical and contemporary symbolic and conventional characterisation as the significant ethnic, religious and sporting 'other' in Scottish society. In itself this represents a story with a difference. The contributions to this new book, Celtic Minded 4, admirably add to the collection.

The Celtic Minded series represents a deeper and more inspective contextual reflection on relevant relations and events. These show Celtic playing a principal role in the socio-cultural, ethnic and religious identities of the multi-generational Irish diaspora in Scotland, elsewhere in Britain and for many Irish in

Ireland and around the globe. This series is therefore also important with respect to the wider story of the worldwide Irish diaspora. Further, it is an addition to other books about football that reflect it as the world's most successful and meaningful professional team sport.

Celtic's quality as a club where diversity thrives is also reflected in the contributions from people in Scotland and elsewhere who are not from the dominant ethno-religious backgrounds of the majority of traditional Celtic supporters. Such supporters and well-wishers of Celtic are critical parts of the make-up of a club and a support that has from its very first days welcomed and embraced anyone who wishes simply to be 'Celtic Minded'. No matter from which continent, no matter the colour of skin, no matter the faith background, or if none, no matter the academic qualifications or job status, all are to be equal, all are to be welcomed: all can be 'Celtic Minded'.

There are several broad categories that won't 'get' Celtic Mindedness. To numerous people throughout society the very notion of Celtic Minded means something entirely different from how those who are Celtic Minded view it. These are to be found throughout the land in every walk of life, where ideas relating to Irish ethnicity, the Catholic faith, Celtic FC, and a host of related cultural practices, memories, symbols, politics, language, morals and nuances are frequently or occasionally represented and perceived as 'the other'.

Amongst these people, groups and organisations are those who ignore the significance and relevance of such narratives, who are unaware, who lack insight and experience, who wish to avoid what they see as awkward questions and answers, and of course, the very many that are to a greater or lesser degree, simply antagonistic and hostile.

For Celtic Minded peoples, it is hoped that the Celtic Minded series allows a space for expression but also self and community reflection. For those who cherish 'Celtic Mindedness', what is valuable doesn't last or prosper without understanding, appreciation, consciousness and effort to give what is good, everyday relevance, and make it a living positive reality.

Sectarianism, anti-sectarianism and Scottish football

Joseph M Bradley

Background

This contribution to Celtic Minded 4 considers use of the term 'sectarianism' in Scottish football and society. This leads also to a reflection on the history of silence around ethno-religious prejudice and discrimination in Scotland since the nineteenth century. This work briefly surveys the recent rise in the use of the term, taking a perspective that the catch-all phrase 'sectarianism' serves little educational, informative, genuine or accurate historical purpose. Indeed, the word/description often provides a source for deception, lies, superficiality, masquerade and concealment in relation to ethno-religious prejudice and discrimination in Scotland.

Close observation helps us recognise that there has been an upsurge in the use of the term 'sectarianism' in Scotland since the 1980-90s. This chapter uses public discourses, mainly press reports over a number of decades, to survey this rise, particularly in relation to football. This also partly facilitates reflection on the historical socio-cultural and political climate that contributed to the evolution of The Offensive Behaviour Act (Scotland) in 2012. This law was, in the main, aimed at dealing with so called 'sectarianism' in Scottish football. Most politicians outwith the Scottish National Party Government opposed the law saying that where 'sectarian' (i.e. religious) offences occurred there was already legislation in place to punish offenders. However for

Crawford, 'the SNP Government succeeded in winning the war over the legitimate right to define the problem of sectarianism, as well as the solution' (in Flint and Kelly 2013). During its short but significant lifespan, there were frequent media headlines about its enactment and calls for a review.[1] In addition, several law judges highlighted a lack of clarity around the Act.[2]

The Act's main football opponents were supporters of Celtic.[3] One fan offered the view that:

> The legislation is solely dealing with what is seen as an unacceptable form of cultural expression in Scotland. The jargon of sectarianism continues to perpetuate a negative interpretation of elements of Irish culture and Irish political identities are being criminalised by this Act.[4]

As the Act developed, and, after its passing by the SNP Government, the club's main fan groups bandied together to protest against it. Many Celtic supporters believe they were the Act's primary focus and were unduly and excessively targeted in terms of freedom of speech and expression, particularly in relation to many of the supports' principal ethnic, religious, political identities and traditions.

Like numerous pieces of modern legislation, it is likely that such an Act could not have passed but for understandings and beliefs constructed as a result of dominant popular media representations of ethnic and religious identities and resultant cleavages and contestations in Scottish society. This work reflects on largely hidden and unspoken (by the governing SNP and other political parties, police, local Government and popular mainstream media) aspects of Scotland's ethno-religious, socio-cultural and political life of which particular manifestations become for some, only visible in football.

Sectarianism in Scottish Football

Although now profusely employed, the term(s) 'sectarian' and 'sectarianism' appear to have been relatively unused throughout nineteenth and most of twentieth century Scotland. Until the 1980s and 1990s it was generally absent in educational, academic, political, media, legal, cultural and political discourses.

1 http://www.bbc.co.uk/news/uk-scotland-scotland-politics-24825094, accessed 1/2/14.

2 http://www.express.co.uk/news/uk/403331/New-blow-to-bigotry-law, accessed 1/2/14.

3 http://www.heraldscotland.com/news/home-news/celtic-supporters-to-release-song-opposing-sectarianism-laws.23342765, accessed 4/2/14.

4 Danny Boyle, St. Patrick's Festival Debate, Coatbridge, 8/3/14.

In public life 'it' (whatever it/sectarianism was or is) was seemingly a topic undisclosed, unmentioned and unrecognised. However, its use has grown exponentially constituting a dominant discursive concept primarily used to express, construct and designate as problematic, various aspects of community identities, and frequently with regards relations 'between' Catholics and Protestants in Scotland. The description has become a common-sense term, popularly and principally used in relation to football, particularly with regards supporters of Celtic and Rangers.

A monumental lack of critical academic works on the subject of 'sectarianism' in the past has partly resulted in Scotland's contemporary media leading the way in constructing the concept as the dominant discursive term covering references – generally negative – to ethno-religious events and identities. Waiton (in Flint and Kelly) believes: 'The focus on 'sectarianism' and the 'Old Firm' was previously limited and appears to have been of little significance as a political debating point before 1997'. An online search for 'sectarian' and 'sectarianism' in Scottish newspapers correspondingly reveals its virtual non-use until a sharp upsurge in the 1990s.

use of [the term(s) 'sectarian' and 'sectarianism'] has grown exponentially constituting a dominant discursive concept

1992	93
1993	229
1994	481
1995	714
1996	1021
1997	more than 3000 and the same for each subsequent year.

For 'sectarianism' the pattern is similar with few if any references until 1992.

1992	20
1993	63
1994	207
1995	325
1996	428
2000	1308
2001	more than 3000 and the same for each subsequent year.

Taken as confirmation for the existence or otherwise of 'sectarianism', this survey suggests there may in fact have been little or no 'sectarianism' evident in Scotland prior to the 1980s and 1990s: not in the 1970s, 1950s, 1920s or the nineteenth century. If there was, might newspapers (and others like the police, politicians, employers, etc) not have commented, reported or addressed it? If not, what might the reason be for such a lack of commentary or 'action'? Was sectarianism a reality but not acknowledged as a problem until the 1980s and 1990s? If so, what was it that was recognised at this time? Where were those affected by it, in terms of employment, politics, housing, media and sport; Voiceless? Silent? Powerless? Did no one speak up for them? Was it a football issue and nothing more? Was it even just an issue for the two giants of Scottish football? Such questions suggest it might be prudent to partly track the upsurge in reports and growing 'interest' in the issue of 'sectarianism'.

Discrimination through exclusion

Since the late nineteenth century, until its hotly contested 'demise' and 're-birth' in 2012, Rangers Football Club had marginally won the most trophies within Scottish football though Celtic's record of European achievement surpasses this success.[5] Rangers is one of the best supported and most successful football institutions in the world, with a social, cultural, religious and political meaning comparable to, and surpassing, some of the most famous clubs in the history of the game. As a result of a number of its fundamental historical associations, identities, and ideological and symbolic links to dominant state and popular notions of Scottishness, Britishness, Royalty, Unionism and Protestantism, Rangers has long been Scotland's establishment club.

Central to Rangers significance is the fact that it was in 1989 that Maurice Johnston became the first Catholic footballer to be consciously asked to sign for the club, breaking a 'no Catholics' tradition going back over a century.[6] Rangers previous history of discriminating against Catholics (who in Scotland are usually from an ethnic Irish background) by only signing and employing Protestants (usually Scots) had, until just a few years before this event, went almost completely without comment or reference in the media: this despite football being the country's most popular team sport, and dominating much of popular culture, radio, press

5 Celtic won the European Cup (later the Champions League) in 1967: this is the most significant trophy ever won by a club from Scotland. After a period of administration as a result of financial mismanagement, massive debt and widespread accusations of gaining leverage as a result of financially 'cheating' to win on the field of play, Rangers was consigned to liquidation on 14/06/2012. Rangers thus momentarily ended life as a Scottish institution but its re-birth shortly after to enter the bottom tier of Scottish football and to rise and re-enter the top tier in 2015, with the same with the same symbols, colours, football stadium and most importantly same fans and cultural attributes, has meant that, despite statutory regulations and most legal opinion considering Rangers as officially obsolete and extinct since 2012, the club can conceptually be credibly treated and conceived simultaneously as a re-constitution and continuation of an unbroken tradition of what has existed since

and television. The absence of public references to the possibility of such ethno-religious prejudice and discrimination in the rest of football or society may be instructive with regards understanding current attempts to address what has come to be termed and labelled 'sectarianism'.

In 1965 one of the first print references to Rangers' practice against Catholics took place when the English-based News of the World newspaper ran a series of articles by former Rangers player Ralph Brand. Amongst criticisms of his former club he denounced its management for its '100% Protestantism'.[7] In a rebuke, the Sunday Mail was the only Scottish newspaper to mention Brand's invective.[8] On a visit to Canada in 1967 Rangers vice-chairman, Matt Taylor said his club's refusal to sign Catholics was 'part of our tradition'.[9] The Scottish Daily Express was the only newspaper to reference this comment as it also did two years later when it criticised Chairman John Lawrence who defended the policy saying that it had always been there. Club director George Brown re-iterated the same view in 1972.[10]

It took until during a period of increasing football hooliganism in Britain, and in relation to Rangers, specifically in the aftermaths of its fans rioting in Newcastle in 1969, then more seriously in the city of Barcelona in 1972 when the club won the European Cup Winners Cup, that the club's anti-Catholic culture began to draw isolated negative comments in Scotland. The latter rioting was shown on television and witnessed by millions across Britain and Europe. More evidently, after rioting in 1976 by Rangers fans in Birmingham at a pre-season friendly match, and in subsequently searching for answers regarding the club's hooligan problem, the Glasgow Herald's Ian Archer asked whether Rangers was 'the only club in the world which insists that every member of the team is of one religion'.[11] The Daily Record joined the condemnation (Murray, 1984).

A week after Birmingham, the club's general manager Willie Waddell publicly used the term sectarianism and announced they were 'determined to end Rangers' image as a sectarian club' (Gallagher, 1987). In 1978 the national (Protestant) Church of Scotland's Glasgow Presbytery's monthly paper The Bush published a strong editorial 'The Blue Barrier' in which it called

[it took until the 1960s and 70s for] Rangers' anti-Catholic culture . . . to draw isolated negative comments in Scotland

1872 (and this is how its fanbase and much of the Scottish media consider the club and sustain a 'same institution' narrative).

6 Murray, B. 1984, 81-84, notes around a dozen largely insignificant and short term exceptions that impinged this policy.

7 'The Lid Off Ibrox', 26/9/65 (3rd, 10th, 17th, 24th & 31st October). See Murray 212.

8 3/10/1965.

9 10/5/1967.

10 Daily Express, 3/6/69, 8-9 and 17/8/1972.

11 11/10/76, p3.

for an end to Rangers policy. Nevertheless, symptomatic of the unusual, radical and hard hitting nature of this article, and somewhat against The Bush's hopes for social justice and equality, a lack of wider socio-political support was evident. Few in wider society rallied. Indeed, 'some parishes cancelled their bulk order of the paper' and before long it ceased publication. (Gallagher 1987)

More significantly, provoked by TV scenes of out of the ordinary on-field fighting between supporters of Celtic and Rangers at the end of the Scottish Cup Final in May 1980, for the first time the Church of Scotland (The Kirk) publicly reflected on, and alluded to, the negative worldwide publicity attracted by Scotland's most popular team sport. Gallagher (1987) notes that at the 1980 General Assembly of the Kirk, a motion calling on Rangers 'to publicly disclaim a sectarian bias in management and team structure', was passed by a majority of 200 but it was an ambiguous result since 400 commissioners abstained (there were around 1250 commissioners in total in 1980). In its annual General Assembly report of the same year, a one paragraph comment in a section on 'Scottish interests' noted:

> Tensions would be eased if all clubs, and Rangers FC in particular, would publicly disclaim sectarian bias in management and team structure, and through integrated team selection, publicly prove that sectarianism has no place in Scottish sport.[12]

Some mention of this match and sectarianism in the Assembly's 1980 Report and more commentary from its Church and Nation Report of 1981 shows that the focus for the Church was 'football, violence and sectarianism'. Despite some evidence to the contrary, reflecting a much more significant largely unrecorded and unspoken wider social and cultural narrative, there was no reference to sectarianism (or ethno-religious prejudice and discrimination) as perhaps existing elsewhere in society. Nonetheless, as an institution, the Church of Scotland made a momentous break with its own traditions and criticised Rangers, in the main a club whose management, staff, players and most supporters were current or token members of the Church, or who at least considered themselves 'Protestant'. This was a comparatively revolutionary development in light of the

12 11/10/1976, 2 & 13/10/1976, 2.

national Church's pre-eminence in Scottish society and, its strident campaign over several decades against minority Irish origin Catholics in Scotland which lasted until the 1950s.[13]

From darkness to light

One purpose in describing some of Rangers discriminatory practices has been to partly reflect its relatively unquestioned status as a bastion of ethno-religious socio-cultural hegemony: a feature which made it popular and extraordinarily well-supported throughout Scotland. Arguably, this also assisted its successes financially and on the field of play. Prior to the 1970s and 1980s there is no substantial evidence of Rangers anti-Catholic practices being reported or referred to in the media and no record of any other conceptually similar word as 'sectarianism' being used to describe this or any other similar practice in Scotland. Rangers anti-ethnic Irish Catholic prejudicial rituals largely existed before the term sectarianism evolved so markedly. Rangers' position as Scotland's establishment football club, as a reflection of the society it came from, and with minority Catholics constituting less than 15% of the population, resulted in a century having passed before dissenting voices emerged. In this sense it is also important to note, that eventual focus on the issue of a 'Protestant only' (how Protestant in terms of Christianity is of course another question) football club also facilitated an illumination of the wider society and this was to become important with regard to subsequent changes in the socio-cultural fabric of Scottish life.

Though small, the relevant collection of academic literature, in the main published from the 1980s, and which specifically or occasionally remarks on the wider historical culture of prejudice and discrimination against Catholics of Irish descent, shows that despite Rangers eventually attracting negative attention, the club was not exceptional and merely reflected and shared the beliefs and attitudes of various other employment practices and institutions in Scotland. Acknowledging this assists understanding wider society's previous complicity with, and disregard of, prejudice and discrimination in Scotland's most popular team sport against its largest immigrant ethno-religious grouping, and

13 Deliverances of the General Assembly, May 1980, 10.

also as to why such hegemony went unhindered. This wider cultural setting also acquires further importance in understanding ongoing contemporary media, police and political constructions of the concept of sectarianism.

It is in this context that it is enlightening to reflect on any significant public examples of contemporary prejudice and discrimination against ethnic-Irish Catholics in Scottish football. In the main this part of the exercise uses mainstream print media to critically reflect on a small number of events, but primarily to recognise how such occasions and hostilities are typically framed and represented in the media. This is important as information produced by the media is a manufactured process and as Reid (in Flint and Kelly) reminds us, 'observations of journalists and the views of other contributors to media narratives are understood not to be neutral'.

The Irish Famine Song

In April 2008 what became known as the 'Famine Song' was publicly sung for the first time by Rangers fans against Celtic supporters. Only its chorus, 'Why don't you go home, Why don't you go home, The Famine is over, why don't you go home', was aired to the 1960s Beach Boys hit 'Sloop John B'. With several verses of the full song disparaging Irish-descended Catholics in Scotland, the song 'invites' them to leave Scotland and go back to Ireland. 'Only' after Celtic supporters complained about the song did it begin to make some headlines. In the tabloid Scottish Sun newspaper, academic Patrick Reilly articulated what he viewed as the song's racist sentiments:

> Can you imagine such a song as the Famine Song being directed at any other ethnic group? Consider what would happen if it was Jews or West Indians who were being singled out for such vile treatment. There would be an outcry.[14]

Reilly's argument was not shared by many others in Scottish football and beyond and a prominent sports and social comment-ator encapsulated much of the antagonism that was to be forthcoming over the following months:

14 Reilly, P. The Scottish Sun, 17/9/2008, 5.

He [Professor Reilly] said of The Famine Song: 'can you imagine it being directed towards any other ethnic group'. . . he can't see that it wasn't directly towards 'an ethnic group'. . . they're Scottish, not Irish and it's time to stop pretending otherwise.[15]

The song continued to be sung in Scottish football over the next few years and was taken up by a number of other supporters when the opposition was Celtic, or an Irish-born or ethnic Irish Scots-born player was a member of the opposition's team, including by fans of Dundee United, Hearts and Motherwell. After an eventual growing public controversy the song's popularity within stadiums ended though its refrain can still be heard in less public settings on the part of groups hostile to the Irish diaspora in Scotland.[16]

Aidan McGeady

Aidan McGeady is a third generation Irish footballer who played with Celtic (2004-10) and represents Ireland in international football. It is commonplace for those of a diaspora-descended community to acknowledge their heritage and to hold social, cultural and political allegiances or citizenship of the nation of their forebears. This can have a particular resonance in sport and representing country of family/community origin is a widespread practice. Indeed, Scotland has a long list of football, rugby and other sportspeople born outside of Scotland but who represent their ethnic homeland/nation in sport. However, McGeady's desire to play for Ireland was met with much negative media comment as well as invective from opposition fans in Scotland. At Celtic Park in 2004, visiting Motherwell fans abused McGeady, subsequently singing the popular Scottish anthem 'Flower of Scotland'. As with many in the media, a Daily Record sports writer supported the abuse of McGeady and revealed part of his and others' rationale when he took the opportunity to vent his anger on Celtic supporters' Irish ethnic allegiances in Scotland.

It's time all Scottish Celtic fans got over their obsession with Ireland. The fact that Glasgow sports shops sell as many Ireland football tops as Scotland football tops is both pathetic and ultimately unhelpful.[17]

15 Leckie, B. The Scottish Sun, 18/9/2008, 11.

16 See http://www.youtube.com/watch?v=eTfFcAQP-dw, accessed 9/11/2011.

17 McKie, J. Daily Record, 1/1/05, 11.

Another commentator made similar comments: 'No apologies. . . this fixation with Ireland which so many Scots have makes my blood boil.[18] McGeady departed Celtic for Moscow in 2010 stating that amongst other factors abuse and death threats played a major part in his decision to leave the club he and his family supported.[19] The player received no similar insult in Russia and to date has not been subject to related negative attention since playing in English soccer.

Pope John Paul II

In 2005 Pope John Paul II died. The Italian Government announced three days of mourning, US President George Bush said 'the world had lost a champion of freedom', UN Secretary-General Kofi Annan described John Paul 'as a tireless advocate of peace' while the BBC reported that tributes arrived at the Vatican 'from political and religious leaders in other parts of the world'.[20] In sport a moment/minute's respect has traditionally been held in recognition of the life/death of such figures. Initially after refusing to join this practice the Scottish Football Association complied and ordered a minute's silence at games. This was prompted by pressure brought upon the body by complaining Celtic supporters, but particularly by 'UEFA's directive' insisting 'on a one minute's silence at all Champions League and UEFA Cup matches'.[21]

However, at the Motherwell versus Rangers match after John Paul's death visiting Rangers fans sang 'No Pope of Rome', celebrating the death of the spiritual leader of one billion Catholics'.[22] Shortly after the Pope's death, at the Dundee United versus Hibernian Scottish Cup semi-final there was some booing during the minute's silence. At the Hearts against Celtic semi-final the following day booing by Hearts fans during the minute's silence was serious enough for the referee to call a halt after twenty-four seconds. The Detroit Free Press reported that 'for the second day, fans jeered during a moment of silence for Pope John Paul II'.[23] The Washington Post used a similar account, Italy's Tuttosport and China's Daily were amongst many across the globe that reported this news.[24] Subsequently the Scotsman newspaper

18 Travers R, Scotland on Sunday, 9/11/97, 13.

19 http://www.dailyrecord.co.uk/sport/football/aiden-mcgeady-i-had-to-leave-celtic-for-spartak-1067324, accessed 1/2/14.

20 http://news.bbc.co.uk/1/hi/world/europe/4399715.stm, accessed 1/2/14.

21 The Herald 8/4/05, 38.

22 'No Pope of Rome, no chapels to sadden my eyes, no nuns and no priests, fuck your rosary beads, every day is the 12th of July' (commemorative date of Battle of Boyne celebrated by Orange sympathising Protestants mainly in Scotland and the north of Ireland). The Scotsman, 9/4/05. In the early 1960s Rangers fans also chanted against the dying Pope John XXIII and mocked a minute's silence on the death of the USA's first (Irish descended) Catholic president, John F Kennedy, see Murray, 1994, 220.

23 11/4/05.

24 The Mirror, 12/4/05, 52, 56

stated: 'The Scottish Football Association decided, in its wisdom, to give bigots and idiots a television platform from which to mock the Pope's memory'.[25] The chief sports columnist of the Daily Record exclaimed:

> Perhaps the SFA should have clung to their belief that they are a secular organisation and ignored calls from Celtic fans to honour the memory of Pope John Paul II.[26]

Although the booing by Hearts fans and the attention it attracted caused a moment of national self-reflection, notably the contextual phrase, 'anti-Catholicism', was virtually absent throughout the Scottish media in describing what occurred. However, a wide range of public commentary demonstrated a media and political awkwardness over the negative attention generated towards Scotland from beyond the country.

The sign of the Cross

In 1996 a Partick Thistle footballer was booked for an infringement during a match against Rangers and then booked again for making the sign of the cross which led to his being sent from the field. Murdo MacLeod, the Thistle manager and his chairman Jim Oliver were called to the referee's room during the interval and it was pointed out that the police had been alerted by some Rangers fans who saw the player make his gesture. The police took no action, but the referee did, although McDonald appeared unaware he had been cautioned. When Jim McGilvray later booked him for his challenge on the Rangers player McDonald turned away as though to continue playing and then looked surprised when he realised he had to leave the pitch. It seems McDonald may have blessed himself after he scored his goal, but it was an action which could lead to his suspension. Presumably the referee, who missed one or two other incidents, felt the player's gesture might have incited some trouble among Rangers' support, but MacLeod and his chairman took a different view. 'Rod blesses himself as he goes on and off the pitch in every game,' the manager said. 'He does it in reserve matches also. I've never seen anyone in Italy, for instance, being cautioned for doing that and so far as Rod is concerned it is normal practice

25 11/4/05, editorial, 19.

26 11/4/05.

for him. It's at times like this you know which city you are in.' Oliver, like most people inside Firhill, didn't see McDonald bless himself, which tends to suggest it was hardly designed to be inflammatory, but he stressed he would be defending the player. 'I understand that after he scored the goal he crossed himself,' Oliver said, 'and I don't think he realised that constituted a yellow card. If he was being booked for his action after his goal then he should have been cautioned at that time, in 35 minutes, and not 10 minutes later. Why this should constitute a foul in football is beyond me, but because we have the Rangers' situation here it seems a different set of rules are invoked. I have to be guarded about what I say, but it is ridiculous.'

In the late 1990s, Mark Viduka, Celtic's Croatian-Australian striker was 'caught' blessing himself by Rangers fans. Subsequently Viduka's actions made headlines in Scotland. One complainant's letter was printed in the Daily Record:

> There is a time and a place for that kind of thing. It is in the chapel on a Sunday and certainly not on the football pitch during an Old Firm match.[29]

Polish internationalist Artur Boruc was Celtic's goalkeeper between 2005 and 2010. He made the Catholic sign of the cross when he played football in Poland and continued this in Scotland. However, in Scotland Boruc's custom evoked scores of negative headlines, letters to newspapers and numerous comments expressed on radio and television. On several occasions Boruc's sign of the cross especially incensed Rangers fans and various Scottish sports journalists. Scotland's main Sunday tabloid editorial demonstrated frustration and embarrassment that his actions, like those relating to the booing of a minute's silence in respect of the death of Pope John Paul II, had made world news:

> Each time the story is retold it is explained how sectarian hatred is a scar on Scottish society. The image of Scotland being beamed around the world is not one we can take any pride in.[30]

Another Scottish journalist spoke of such incidents as 'ruining our reputation'.[31] The Scotsman, reported: 'last night a Rangers fan spokesman accused the Celtic goalkeeper of trying to incite the crowd by blessing himself during yesterday's game'.[32] The

27 Daily Record, 12/12/94.

28 5/2/96.

29 Scottish Catholic Observer, 25/8/06.

30 Sunday Mail, 27/8/06, 24.

31 Sunday Mail, 13/8/2006, 69.

32 Scotsman, 18/12/06.

same broadsheet was the subject of a complaint on the part of the Catholic Church in Scotland for its front page story, with accompanying picture of Boruc blessing himself and specifically framing the footballer's practice as an unacceptable 'sectarian' act in Scotland. The Scotsman stated:

> Last week the First Minister Jack McConnell hosted a summit on stamping our sectarianism. Officials from Celtic and Rangers attended. . . **But** (author's emphasis) for the second time in a year during yesterday's Old Firm match, the Celtic goalkeeper Artur Boruc provoked Rangers fans by making the sign of the cross.[33]

The Polish international goalkeeper departed Celtic for Italy in 2010 before returning in 2012 to play in England. His continued making the sign of the cross did not attract any abuse or media headlines amongst supporters of clubs in Italy, England or wherever he has represented Poland in internationals.

Prejudice and discrimination against Catholicism

These few examples of recent ethno-religious controversies in football point 'at least' to the problematisation of minority Irish and Catholic identities in Scotland. Gallagher (1991) states that historically, 'Presbyterianism was not just a state religion but, for more than three centuries, defined the Scots to one another and to the rest of the world'. Muirhead (1973) opines that 'in Scotland anti-Romanism had become a religion and a way of life'. Another commentator relays that in late eighteenth century Glasgow there was only thirty-nine Catholics but forty-three anti-Catholic societies (Gallagher 1987. Devine in Devine & Mitchison 1988).[34] Davies (in Flint and Kelly) notes:

> Irish Catholics were treated with disdain by many Scottish Protestants on grounds of both religion and ethnicity and suffered widespread discrimination in the labour market.

Prejudice, racism and bigotry are as significant for its victims as for those that have gained commensurate social, political, economic or cultural advantage. Therefore, it is fundamental for any study critically examining the contemporary utility of the

33 Reported in Scottish Catholic Observer, 5/1/2007, 3.

34 In the wake of composer James MacMillan's very public complaints with regards anti-Catholicism in Scotland in 1999 a relative explosion of publicity was generated resulting in hundreds of media and numerous academic articles within and beyond Scotland. See http://www.independent.co.uk/arts-entertainment/podium-james-macmillan—the-bigotry-that-shames-scotland-1111793.html.

term sectarianism to consider the historical environment and background of religious, national and ethnic prejudice traditionally faced by minority Irish Catholics in Scotland. Likewise, it is important to be cognisant of the role of power in discriminatory unequal relationships: and Catholics being a religious minority in Scotland. It is with such a reflection that we may find an enhanced understanding of some of the roots of the high profile events and incidents that have occurred in recent years in football as well as the evolution of the catch-all omnipotent term 'sectarianism'.

In relation to Celtic, regardless of its ethnic-Irish Catholic roots and identities, the club has always employed non-Catholics, including some of its most coveted players and its greatest ever manager, Jock Stein. In addition, surveys show that although the vast majority of supporters are Catholic (practising and non-practising), approximately 10-15%, are Protestant, other religions or non-religious (Bradley 1995). During over twenty years of researching Celtic supporters, it is striking that all hostile references to religion have related entirely to complaints of perceived anti-Catholic bias and bigotry.[35] More indicatively, there are no comparable examples of anti-Protestantism as there are for anti-Catholicism in Scottish football.

Such 'contextual facts are vital, not in any attempt to unfairly single out Rangers, or to praise Celtic, but for any genuine attempt to understand the construction of dominant mainstream discourses and narratives around relationships between both clubs. The absence of organised or significant anti-Protestantism in football raises significant questions regarding the meaningfulness, utility and application of the term 'sectarianism'. Similarly, as to why Celtic, after over a century of employing and playing Protestants as well as having members of that faith based within its support, might be frequently described as the 'sectarian' opposite of Rangers: 'the other side of the same coin'?[36]

Celtic and the Scottish media

It is such an enquiry that can assist understanding why Celtic supporters became the most vehement and sometimes most

35 Research carried out since 2003 by author amongst Celtic supporters in Scotland, Ireland, USA, Canada, Australia, Jersey and England. As yet unpublished.

36 This term is used liberally in the mainstream media, but is observed most frequently on numerous fan websites, for and against, when discussing Celtic and Rangers. The classic examples of the use and propagation of the term is to be found in Bill Murray's influential 'The Old Firm' – as the first substantial book written on the subject.

visible opponents of the 2012 Act. In 2014 Celtic Football Club responded by calling for an early review of the legislation.[37]

Celtic is an iconic diasporic football club with a multi-layered hybrid identity reflecting its birth from, and its crucial cultural role within, the Irish community in Scotland. Celtic's defining and unique roots, identities, links and associations with Ireland, Irishness, Catholics, Catholicism and its underlying charitable ethos, have traditionally provided the club with its most appealing attributes for Irish immigrant-descended Catholics, whilst also making the club and its fanbase conspicuous in Scotland. This in a society that was for many centuries defined by its Protestantism and as part of Great Britain, conquered and colonised, among other countries and territories, the island of Ireland. For Scots, this is particularly obvious with regards the northern Ulster province (see Bradley in Flint and Kelly) over the course of several centuries.

Examples of anti-Catholicism and anti-Irishness within Scotland's most popular media-saturated team sport indicates that public manifestations of an Irish Catholic presence in Scotland, particularly evidenced in Celtic's history and manifest-ations of its supporters' core identities, remain contentious. The role of the media in creating and reflecting this perception has been critical.

Embedded, dominant, orthodox and conventional rhetorical discourses existing throughout Scottish football, amongst fans, authorities and the sports media in particular, are adversarial towards Celtic and its supporters' Irish and Catholic identities. Aberdeen fans sing to Celtic supporters, 'Can you sing a Scottish song'? Dundee fans boo Celtic's supporters' Irish ballad 'Fields of Athenry', as also have Dundee United fans.[38] A former Young Scottish Journalist of the Year criticised Celtic supporters:

> They flap the Irish tricolor and sing sad Irish songs and roar of the Irish struggle. There's a country called Ireland for goodness sake, why don't they go and live there?[39]

As well as Celtic supporters' Irishness, Kelly notes how prejudice and hostility against associations with Catholicism extends beyond Rangers. He highlights a Sunday Herald

37 The Herald, 5/3/14, 3.
38 28/1/06.
39 MacLeod J, The Herald, 18/2/2002.

29

journalist's 'trivializing Catholic rosary beads' and a Scotsman reporter making negative references to the formerly significant Catholic practice in Scotland of fasting on Fridays, both in the context of Celtic (Kelly 2011).[40] Another sports journalist referred mockingly to Celtic's Chief Executive going around 'the [Catholic] chapel halls of the country. . . to outline Celtic's future'.[41] In 2013 Motherwell fans disdainfully sang to Celtic supporters, 'You only sing in the Chapel', a song frequently sung by Rangers fans.[42] Denigrations of Celtic and its supporters Irish ethnic and Catholic identities and outlooks are ubiquitous in Scottish football, including within the sports media.[43]

Equivocation and the 'Old Firm'

Despite the commonly used descriptive term, 'Old Firm', each club comprises distinct identities. Rangers' fans have a number of important divergent features (particularly support for British Unionism and politico-cultural Protestantism in the north of Ireland), but also shares numerous identities and variations of these identities with other clubs in Scotland and society generally, mainly in terms of history, heritage, culture, national and religious outlooks and attributes.[44] Celtic and its supporters are largely integrated into Scottish and British societies while their diasporic Irish and Catholic identities mean that they also preserve a noteworthy and significant distinctiveness – 'otherness'.

It is in the context of each club's uniqueness that reflection on the idea of 'equivocation' can provide insight into understanding how the Scottish media has served a primary role in creating and/or reflecting a common sense view, a momentum and a social and ideologically manufactured perspective, that has facilitated a framework, appetite and desire for the construction of the term 'sectarianism'. This is especially relevant to understanding the interpretation of many Celtic supporters who saw themselves as the main target of the 2012 legislation. Such reflection can show how each club and their supporters' distinct communal personalities and ideologies are disguised, omitted or misrepresented amidst rhetorical narrations that refer to them in concert. This equivocation not only characterises the popular media, but permeates various levels of society. A brief focus on

40 13/4/2008 & 31/5/09.

41 Waddell G, The Sunday Mail, 23/5/2010. Celtic's Chief Executive did not visit even one Catholic 'Church Hall' and would not have been expected to by Celtic supporters or Catholics in general. This was of course a classic case of detrimental Irish Catholic stereotyping and labelling on the part of this sports reporter/journalist. As this work demonstrates in Scotland this kind of reporting and representation has particular negative resonances.

42 21/12/03 & 27/2/13.

43 See Bradley J M, 2008, 96-110.

44 There is much obvious correlation for example between many members of the Orange Institution in Scotland and Rangers fandom. See Bradley 2004.

some examples of this preferred narrative shows that the concept is critical to many if not most popular media references to 'sectarianism'.

As an illustration, despite Celtic not being involved in the match, in the wake of the Birmingham riots on the part of Rangers fans in 1976 the Daily Record tempered its editorial criticism of the rioting supporters stating that Celtic, should be: 'willing to be recognised as a sporting bastion of Catholicism. They must bear a share of the guilt'.[45] Likewise, when a prominent Daily Record journalist reported that a Rangers fan fatally stabbed a Celtic supporter, she wrote: 'Celtic and Rangers have become an excuse, a vessel, for a degree of barbarity and evil in our society which disgraces us all'.[46] When a Catholic footballer and known Celtic supporter was abused because of his religion when playing for Hibernian against Rangers, a Daily Mail sports writer brought Celtic into his report stating:

> There aren't enough police cells in Glasgow to accommodate all the bigots who pollute Rangers' ground – or the one on the other side of the city, for that matter [at Celtic].[47]

A Daily Record and popular radio football commentator frequently refers to both clubs within a single unequivocal 'sectarian' bracket, referring to their supporters as together inhabiting 'a small planet called Scotland'.[48] A Scottish Sun columnist (who also mocks Celtic supporters' Irishness) habitually refers to Celtic and Rangers as the 'Bigot Brothers'.[49]

Again, although Celtic had no involvement in the match, in the wake of Rangers fans rioting in Barcelona in 1972 the Daily Express challenged 'both' Rangers and Celtic to 'stamp out the bigotry', and backed the Glasgow magistrates request that Rangers 'make a public statement saying that Rangers were not sectarian, and that Celtic take down the Eire flag'. The Glasgow Herald later condemned Rangers for not issuing a statement about sectarianism and Celtic for not taking down Ireland's flag.[50] The SFA was also equivocal in the wake of the Barcelona riots criticising 'both clubs', saying their sectarianism was 'the root cause of the hatred and bitterness [that] existed between the two sets of supporters for decades' (Murray 1984).

45 Daily Record editorial, 13/10/76, 2.

46 21/11/99, 23.

47 Daily Mail, 1/3/97, 76.

48 Radio Clyde Superscoreboard, 1/2/13.

49 Scottish Sun, 15/7/09, 54, 18/11/13, 24, 20/4/09, 24. For but one example of the same journalist mocking Celtic's Irishness see footnote 22.'

50 23/8/72, 8.

In relation to the Irish national flag the Scottish Football Association also ordered Celtic to remove this from its stadium twenty years earlier: the club rejected this on the basis that it was an attack on its heritage and identity.[51] After a 2019 League match played at Celtic Park, when several Rangers footballers were sent off and some Celtic supporters were attacked in the hours after the game, the popular print media in Scotland once again generally equivocated in its 'condemnations'.

These few examples demonstrate that even when Celtic or its supporters have no obvious role in a perceived or socially constructed sectarian event or practice, a convention exists which acts to draw in and locate both clubs and/or fans within the same conversation. It is in this context that the term, the Old Firm, becomes most popular and is seen to acquire some of its most disabling effects in understanding cause and effect and power and powerlessness in relation to ethnic and religious prejudice and discrimination. It is here also that we can see that important social, cultural and political outlets and sources of information 'blame' Celtic and Rangers together for what is called, 'sectarianism'.

The works of one 'Old Firm' popular historian (Murray 1984) in the 1980s and 1990s demonstrates a predisposition for Scottish writers/reporters to use ill-defined, indistinct and ambiguous language when 'considering' ethno-religious history, identity and cleavage. For example, he describes anti-Catholic rioting in Edinburgh in 1935 as 'sectarian riots', adding that they were of 'a kind more disgraceful than any that dishonoured the terracings of Ibrox or Parkhead stadiums'. Apart from questioning why Celtic is referenced at all, these serious anti-Catholic riots of the 1930s in Scotland's capital city were not as might be interpreted, a result of inter-communal frictions 'between' Protestants and Catholics, but were an expression of prevailing overt socio-political and political anti-Catholic antagonisms, including a campaign by Scotland's national Church of Scotland against Catholics of Irish descent (Gallagher 1987).

As with many of his contemporaries in this instance the author calls this 'sectarian', but not more accurately, anti-Catholicism and anti-Irish racism. This partly reflects the underlying persistent

51 The Association, which represented all football clubs in Scotland, considered the display of the flag as having nothing to do with Scotland and an incitement to 'sectarian acts and behaviour'. See Brian Wilson, 1988.

rhetorical insinuation that two equally weighted tribes exist, that 'each is as bad as the other' and that they are 'two sides of the same coin'. That 'each side' is constructed as 'sectarian' is illustrative of the privileged explanations and representations of Scotland's anti-Catholic and anti-Irish culture that dominates within the Scottish media. Significantly, for Flint and Kelly:

> In Scotland sectarianism is often anchored in public and media discourses as a non-hierarchical dualism constituting Protestant Rangers and Catholic Celtic ('the bigot' brothers), thus stripping it of its central power dynamics.

Conclusion

To begin to understand 'sectarianism' in Scottish society, and to attempt to address relevant ethnic and religious prejudice, discrimination and bigotry, one requires consideration of its history: such analysis, on the part of the media or otherwise, is virtually absent in relevant accounts. It is in this light that this essay has reflected upon some of the dominant discourses and narratives critical to the construction and sustenance of popular beliefs with regard to ideas about 'sectarianism' in football and society, especially in terms of football in Scotland. In reality, the use of the word 'sectarianism', particularly on the part of the Scottish media, says little if anything of substance about ethnic and religious discrimination and bigotry. This omission is critical in the construction of frames of reference and is largely unquestioning of the cultural power of language. In Scotland 'sectarianism' is a catch-all term that ignores and disguises the history of ethno-religious prejudice and discrimination, while creating the 'sincere fiction' that 'sectarianism', whatever that may be, is being addressed. (Kelly 2011)

In recent decades Scotland has become less Protestant, more secular, less British, more Scottish, less Catholic and less Irish: also, more Polish, Asian, Muslim, and more anti-Christian. Anecdotal evidence also suggests that many in Scotland who practise their Protestant faith are much less likely to be anti-Catholic than previous generations. The Catholic Church in Scotland has become less insular and more ecumenical. The

> To begin to understand 'sectarianism' in Scottish society. . . one requires consideration of its history: such analysis, on the part of the media is virtually absent.

Church of Scotland has made an apology to its fellow Irish-descended Catholic community for the intense prejudice and discrimination it helped visit upon them during the twentieth century (Gallagher 2013). This work also acknowledges that not agreeing with or believing in some of the practices and beliefs of Protestantism or Catholicism does not equate with being prejudiced or discriminatory against these faiths and that these can be fair and legitimate perspectives (although they can very much also be motivated by other ideological 'educational' intentions, bias, intolerance, ignorance, etc).

This essay has utilised a contextual exploration to reflect on the problematisation and othering of Irish/Catholic/Celtic identities. Opposition towards Irishness and Catholicism has long pervaded football in Scotland. There is little or no evidence to suggest that this is acknowledged or addressed in any significant cultural, educational or political setting. As this work has demonstrated, the media, particularly the sports media, has played a central role in creating and reproducing the discourses and narratives that have constructed Celtic and its supporters Irish and Catholic identities as intolerable and appalling 'others' in Scotland. Critically, in constructing widely opposed (now rejected) legislation, a question can be raised over whether some notions of Scottish political and cultural nationalism, particularly within the SNP, but also on the part of Scotland's other political parties, drew upon and reflected more than a century of hostility and prejudice towards Scotland's Catholic minority of Irish descent. A previously dominant Labour Party's record against anti-Irishness and anti-Catholicism in Scotland is also hardly worth noting, despite most Catholics traditionally joining or voting Labour.

Reid's (in Flint and Kelly) assertion that public discourses can reinforce and naturalise dominant ideological systems of 'othering' is relevant. 'Sectarianism' has become a ubiquitous term and constitutes the dominant discursive descriptor of whatever is construed as socially and culturally different or discordant with regards Catholic or Protestant identities, which can also often encompass Celtic and Rangers.

One example outside of football shows how uninformative, superficial and political the term is. When talking of people 'choosing' either a Catholic or Protestant marital partner, Rosie calls this often complex act (if indeed it exists as stated) a 'sectarian preference' (in Flint and Kelly). Even more seriously misguided, is that with all due respect to the central importance of real or imagined religious faiths to the identities of Rangers, Celtic and their supports, it is uniformed, limited and biased to state as one author does that they are 'championing' the 'causes' of Protestantism and Catholicism. Such superficial and anti-intellectual labeling creates and sustains ill-founded commentary and supports the widespread use of the negligent omnipotent term 'sectarianism' (Murray 1984).

In 2014 a Labour MSP stated that he believed with regards Celtic and Rangers and their cultural and political identities that 'this [SNP] Government has something about equivalence. . . if you're going to do something about one lot you've got to do something about the other'.[52] Historically, examination, recognition or disapproval of discrimination and prejudice against Irishness and Catholicism in Scottish football, as with society at large, has been largely absent in the Scottish media. In fact, it has frequently only been in recent years when the world's media have looked in Scotland's direction that a feeling of embarrassment or shame has been apparent and an urge to change such an image has been provoked. Such change is positive, however in being embarrassed and ashamed of the attention Scotland's anti-Catholic and anti-Irish dimensions have on occasion attracted, 'the other side' – i.e. Celtic and its support – has been manufactured as part of the relevant discourses.

This narrative was exemplified by the Scottish Parliament's Justice Committee convener, SNP member Christine Grahame, when chairing consultations prior to the institution of the 2012 Act. She was explicit about the 'quest for balance' and equivocation, saying:

> . . . prosecutions under the 2003 Act will be more successful in relation to Rangers supporters singing – notwithstanding the point that the songs are not all sectarian – than Celtic supporters singing, behaving in a certain way or chanting because that would not be deemed sectarian and would be more likely to be deemed political?

52 St. Patrick's Festival Debate, Coatbridge, 8/3/14.

Panel member Professor Tom Devine responded, 'I do not understand your point', to which convener Grahame clarified, adding, 'My point is that it is not even'.[53] It seems that even amongst the country's political leaders and law makers that the argument of 'one side being as bad as the other' dominates and, to the point that it can hinder progress in terms of ethno-religious justice and equality in a multi-cultural society. Indeed, in itself this perspective can represent institutional ideologically-laden prejudice and bias.

Ethnic and religious prejudice in Scottish football and society has been dominated by demonstrations of hostility towards public manifestations of the identities of the country's longest established ethno-religious minority.[54] Antagonism towards making the sign of the cross, representing Ireland in international football, campaigns and demands made against the presence of the Irish national flag at Celtic, or singing of the Irish national anthem and other Irish songs are frequently manifest amongst football fans and the media. A historically significant popular ideological anti-Irish and anti-Catholic thread is clearly manifest in Scottish society. This is particularly identifiable in relation to the mainstream media which is a primary source of socio-cultural and political information framing and narrating these as problematic. In relation to the Act, examination of numerous mainstream media sources illustrates that it is Celtic and its supporters' ethno-religious identities that are represented as the principal 'offenders' in Scotland and the 2012 Act can be seen as a culmination of many decades of a discursive prejudice that ultimately assisted in its construction. Central to relevant discourses, and to the perpetuation of ignorance, or a desire to 'actively' forget, about the roots and manifestations of prejudice, discrimination and inequality, has been a widespread utilisation of the term 'sectarianism'. This has contributed towards an ideological framework of interpretation, understanding and categorisation that functions to conceal and distort the history and reality of ethno-religious identities, racism, chauvinism and injustice in Scotland.

In 2006 a question was asked in the Scottish Parliament by renowned independent (former Labour MP) member Denis Canavan.[55]

53 http://www.scottish.parliament.uk/parliamentarybusiness/28862.aspx?r=6439&mode=pdf, accessed 1/2/14.

54 The presence of antagonism and hostility towards people perceived as anti-Irish and anti-Catholic exists in Scotland. Davies refers to 'gestures of defiance' on the part of Irish Catholics in the face of anti-Catholic Orange Walks, Flint and Kelly 50-64. Also see for discussion linked to language, ideas and abuse, Davis chapter in Flint and Kelly, pp. 115-129.

55 http://www.scottish.parliament.uk/Apps2/Business/ORSearch/ReportView.aspx?r=4688&i=37710&c=883683, 23/11/2006, accessed January 2011.

It is a national scandal that the Scottish football authorities turned a blind eye to anti-Irish racism in Scottish football for many years. It was not until UEFA took action that certain people were brought to their senses. As well as using the law to prosecute those who are guilty, will the Lord Advocate urge the Scottish football authorities to take strict disciplinary action against any guilty players, supporters or, if necessary, clubs, to stamp out all forms of racism and sectarianism, which should not be tolerated in a multicultural, multi-ethnic Scotland?

Subsequently, there was no debate on this matter and no one in the sports or wider media publicly reflected upon or reported Canavan's enquiry. As this essay significantly reveals, such questions have been largely ignored and often only 'addressed' when attention from beyond Scotland has been provoked.[56] This essay re-affirms Kelly's (2011) perspective that:

> There is a powerful and longstanding ideological 'framing' of sectarianism in sections of the Scottish press [and media generally] that is latently power-laden. . . [and that this media] treatment of sectarianism is shown to lack sensitivity to the historical, hierarchical and relational aspects of religious, political and ethnic identities in Scotland.

Incisively, Flint and Kelly (2013) talk of:

> The sleepwalking prejudices of sections of Scotland's football fans, its media and its governing bodies, who continue trying to solve ethno-religious prejudice by inadvertently engaging in it themselves.

This composition points towards the use of the term sectarianism as an ideological construction that does little if anything to address historical, or challenge contemporary, ethnic and religious discrimination and prejudice. It also reflects the discursive power of the label and the hegemonic political cultural and social jurisdiction and domination held by those that use it to assert and impose an insincere and deceptive picture of what ethnic and religious prejudice, discrimination have been and are in Scotland. Its popular and common-sense usage has served to disguise and deny a history of anti-Catholic and anti-Irish prejudice while assisting in the reproduction of re-cycled forms of these very notions. If society in Scotland genuinely desires to rid itself

56 During consultations prior to the institution of the 2012 Act Professor Tom Devine stressed how different Scotland had become with regards its 'sectarianism' in recent decades, pointing towards the stare of the outside world as one significant reason for this. He said: 'We now have different expectations, partly because the attention of the world is on us. CNN was in the country two days ago [to note discussions on the Bill], and it might well have interviewed members of this committee. Its report will go out in 200 countries during the next couple of weeks. The bill process is still going on, so the world is still very interested. The international factor has been relevant'. http://www.scottish.parliament.uk/parliamentarybusiness/28862.aspx?r=64398&mode=pdf, accessed 1/2/14.

of its deep and profound ethno-religious prejudice and antagonism it first requires to hold up a mirror to see what the issues have been and are in the first place.

References

Bradley, J. M. Ethnic and Religious Identity in Modern Scotland: Culture, Politics and Football. Aldershot, 1995.

Bradley, J. M. 'Orangeism in Scotland: Unionism, 'Politics, Identity and Football', Eire – Ireland: An Interdisciplinary Journal of Irish Studies, 39 (1 & 2), 2004, 237-261.

Bradley, J. M. 'Celtic Football Club, Irish Ethnicity, and Scottish Society', New Hibernia Review, 12 (1), 2008, 96-110.

Bradley, J. M. 'History and Memory in Scottish Football', in Flint and Kelly, 65-81.

Davies, A. 'They sing that song, Football and Sectarianism in Glasgow in the 1920s and 1930s', in Flint and Kelly, 50-64.

Devine, T. M. in T. M. Devine. & R, Mitchison. People and Society in Scotland, vol 1, 1760-1830, John Donald, Edinburgh 1988, 154.

Flint, J. and Kelly, J. Bigotry, Football and Scotland, Edinburgh University Press, Scotland, 2013.

Gallagher, T. Glasgow: The Uneasy Peace, Manchester University Press, 1987.

Gallagher, T, 'The Catholic Irish in Scotland: in search of identity', in T.M Devine Irish Immigrants and Scottish Society in the Nineteenth and Twentieth Centuries: Proceedings of the Scottish Historical Studies Seminar (Strathclyde: John Donald Publishers,1991, 19-43.

Gallagher T, Divided Scotland: ethnic friction & Christian crisis, Argyll Publishing, Scotland, 2013.

Kelly J, 'Sectarianism and Scottish football: Critical reflections on dominant discourse and press commentary', International Review for the Sociology of Sport, 46 (4), 2011, 418-435.

Muirhead I A, 'Catholic Emancipation in Scotland: Scottish Reactions in 1829', Innes Review, 1973, 24 (2).

Murray, B. The Old Firm'; The Old Firm: sectarianism, sport and society in Scotland, John Donald, Edinburgh, 1984.

Murray, B. Glasgow's Giants: 100 years of the Old Firm, Mainstream, Edinburgh, 1988,

Murray, B. Bhoys, Bears and Bigotry: Rangers, Celtic and the Old Firm in the New Age of Globalised Sport, Mainstream, Edinburgh, 2003.

Reid, I, A. 'He's back! But Scotland's National Demon Never Left: Revisiting Media Representations of Neil Lennon and Narratives of Bigotry', in Flint and Kelly, 145-159.

Rosie, M.'Perspectives beyond the Old Firm', in J Flint and J Kelly, 19-33.

Waiton. S, 'The New Sectarians', in Flint and Kelly, 99-114.

Wilson, B. Celtic: A Century with Honour, Glasgow Willow Books, 1988.

The Beattys': a special part of the Celtic family

A Special club for a really SPECIAL Bhoy

Martin Beatty

Craigavon Area hospital. . . 23rd December 2003, 6:10pm local time. Panic, fear, numbness, tears and complete helplessness. Craigavon Area Hospital. . . 23rd December 2003, 7:12pm local time. The realisation that the wee bhoy in front of me fighting for his life was my wee bhoy and a promise was whispered in his ear that if he made it I would do everything I could to protect him and to make his life as special as he was. Celtic Park, boardroom 20th June 2015, 12:05pm local time. Numbness, tears and a heart bursting with pride.

In my wildest dreams I could never have imagined what lay ahead for our son. A son born with Down syndrome and a serious heart defect, the odds were well and truly stacked against him but little did we know that a football club in the east end of Glasgow would transform his and our lives forever.

Jay was born into a family in Lurgan, Co Armagh, which was steeped in Celtic football club. He never had an option, it's who we are and what we are and that made Celtic a big part of our lives. In 1969 my parents and brothers and sisters returned from Glasgow to Ireland and settled back in Co. Armagh. My parents' timing may not have been the best as at the same week we moved back the so-called Troubles in Northern Ireland broke out. Basically they were now living in a war zone. I came along in June 1970 to complete the family of five Bhoys and two Ghirls (twins). I had a great childhood as my mother and father worked hard to provide for us in very tough times.

From as early as I can remember Celtic was a passion in our home. All my family supported them as it seemed did the whole town I lived in: well one half of the town as the other half would have followed Rangers. Growing up following Celtic in Lurgan gave us limited access to actually seeing them, although we had a large Celtic supporters club in the town that on occasion ran trips over on the ferry. However, my parents' money had to be spent on more critical things. Each Saturday night my mother and father and I would have sat in front of the TV while my mother watched 'Knots Landing' and my father and I waited on 'Match of the Day' in the hope they would show 30 seconds of Celtic after the English games. Despite this poverty of actually seeing my team, I was Celtic daft. I loved everything about them and this has continued throughout my life. I met my wife Aine in school. She was my best friend, but I had always fancied her anyway: I just didn't have the nerve to tell her. We married and bought a house in Lurgan and along came our daughter Olivia who we thought completed us. But we weren't there yet. We were all so happy when we found out Aine was pregnant again and on the 23rd December 2003 our so called perfect wee world was about to change but little did we know then how much: nonetheless, our family was now complete.

When Jay was born we knew there was a problem within the first five minutes as several doctors and nurses were attending to our bhoy and things did not seem right. After an hour we asked 'was all ok', only to have a young doctor with tears in her eyes telling us 'we believe your son has Down syndrome'. We were devastated, panic set in, certain images went through our heads: fear and worry immediately ensued. The doctor then followed up with 'and he has a serious heart problem'. From that moment on Down syndrome was forgotten about as it was now a fight to save our son's life. Following the ambulance with the siren on down the motorway to the RVH children's heart hospital was the journey from hell. The Clarke clinic became our home for the next 7 months and it was not easy. Jay had it tough and on a number of occasions we thought we had lost him, and, after an eight hour heart operation and through his own determination to live and everyone's prayers, in July 2004 we were finally able to take him home for the first time.

Jay had a tough start to his life but he was our wee Bhoy and we now had a promise to fulfil. While in hospital we spent seven days a week, eighteen hours a day by his bedside, reading to him singing to him, and praying for him. My wife was an inspiration of how a mother should be and while I had to travel back to London after a few weeks to work, as bills had to be paid, my wife was there every day reading up and preparing for when he would come home. She never once doubted and was and still is an inspiration to me. At the weekends I would come home and go straight to the hospital and spend my time there, as Jay lay in his little incubator with what seemed wires coming from every part of his body, I would read Jay stories from the 'Celtic View' and Celtic books, not knowing if he could under-stand: but it passed the time and we could see him smile. It was my way of letting him know that I was there. My time spent reading also gave me deeper insight into our great club and its formation, its values and history.

With Jay now home we went about our lives promising to make a difference to try and break down barriers, stigmas and to change many people's negative attitudes to Down syndrome. Being a Celtic supporter had changed over the years and we were able to attend games more frequently. With Sky TV we could watch them live on a near weekly basis. From an early age Jay would have sat in his chair watching Celtic with me and no doubt hearing a few choice words being shouted at the TV. It was evident that he loved watching them and instead of Barney dvds he was watching more and more Celtic dvds, cheering at every goal. Which, when the dvd is titled Celtics greatest goals, can become tiresome when it's on all day – every day.

January 2nd 2011 changed everything for Jay and started an obsession that has not faltered. It is something that I have never seen before. It is an obsession that has taken over our lives: it has changed our lives for good and unfortunately, also for bad. Celtic took to the field against Rangers at Ibrox and with Rangers favourites to win up stepped Mr Samaras who scored two goals and sent my wife and I into complete delirium, with Jay sitting watching on in awe of what he was seeing on TV and what he was witnessing in our living room. From that day on Jay's life changed forever. He had one focus and nothing else mattered in his life bar Celtic football club: and I mean it has been relentless morning, noon and night. I do not believe I have ever had a conversation with Jay that in some way has not been turned by him into something about Celtic: he lives and breathes it.

Following Jay's birth my wife threw herself into a support group she had set up called 'Downs & Proud', and through social media we started to post up photos of Jay and short videos with the sole purpose of showing others that we were proud of our son. We hoped that photos of our son and little stories about him would make people smile and that it would show others the pride that we had in our Bhoy and our pride in that he had Down syndrome.

These photos and videos started to be shared amongst Celtic fans and over time it was evident that people were falling in love with our Bhoy. From an early age Jay's image was being used more and more to help promote Down syndrome inclusion, a family photo with his sister in their Celtic tops when Jay was only two years old was used to promote Down syndrome awareness in North America and his image was beamed on a large screen in Times Square. This gained a lot of publicity in Ireland and America and Jay's story was covered on the local news and newspapers. We travelled to New York City to be part of this amazing experience and the following year Jay's image was again used on posters in NYC to contest the stigmatisation of Down syndrome, and indeed, promote it positively.

My wife's support group was beginning to expand as more and more people from the mid-Ulster area started to join. It was now a thriving cross community charity and a lot of hard work, but was worth it as she was making a difference in the lives of many families. As a family we were getting on with our lives following Celtic on TV and supporting our local Lurgan Celtic No 1 team where Jay had become the mascot. I had brought Jay to Celtic Park on several occasions which he loved, the noise, the colours and that feeling of happiness when we scored. Neil Lennon lived close to us in Lurgan and we had gone to school with him. Jay just loved him and on occasions we would meet Neil at his home or at the stadium and I think he was taken back by the love and warmth that Jay had for him. Through Neil we had got to meet the players and of course Georgios Samaras who was Jay's idol. Samaras was a laid-back kind of person with his long black hair and beard while Jay with his skinhead and big glasses was always beside himself with excitement when he saw him: they instantly hit it off.

May 11th 2014 started off as any other day supporting Celtic. Jay and I were up early to be at the Celtic supporters club in Lurgan to catch the 6am bus to the boat and onwards to Celtic Park for the final game of the season. We were seated in the North Stand and at the final whistle we went and stood at the wall that surrounds the pitch to cheer on the team in their lap of honour. Jay was just so happy but what happened next would change our lives.

Neil Lennon spotted Jay in the crowd and came over to him and placed his winner's medal around his neck: at the same time his hero Samaras lifted him out of the crowd and into his arms and took him around the pitch on the lap of honour. At the time I was in shock at what was happening and hearing the crowd and panicking that Jay would drop his medal on the pitch. At the time I was unaware that anyone had seen this moment bar those around me as I forgot about the images being shown on the large screens in the stadium and the millions that it was being beamed to around the world including Aine and Olivia who were watching with tears in their eyes back in Lurgan.

Leaving the stadium was surreal with so many well-wishers hugging Jay with me still wondering how they all had seen it. Getting back onto the bus and a phone call to my wife with the words: 'you're never going to believe what happened' only to be told 'we just watched it live on TV'. It then dawned on me what a big event it had become. Within an hour the phone calls from the press around the world had started and have really never stopped. Jay's story was now being beamed around the world and his image was being shown everywhere. While we were delighted we were also very overwhelmed as this was something difficult to control and take in.

The summer of 2014 was the World Cup in Brazil. Ireland had failed to qualify as also did Scotland. So, for me, the World

Cup really meant nothing. However, for Jay it was a chance to hopefully see Samaras on the TV. A month after being carried around Celtic Park Jay's life was going to go into the spotlight again. Samaras scored a penalty to put Greece into the last 16 in the dying seconds of the game. It had been played through the night but we had recorded it for Jay and allowed him to watch it the next day after school, I filmed his reaction when Samaras scored and put it up a 30 second clip of it on my social media page: this went viral and worldwide.

Greece had gone into meltdown over this clip and within the space of 24 hours Jay's story was headlines across Greece and other parts of the world. Soon we had the press and film crews outside our house. Two days later we were to travel to Dublin to fly to Boston for our family holiday. The interviews and phone calls had not stopped and while sitting on the plane with the doors closing my phone went again much to my wife's disgust as she was saying 'turn it off, we are on the plane'. I took the call and it was an invite from the Greek side to fly to Brazil to follow the remaining matches in their World Cup campaign, I could not take this all in and had to quickly explain that we were actually on a flight to Boston and could not attend, much to the dismay of the caller. We took off on our family holiday with not a word being spoken. When we landed in Boston we believed we had left all the madness behind only to start receiving call after call that we were going to Brazil as somehow it was all over the news that we had been invited and had accepted. Samaras had done a press conference confirming he could not wait to see Jay. We were in a real panic on this but thankfully the situation was corrected. While in Boston we could not believe the people who knew of Jay and Celtic that were stopping us in the streets.

One morning Jay and I were having breakfast in our hotel, waiting on his mummy and sister to come down. It was a large dining area with a large TV mounted on the wall. I had my back to the TV and Jay was facing it playing Celtic on his iPad. I could see people in the dining area looking over and then looking away but that had sort of come the norm by now. It was only when Jay said, 'daddy I am on TV' that I realised why people were staring. I turned round to see Jay's face and video clips and people talking about him on a US morning show for around two minutes. I did not hear what they were saying as the sound was turned down but it was now evident that his story was going global. While in Boston we were invited by some Greek scholars to Harvard University for a tour and to watch the Greece game against Costa Rica. There we were, a family from Ireland on our way to one of the top university's in the world because of our son. It would be the first time any of the Beatty family would ever get to look inside a university.

Through all of this madness Jay was unfazed. He did not appreciate how sensational and big his story had become: indeed, he showed no interest in this development in his life. He had Celtic on his ipad and that was all that mattered. Greece were sadly knocked out of the World Cup and we continued with our family holiday.

Around November 2014 we received a letter from the Greek sports personality of the year awards which are the oldest sporting awards in the world. They wanted Jay to attend as guest of honour. Jay and Georgios Samaras were to be awarded on the night. We could not take this in and really were humbled by the whole scenario. In December we flew to London then to Athens airport. On arrival we were met by camera crews and photographers and there it seemed Jay's image was everywhere; TV, magazines and newspapers. This was really overwhelming and actually frightening as everywhere we went there were photographers taking pictures of Jay. The award ceremony was a very emotional night as Samaras's grandfather had died that day. But he would not let Jay down and arrived to take to the stage to receive an award with our Bhoy: we will always be so grateful to the lovely people of Greece who have been so kind and loving towards our son.

We were not used to what was going on and believed that Jay had had his fifteen minutes of fame. But then, a goal that Jay scored while on his first Celtic away game at Hamilton would again make the headlines and result in Jay receiving a SPFL goal of the month award and further newspaper headlines around the world.

We were just so proud of our son. Played once for Celtic and scored once.

This lead to further awards in Barcelona, Ireland and Scotland. However, with all this kindness and love a dark side started to raise its head and has continued since. Internet abuse was something that we were unaware of and never once thought that we would have to deal with. While so much positivity was going on we started to learn of disgusting comments being made about Jay on social media. This was universally condemned but has continued on a daily basis ever since. The abuse, the threats and the language directed at Jay and our family on a near daily basis has been staggering and has had a very adverse effect on our lives. The comments are shocking and disgusting and have sickened hardened police officers who have had to deal with it.

Jay is an Irish Catholic Celtic supporter from Ireland who has Down syndrome. For some this mix is the perfect excuse to lodge a hate campaign against him which has resulted in numerous arrests and charges. As a family we struggle daily with this as Jay is the most innocent loveable child that you could ever meet: thankfully, we have been able to shield all this from him. Nevertheless, as a father and husband it has been heartbreaking watching my wife and daughter reading and hearing these threats and vile abuse. This has put a serious strain on our family life and our health. However, this is only a small minority and the love and affection that has been shown to Jay throughout the world is so humbling and overwhelming. The fans are the heartbeat of Celtic FC. They are fans like no other and thanks to the kindness and love of these fans and fans from other clubs it far outweighs the hatred and bile that is thrown at us.

This leads to 12pm on 20th June 2015. Walking through the doors of Celtic Football Club holding my son's hand with my heart about to explode, my stomach turning and trying desperately to keep my emotions under control, being guided into the Celtic boardroom and to watch my son sit at the directors' table along with the Celtic Foundation CEO Tony Hamilton. There, he signed his name to a contract to become 'Ambassador for the Celtic Foundation': a moment that will live with me forever. I could no longer hold it together and the tears flowed down my face. How did a wee Bhoy with no hair, big glasses and Down syndrome end up signing for Celtic. . . ? Well it is Celtic, 'A Club Like No Other': founded out of oppression and for charity. Founded to provide food and a focus for poor Irish immigrants and their offspring.

The supporters are the lifeblood of the club and most Celtic fans have never forgotten what our club is about with a history of pride and a history of giving people a chance. My son has become one of those who was given that chance and for that we owe Celtic and its fanbase a great debt. We know we will never be able to repay this. We are so proud to support Celtic FC and are proud of what our club was, is, and has become: from having nothing to becoming one of the most iconic football clubs in the world. We want to thank you all and hope that in some small way that Jay has made you all happier and proud.

We never thought stuff like this would ever happen to people like us and thinking back to 6:10pm on 23rd December 2003 still fills me with so much sadness because of how I reacted when I heard the words Down syndrome; the panic, fear, numbness, tears and complete helplessness. These have been replaced with tears of joy and happiness. This is what my bhoy and a team from the east end of Glasgow have done and I thank each and every Celtic supporter for making him the person that he is. A SPECIAL Bhoy who supports a very SPECIAL Club.

'The Good News':
Celtic FC Foundation

TONY HAMILTON

According to the social mission statement, Celtic tell us: 'The Club always has been and always will simply aim to be the team of the people.' Reflect on this for a moment, think it through: The team of the people. You and I know, however, we are not actually 'the people'.

But 'Celtic-minded'? Emphatically so. The people. . . not so much. We've been conditioned to accept that fact through generations of indoctrination, propaganda and the odd gentle nudge from some elements within the fourth estate. But I'm okay with that. I'm okay with how this football club of ours conducts itself generally. And, if I'm honest, I'm immensely proud of who we are and, consistent with who we are, who we are not.

I'm in a privileged position at Celtic. I ran the multi media side of the business for close on ten years. . . and since summer 2013, I've headed up the charitable arm as chief executive of Celtic FC Foundation. And, in those past few years, we've tried to make progress, make a difference, and we've tried to do the right thing with and for those around us: while accepting that we can't boil the ocean on our own. We know our limitations, that's for sure.

Nevertheless, this Foundation isn't a gimmick and it's not something we're doing simply because that's what others expect of us, or many other football clubs to do these days. It's actually in our DNA and not a corporate add-on. The Celtic story fascinates me. It always has done. I've been lucky enough to cover it in film and in print over a long time and to now have this opportunity to continue to do what this club was formed to do in 1887 is an honour for me and one which I will never take for granted.

For many a long year the club, without much evidence to substantiate it, dined out on the 'charitable roots' angle. That changed forever when Fergus McCann wrestled control from the so-called 'old board' on March 4th, 1994. McCann brought charity and charitable giving back to this club. However, the truth is, it still lurked beneath the surface in the period from Brother Walfrid's departure to the Kellys and the Whites being deposed: this was especially true for the support for whom charity giving was ingrained. But in that intervening time, it was done quietly, privately.

Each to their own, I suppose. Yet why it was a secret perplexes me to this day. My view of altruism and community-type work is different from that. I deploy a commercial solution to a third sector problem. I do that because my background is commercial media and I worked in a hugely competitive and demanding space at the football club. I didn't know much about charity when I took this on and I'm not sure I know a great deal more now. But I know what works and what doesn't work and that is more important. We employ commercial means at Celtic FC Foundation to generate a surplus, but we use that surplus for the greater good: not to add financial value for shareholders. And we learn from those who need our help. We do things with people, not to them.

In general, and, as an example, and in contrast to how the football department is run, we do things in public these days. But importantly, not for the headlines. Never to exploit people. And certainly not so anyone will say 'look how good Celtic are'. We publicise (most of) our charitable activity for two main reasons. The obvious one is so that people who need help can participate – we offer help to marginalised groups and individuals and we need them to be aware that such help exists.

The second reason is that we want to be able to do more of

it. So, with the publicity generated through our in-house and external media channels, we not only catch those who might benefit but we also catch those who might be benefactors, the philanthropists out there. It's win-win. And often the bi-product is that we are then able to do more of the things which we believe are adding value for communities that need it.

The truth of the matter is that charity is wholly and genuinely in our DNA. Although there is this long period of charitable semi-abstinence, which we have recognised, charity in modern Celtic times takes its place alongside football (the reason we are all here) and the commercial expertise we use to fund it, and to try and gain a competitive edge on our European counterparts many of whom are aligned to football leagues where wealth and riches are the rule, not the exception.

Celtic FC Foundation focus around four key areas under the banner of HELP: Health, Equality, Learning and Poverty

What we're aiming for here is to alleviate poverty for as many people as we can, so that element, for me at least, stands head and shoulders above the others. In many ways Poverty and Health, Equality and Learning serve separate purposes. Poverty is what we are fighting and the other three are often the tools we use to fight it with. Health is important because without it people are less likely to secure employment or manage to maintain it. So we work with people who experience long-term barriers through health reasons and we also work with people who suffer from chronic illness and try to improve their quality of life, even although work may no longer be an option for some of them.

We use football as the hook but we don't teach anyone how to play. Instead, we use our expertise in physical activity delivery to improve a person's fitness from the time of coming to us to the time they leave, often 12 weeks later. We monitor, measure and evaluate all of that and we adapt and tailor projects to suit each individual's needs and circumstances both in terms of theory in the 'classroom' and physical activity in the gym.

Equality is key because we are a club, as always, open to all. In this regard we work with children and young people (as one example) who can be excluded from simple things such as recreation ('play time') because they have complex physical disabilities such as Down syndrome or autism. In some cases, it's a multiple of two or more. Our award-winning 'Ability Counts' project covers all of that and we actively fundraise to continue to deliver it because we know it resonates with young people and their families.

And we treat ex-offenders as equals once they have demonstrated they want a second chance. We offer our employability expertise to help them stay out of jail. However, jail for many is a symptom of something major that's gone wrong in that young person's home life, so we try to address other issues such as addiction and mental health, and simpler issues such as numeracy and literacy. And if we don't have the competence inhouse, we hire in professional resources as part of the project delivery.

Learning opportunities are funded through private benefactors – not the wider Celtic support – and we aim to create opportunities for children and young people who would otherwise be passed by, often because of where they live. This work is vital for us and we invest those private funds heavily around music and digital education, masterclasses and opportunities that would not exist otherwise.

The work we do in Poverty is more obvious. We have a foodbank partner, which offers more than food, and we have an annual Christmas Appeal for the poorest 300 or so local families, 100 single vulnerable OAPs and a dozen or so charities who look after people who lead chaotic lives such as the homeless, refugees and women and children in refuge. Once out of the Glasgow area, we can talk about our social inclusion work in Tower Hamlets, building kitchens in Africa and providing ambulances and emergency supplies for refugees escaping war across the Middle East. It's all go. I was once asked if this is a full-time job . . . I laugh as I think about the live projects we have on the go today.

There are many other examples of the work that we engage in but suffice to say we have no interest in duplicating services, which other organisations are already delivering effectively. And we have even less interest in passing people from project to project. We are interested only in making a sustainable difference and to do that we need a positive outcome, which in many cases is gainful employment.

And while Fergus McCann might be seen as being responsible for officially returning the concept, and formalising the giving of charity to Celtic, the current custodians, through the stewardship of the football club's chief executive and the plc board, brought the qualities back to Celtic that give charity substance and meaning; compassion, empathy and humility. And, that is delivered across the club with the sharp end being Celtic FC Foundation – a registered charity in Scotland in its own right. We're deadly serious about charity at Celtic.

Late nineteenth century Victorian Britain was a foreboding place. Especially in the east end of Glasgow. Or the east end of any industrial city for that matter. Today's youth may find it difficult to comprehend the hardship of those times. However, sadly (well, actually much more than 'sadly' as this is such an inadequate word in such circumstances) there are many people living among us, as our neighbours, fellow parishioners, friends, relatives, who don't find it difficult to imagine at all. They are living it today: in 2019. The more things change, and all that. . . Yes, in 2019, there are many homeless, many hungry, many neglected and many individuals and families living in abject social conditions and in extreme poverty. There are hundreds of houses, visible from atop Celtic Park, in the north and east of this city where occupants are living without employment, electrical power or hope.

And it's the hope we have to restore first. When I say 'we' I don't mean Celtic FC Foundation in isolation. That would never work. We're not grand in any way and I would never wish to be sanctimonious. When I say 'we' I mean you and me and everyone else in between.

We require to look outwards across the city and across the Third World and many places in between. Our work starts in the north and east of Glasgow, but it doesn't stop there. Areas such as Inverclyde and North Lanarkshire are priorities for us because life for many in those places is atypical as you look at national deprivation statistics. If everything, however, is a priority then nothing is, so our main focus in Scotland is in the west. We also deliver funded projects in the east end of London and we are raising our game to do more in Ireland, our spiritual home.

The overall concept of Corporate Social Responsibility (CSR) as I understand it in the world of business is not for me. Perhaps I'm overly cynical but CSR (notwithstanding the fact that Celtic FC Foundation recently won an award for it) doesn't do it for me. My experience, albeit limited, suggests CSR for many organisations can be a cheap and easy way of easing one's conscience: and that's not 'charity' – beneficial in some sense and worthwhile and needed though it may be. A lot of organisations tick the 'giving back' box by throwing a few quid at community projects, which they know nothing about, have even less interest in and have no way to monitor and evaluate performance. Then, they move on and sleep well.

However, it's different here. It actually needs to be different if 'change' is the watchword. Yes, we have a social conscience but we partner with organisations who support us and share our values. Commercial partners including Dafabet, Magners, New Balance and Fleet Alliance all support our efforts considerably and all work extremely hard improving their own communities too. As do others. A recent University of Strathclyde, Fraser of Allander Report stated:

> The work of the Celtic FC Foundation is quite unlike standard football club foundations in scale and scope, with its focus on improving health, promoting equality, encouraging learning and tackling poverty.[1]

So CSR is not for us. For the same reasons we're not in this space for headlines, we're not in it to be seen to be doing the right thing from a corporate perspective. In many ways I find the whole thing quite insulting. And, ordinarily, I'm not the easiest guy to offend.

I'm often asked 'but what do the club contribute'? My answer is simple. In cash terms it's a very significant six-figure sum. Then, there's the value of premium office space at the heart of Celtic Park and use of everything and everyone else employed

1. Report on Celtic's contribution to Scotland's economy, researched and written by Fraser of Allander Institute, University of Strathclyde, 2018

55

here – the exact same as every other part of the club enjoys. But they also give their heart and soul to make this work and I can't put a price on that.

We are a broad church. We hold appeal for many constituent parts. All faiths and none. A wide range of political views and parties. However, a few things in my mind unite us. A love of this football club for one. A love of why it was formed and a common desire to help people. And, we help people because we can. Sure, it's a government problem, a problem of financial systems and arrangements, of ideology, of morality, and, of wider society. Nevertheless, it's our problem and yours too, and we're taking it on. I'm not in a position of objectivity to judge our performance or comment on it. That's down to you, our partners and those people whose lives we strive to improve. However, this Celtic thing we obsess over sounds very much like a team of the people to me. Charity's only one wee part of the story: but it's a core part after all.

Celtic, Celtic
– that's the team for me!

JOHN PAUL TAYLOR

I was born in Glasgow in Robroyston Hospital on January 3rd, 1965. My parents, John and Rosemary at that time resided in Winifred Street in Robroyston along with my older sister Ann Marie. My father, a fitter to trade, had worked in the Caledonian Rail Works in Springburn before becoming a Glasgow taxi driver, the only other job he would hold until his sad passing in 1999 at the age of 63. My mother worked in the British Linen Bank before moving onto the Post Office first in Barmulloch and latterly Millerston, where we eventually found ourselves living from 1969 and my mum still lives in the same house today.

We had a modest income and both my parents worked hard to ensure that we were afforded life's essentials and where possible some added luxuries. We moved to Cumbernauld not long after I was born, residing in Glenacre Road in Carbrain and it was within that very house my dad watched Celtic's victory against Inter Milan on May 25th, 1967.

It was way before I had any comprehension of football but I can still recall that house and can picture my dad and other family members celebrating in style. My mum had five brothers, one of them, Ronald sadly passing away as a child but William, Alex and Edward were all around the age of my dad and they had a really close family bond, the same as the one that I would later share with the youngest of the brothers, Gerard, who was just four years older.

By far and away the most influential person over everyone in this group though was my grandfather, Ronnie McDonald. Big Ronnie was born of a Garngad father and a French mother, quite unique. Big Ronnie was also employed at the Caledonian works as were most of the other family members with the exception of Alexhey – all had a spell with varying degrees of success.

As you may have gathered there was heavy male influence throughout the family, the men worked hard and like many others in those days they enjoyed a drink at the weekend, enjoyed a bet and the football. More than anything they enjoyed the football. Our family was Celtic, although my granda had a strong connection to St. Roch's juniors and on many occasions went round the doors to raise funds to keep the club alive. I'd say my granda's first love was for 'The Candy' but there was a close tie in those days with Celtic and he often managed to find a way to get players on loan or old kit or footballs, anything that would save a bit of money for St. Roch's. He did of course have a passion for Celtic like the rest of the men in the family and this would rub off on Gerard and I as we grew up.

My grandfather on my dad's side was non-Catholic, in fact he was non-denominational, a lovely quiet man who never really demonstrated a real passion for football that I can recall. The rest of the family were all Catholic. Was this a factor in whether we supported Celtic? I suspect it was to a degree, however I do think there was more than that. Our family were in the main practising Catholics. I never saw them demonstrate any intolerance to anyone. Sure they were proud of who they were, they were proud Celtic supporters but it didn't negatively influence their thoughts towards others. My dad would always say there's good and bad everywhere – as a cab driver he encountered all sorts of folk every day, Glaswegians from every social background. In truth he'd generally make judgements on whether people gave him a tip and many a time he would share a story of some TV celebrity or footballer who didn't tip. These were affectionately known as a 'berry' – this meant a bare hire. If you were a berry he never forgot it and nor did we. He would ridicule them any time they appeared on TV – with my Da, it was personal!

The key point here, though, was that he always judged people as he found them. I know he would occasionally pick up footballers from Celtic and Rangers and he used to tell us about them at the dinner table. He would be perfectly straight – they were nice or not nice. The team they played for wasn't important to him, it was about the person and there were players from Rangers that he would have a genuine liking for because he found them to be so pleasant or they gave him a good tip. Don't get me wrong, he never wanted Rangers to win but he retained a personal liking for certain players, some that spring to mind were Jim Baxter, Sandy Jardine and Colin Jackson – he would never say a bad word about any of them.

My da was the most fair minded guy I ever knew and I think on balance if he hadn't been a Catholic he would still have been a Celtic supporter. Why? Because he was Celtic minded. My da was a great man for social justice and equality, he was always open to new cultures – he welcomed immigrants into Glasgow and celebrated their culture. He loved a curry so I think he could see the benefits. Seriously though, he was a great supporter of the missions and he donated every month of his life in the hope that his contribution was helping to make a better life for someone less fortunate. He never once displayed any sense of entitlement, he worked hard and he was grateful for any good fortune that came his way. He was a man for the people, a working man albeit he wasn't overly political. He was a simple guy that lived for his family, his faith and his football. I know that phrase has been used before but I can't think of any other that would fit my da. That was his life and I'd like to think those values have been passed on from him to me.

Looking back, for families like ours when it came to following a football team I pointed out we were a Catholic family from the north east of the city so geographically Celtic were our local team. The other major club in the city had put the shutters up for families like us, we were not welcome and this didn't fit with our values as a family – we were inclusive not exclusive, we were open not closed, so in that sense Celtic were the perfect fit both in terms of location and values.

As I got older I started attending matches at Celtic with my dad. This would have begun around 1971 so some of the memories are sketchy but I recall my first European match against Ujpest Dozsa when Lou Macari scored. There were other matches during that season but none so remarkable that I could pick out any key moments. Saturday was a busy day for my dad so games were dotted around occasional Saturdays and midweeks. The big game from that 1971/72 season was the Scottish Cup Final. By that point I'd got a taste for it so the match against Hibs was in my sights. Naturally he couldn't commit, the priority was always putting food on the table and paying the bills so work came first then if possible we'd go to the football – it was all about priorities though. Thankfully on the day he arrived home after his morning shift he had Main Stand tickets for the Cup Final and we made our way to Hampden. I don't recall much about the journey. Our neighbours the McAlpines were big Celtic fans and I've a feeling we went with Jimmy next door in his Vauxhall Ventora, blue with a black vinyl roof, a class car. Having arrived at Hampden we made our way to our seats, bang on the halfway line and what felt like touching distance of the Cup. Billy McNeill put Celtic in front with Alan Gordon equalising for Hibs, before Dixie went on the rampage, scoring one of the all-time great Cup Final goals, while Lou Macari grabbed the other two.

From then on that was me, I wanted to go every week. I knew it wasn't going to be possible but in the coming years I made it to hundreds of matches either with Gerard and I getting the old Football Special trains, or with my cousin who by that point had a car. I especially loved away games – there was always something a bit extra about going to Morton, St. Mirren, Hibs, Hearts or Motherwell by train. Looking back I've no idea where we got the money from but one way or another we just found ourselves at the match. Our favourite games would be in Edinburgh purely for the fact that you got salt n' sauce on your chips. Gerard and I loved salt n' sauce. In fact the chip shop that we used when we went to Tynecastle is still there.

Going to Celtic just became a way of life as I got older. There were times when we couldn't get to the match and we would go to see St. Roch's, who were always our second team. I even recall a period when I went to matches at Shawfield to watch

Clyde. This came about after a particularly unpleasant experience where my fiend Mark Wright and I fell victim to some bad lads in Barrowfield. That ended with a trip to Glasgow Royal Infirmary but it was part of growing up in Glasgow. Everyone took a beating at some point but mine had wider consequences. I was banned from going to Celtic on my own for a while so went to Clyde with Gary and John McGuire for a few months But my heart was with Celtic and we used to take a radio so we could follow the Celtic score.

Naturally as you get older you develop other interests – in my case music was a big thing but the football was never far away. I attended St. Pat's secondary in Coatbridge and this opened up a whole new social scene for me. There were plenty of boys who were equally immersed in Celtic – I actually still see some of them at matches to this day. The Whelans from Moodiesburn have always been steeped in Celtic and I occasionally see Jim and Gerard at games. St. Pat's though, brought me into contact with boys from places like Glenboig, Moodiesburn, Chapelhall, Calderbank and Coatbridge and lots of these boys were as hooked on Celtic as me. I can recall we used to try to outdo each other with what games we were at, what kits we had and even who had the most badges. School was more about being the biggest Celtic fan than actually learning. Well it was for me.

In 1980 I trumped everyone, Celtic were drawn to play Real Madrid in the European Cup and my dad decided we were going, not only to Celtic Park but also to Madrid. Europe away was a first and I have to say the boys in school, whilst obviously wishing it was them, were all great about the fact that one of their mates was going to an away game in Europe. I understand that travel is much easier these days but back then this was quite a big deal. Many of the boys gave me scarves or some other Celtic item to take for them just so they could say it was in Madrid. I recently found a photo of myself at the match and I was completely bedecked in green, white and gold. I even had a flag that had been in Lisbon given to me by my old neighbour and friend, Willie O'Malley. I look completely ridiculous but at the time I felt ten feet tall. We went to Madrid on the Provan CSC bus which left from the old Provanmill Inn.

We travelled by bus to London and flew from London to Madrid. I can recall that on the day of the match, March 19th, it was St. Joseph's feast day and of course my da had to get to Mass which meant I had to get to Mass. I was like, surely not da, we can give it a miss. But no way – it was Mass for us – that was just him. As soon as he landed in a foreign country his first mission was to find the chapel and get Mass times. I wonder how many families still do that? Ultimately we failed to go through in Madrid losing 3-0 after a 2-0 first leg victory, but the trip opened my eyes to a bigger picture – Celtic in Europe – that was taking it to another level. I met some weird and wonderful characters on that trip some of whom I still see but the whole experience just strengthened my bond with Celtic and my da.

As it turned out it would be a few more years before I was able to follow Celtic in Europe. In the meantime it was a case of the domestic scene and getting to as many matches as I could. We travelled the country following the team home and away. The team's fortunes fluctuated as we witnessed the emergence of Aberdeen and Dundee United as real challengers.

Around this time my sister was going out with a local boy who was really good at football, he was also a non-Catholic and his brother played for Rangers. How would this all turn out? Of course there was never an issue. As I highlighted earlier my Dad just wasn't like that, all he was interested in was the fact that Ann Marie was with someone who would look after her. The religious aspect was never in question and nor was it for Graeme Sharp. As it turned out they were married and Graeme went on to have a wonderful career at Everton and ultimately my da started following him and his career more closely. I think he thought he played for them himself at times the way he spoke about the first team players, calling them all by their nicknames – it was funny but he loved it. Again the key point was the fact that both he and my mum welcomed Graeme and his family into our family. It made no difference to us that they were from a different faith or background. All that mattered was that he was a good person. We did of course set about trying to convert him into a Celtic fan, with some success, as my nephew Christopher is Celtic, his first Glasgow derby being the 6-2 match.

So when looking back at the early stages of my life it was punctuated by great Celtic occasions – the Cup Final in '72 followed by victories against Airdrie and Dundee United. Ten men winning the league in '79 and Madrid in 1980, the centenary year in 1988, all great times which in hindsight, helped form an unbreakable bond between me and my da. Football was every-thing to us – Celtic naturally – but we also had the added interest in Everton through the family connection. The added bonus on that front was the fact that even Everton ticked the boxes for us in terms of their status as underdogs and a long way from being the establishment club on Merseyside.

As time moved on I became settled in my job as a betting shop manager with Ladbrokes, a job I loved although it hindered my weekend opportunities to get to football. It allowed me to meet a variety of Glasgow characters and establish friendships with many great people. All of the men were football mad – the betting on football in Glasgow at that time was more than the rest of the UK combined. In Glasgow everyone was an expert when it came to football. What struck me was that the men who shared the same values as me were Celtic fans, men with the same political beliefs, men with social justice at heart. Now that's not to say that fans of other clubs didn't share these values, saying all Celtic fans were saints – I just found that those who I struck a real kinship with were men like my da and for me there was a difference. Whether it was just a perception or otherwise I'm not sure, but I sensed it and if I'm honest I liked it. I liked the fact that we were different, that we were minority, I liked the fact we were successful against the odds, I liked the fact that I identified with these men and our values were reflected and shared in those of our fellow fans. We were Celtic for a reason.

In 1993 I got a phone call that would change everything. It was a chance to go to Celtic Park to speak to someone about the possibility of a job at the club. I can't explain how excited I was and to be honest gave a pretty poor interview but thankfully my future boss, Mary, asked me to come back the following week when I did much better. I was successful and on October 3rd, 1993 I started work at Celtic FC. As I say it changed everything.

When I joined Celtic as Ticket Office Manager we had 7300

season ticket holders, most of whom were for the terracing. The stadium wasn't in great shape and we were struggling on the park. We hadn't won a trophy since 1989 when Joe Miller scored against Rangers. Liam Brady was in the last throes of his term as manager and I guess from a fans' perspective things looked a bit bleak. For me, however, this was a dream come true. In those days there was still quite a bit of interaction with the first team and backroom staff. The guys were all very friendly and essentially just like work colleagues who would often come into the office to get a catch up and of course use the phones. Old Steely was still about and he used to create havoc when he came in. He always had a story and had us all in stitches with his tales of the old days either with Celtic or Scotland. Neil Mochan was still at the club and was another who had a million stories. Neilly had a really dry sense of humour and was a great character. To get the chance to spend time with these men was wonderful.

My job also brought me into contact with Celtic supporters from far and near, many of whom I still see. It's been an interesting time watching the old guard slip away to be replaced by the young fans, old gentlemen switching places with the Celtic jersey-wearing young team who have now been moved on by the new breed of fans with an Ultra style – no colours – flag waving raised on a diet of titles and trebles. I wonder what will come next.

In the subsequent years I saw and worked through some crazy times. I was on site on the day of the famous takeover when Fergus swept to power, I walked into stationery cupboards that day to witness share deals taking place. Everywhere you went there was someone in a room or an office or a cupboard with their lawyer. That was a crazy day. When it was all over the future of our club had been secured and that was all that mattered.

Working for Fergus was an amazing experience. He was a visionary with the heart of a lion. He was scared of no one, and he wasn't afraid to take on any challenge if he believed he was right. Sure he could be abrasive, but there were sharks all around and he needed to be single-minded to achieve all he set out to do.

Under Fergus we saw a few managers. Lou Macari came and went and Tommy Burns replaced him. What a wonderful guy Tommy was. There has been so much said and written about Tommy there's nothing I could add other than to say he was a thoroughly decent man who had time for everyone. He deserved so much more during his time as manager.

Over the years I worked under Kevin Kelly, Fergus McCann, Allan MacDonald, Iain McLeod, Eric Riley and Peter Lawwell. I've seen Liam Brady, Frank Connor, Lou Macari, Tommy Burns, Wim Jansen, Dr Jo Venglos, John Barnes, Kenny Dalglish, Martin O'Neill, Gordon Strachan, Neil Lennon, Ronny Deila, Brendan Rodgers all come and go as managers (and the very odd one comes back again of course). You might have noted that I omitted Tony Mowbray as I wasn't here during that time. In 2008 I took the decision to look for something different, I was exhausted after fifteen years at the ticket office. The business had moved at breakneck speed since Fergus arrived. I'd been involved in title-winning days, cup finals, Glasgow derbies, last day league winners, last day league losses, cup final defeats, a UEFA Cup Final and umpteen marketing campaigns for season ticket sales. I was part of the team that made the switch to Hampden and back again whilst we set about rebuilding Celtic Park piece by piece. In the end I just needed something different. I was burst.

I spent five years working in retail finance in Edinburgh but my heart never left Celtic. I still attended every game home and away and I have to say those years were among the most enjoyable I can remember as I had no pressure. I could go as a fan with no responsibility. I loved that. In 2013 I was given the chance to come back to the club in a Supporter Liaison role. I have to be honest and say I didn't give it a second thought. I had never really left Celtic Park and I'm delighted to be part of everything that's happening at the club right now, we have a great team, a wonderful manager and an executive team who have done a remarkable job to put us in the position we are right now.

Things have gone full circle since I first started going to Celtic Park with my da. We are now the dominant force, we are the Champions but most importantly our values remain through the Foundation and the great work of Tony Hamilton and his team. We are a force for good and do more now for charities and good causes than we have ever done. For many that is the most important thing because that's what keeps us different. Our values and our beliefs and as long as we stay true to those we will always be Celtic, a Club Like No Other.

Faith in Football

Canon Tom White

The invitation on August 15th to contribute to Celtic Minded 4 was warmly appreciated and accepted. Then, panic struck: what should I write? With this very question lies both my motivation and the obvious agenda that I wish to pursue: I am keen that the spiritual, cultural and historical origins of Celtic Football Club are not consigned to the past, nor seen as out of step with modern 'inclusive' Scotland.

For some the date mentioned above will have significance as on the 15th August the Catholic Church throughout the world celebrates the Solemnity of the Assumption, when Our Lady, Mary the Mother of God, was assumed into heaven to the rejoicing and praising of Angels, as states the inscription just above the High Altar of St. Mary's, Calton, the birthplace of Celtic FC.

St. Mary's is dedicated to the Assumption and the 15th of August is not only the parish feast day, but also the anniversary of the church's opening and dedication. 2017 was St. Mary's 175th Anniversary, and, after the Cathedral, St. Mary's can boast of being the second oldest and continuously used church in the Archdiocese of Glasgow: the main area for modern Catholicism in Scotland. This was a milestone for our parish and I was most grateful to Archbishop Conti for celebrating our Jubilee Mass that evening. It was only fitting that he did so because during his time as Archbishop he elevated St. Mary's to the status of Pro-Cathedral at the same time as the renovations at St. Andrew's.

I recall the morning of the anniversary quite poignantly. I was in a particularly reflective mood as I considered our parish and its history. I sat in our magnificent church and contemplated Father Forbes, the Banffshire man who toured Ireland and raised the money to found the parish and build the Church. His body along with Bishops Andrew Scott and John Murdoch are in the parish crypt, along with 14 young priests, mostly young Irishmen who lost their lives while tending to the diseased sick of Glasgow, most themselves being Irish immigrants.

My prayers were not only for them but looking at the Stations of the Cross in the Church, which were brought by Canon Fitzgerald from Paris, all my predecessors were in my prayers. The parish records show that Canon Fitzgerald stayed with his friend Father Vianney whilst in Paris. The very same friend was beatified in 1905 by Pius X, and twenty years later canonized by Pius XI. St. John Vianney is the patron saint of Parish Priests and it is therefore of no surprise that as I prayed for those in my care at St. Mary's, I turned to St. John Vianney to give me all that I need to be a good shepherd after the image of these great and good men whose legacy I have inherited.

I have now been in St. Mary's for fifteen years and I think this gives me quite a unique insight into a certain club whose fans laud the need to 'know your history'. Part of the legacy of St. Mary's is the work undertaken by the then relatively new arrival at the parish, Brother Walfrid, the deputy headmaster of St. Mary's Primary School, and other founding fathers of Celtic Football Club. It is a legacy and link that I defend and celebrate more profoundly as my tenure in the Calton runs its course.

There is the strong and often compelling narrative that faith and football/sport should never mix, and I certainly am aware of those strong arguments. That said, such arguments are not by any stretch of the imagination universal truths. Indeed, I would say that to hold such a position is almost as absurd as saying that Catholic schools cause division! Why does the faith foundation of Everton, Southampton or Manchester City and other clubs around the globe cause no issue, just as Catholic schools abroad in every corner of the earth aren't problematic? To hold such a view and not reflect on why it is almost a uniquely

Scottish phenomenon, compounded with a failure to challenge some dominant aspects of Scottish culture and national psyche, will serve only a short while. Maybe until the scapegoat of Catholic schools or indeed a culturally Irish and Catholic Football Club dies and society goes on to pursue yet another scapegoat.

At this point I must admit that during my first five years at St. Mary's I was indifferent to the 'Celtic' dynamic of our parish's history. Relations with the club were not dead, just indifferent. There was always the understanding that perhaps if there was an hour of need the club may help. We had the odd parish fundraiser at the Kerrydale Suite, but I am not sure we received 'family and friends rates' either! It was at these fundraisers that the parish's most famous and arguably most treasured son, Tommy Burns, would want to support us with his presence and his legendary singing of Mack the Knife! Everyone with a depth of following of Celtic will know of Tommy's heroic but ultimately failed battle against cancer. It was through this tragic loss for his family and club that something was awoken in me.

I had often seen Tommy at weekday mass in St. Mary's but I, like many of the parishioners much to their credit, would say no more than 'hello Tommy', and leave him in peace to get on with his prayers. Now Tommy was dead, and was making one last journey to his spiritual home of St. Mary's. The vast crowd which gathered outside for the Requiem Mass eventually closed Abercromby Street as the Celtic Family gathered to mourn and pray for one of their own. With St. Mary's packed to capacity (circa 1600), treble the number outside, and yet more at the stadium, it became obvious that Glasgow was burying one of its giants. Not since the funeral of the late Cardinal Winning had the Catholic Church witnessed the faithful gather in such numbers for a funeral. Just like the crowd outside St. Andrew's Cathedral on the morning of Cardinal Winning's funeral, those who gathered outside St. Mary's gathered with sincerity of heart and clarity of purpose: they were here to pray for the repose of Tommy's soul and the comforting of his dear wife Rosemary and their family.

From that day on I was aware more than ever that the Catholic identity of Celtic was not simply a thing of the past, but was something alive and active. No other football club in Britain could, along with huge numbers of its support, come together and actively and genuinely be part of, participate in, and share in the celebration of Mass for one of their own: this was a clear demonstration of Celtic's uniqueness – at the very least, in Scottish and British football society.

My spirits were lifted when I saw 'the faith' was still an intrinsic part of this football club. Previously I'd had various discussions with some officials at Celtic over the years who seemed keen to support a narrative that the Irish and Catholic identity of Celtic and its support is a thing of the past, or certainly not a defining characteristic. They would often pose the rather sometimes simplistic question, 'how many go to Mass?' To this question I am happy to counter with my own question, 'where do they go in time of trouble or need?' These kinds of Catholics I have heard being referred to by a colleague as 'Taxi Catholics', as the practice of their faith seems little more than arriving in a limo for their first communion and then their wedding, and a hearse and limo at their Requiem. As saddening, imperfect and shallow as this may be, it certainly demonstrates that they still identify in some way with their Catholic faith at some of the most important points in their life: and I like to think the title 'Catholic' sticks as much to anyone as the more negative titles that are given to others in society. Baptism quite simply cannot be undone. Fact!

For those of us that do live our faith as the centre of our lives, Catholicism/Christianity might be considered in many ways a 'missed opportunity' with regards those people who seem to 'give it up' and become secular in their lifestyles: their lives taken up, trapped sometimes even, by things that will pass, often at the expense of things that really matter. In other words, the old battle between good and evil in the eyes of many with faith.

In addition, as the editor of Celtic Minded points out elsewhere, in his capacity as academic researcher who has carried out work in the area of the socio-cultural and religious lives of Celtic and other football supporters, he has found that there is in all likelihood more Celtic supporters attending weekly Mass than any comparable group of Catholics (around 90% of Celtic supporters consider themselves Catholic) in Scotland. This is even if we take it by Scottish towns, cities, schools, even Catholic parishes themselves.

So another way to see the Church attending Catholic-Celtic connection is as follows; we should remember that all Celtic supporters are not Catholic, and, with respect to those that are, in Scotland (varyingly as with numerous other countries) all Catholic Celtic supporters do not attend Mass. However, and this is critical to understanding Celtic fans in a wider context, Dr Bradley's research shows that a significant number of Catholic Celtic supporters do attend Mass regularly. Indeed, amongst all groups of football supporters in Scotland, club and national, Celtic supporters stand out a proverbial mile for being a group where Church attendance (as well as being Catholic and Christian) remains important and significant.

Give or take a few percentages here and there, around a quarter of Catholics in Scotland attend Mass every week or more. Around a quarter go from time to time. Around 50% don't have much contact with the Church except through marriage, funerals and other sacraments occasionally (and undoubtedly some think supporting Celtic is a Catholic connection). Many of these nonetheless have attended Catholic schools, have some rudimentary understandings of Jesus Christ and more. Many see a great deal of the issues in the world – poverty, abortion, migration, war, etc, through Catholic or partially Catholic eyes. Even some post-Catholics, atheists that were previously Catholics, can retain elements of what they see as values, morals and rights with respect to Catholicism/Christianity. Some Catholics are also of course deeply anti-Catholic, including a very small number of sometimes vitriolic and vociferous Celtic supporters. Interesting though such discussions can be, especially in light of Catholic community debates around a perceived declining faith in Scotland, I'll leave more of such observations and notions to the sociologists that explore these matters more fully.

Whilst the previously referred to funeral rites of Tommy Burns awoke in me an awareness of a facet of the support that was still very much alive, at the time I made no real move to build on it, not because of any indifference, but simply the pressures of everyday life and ministry push such initiatives to the back of the queue. As important as Tommy's funeral was, the next week brought another few funerals with other families equally hurt and devastated.

Strikingly, there have been other occasions when those associated with Celtic and the Irish community have sought welcome and support at St. Mary's: when fans in recent years were illegally and unjustly 'kettled' by Police on the Gallowgate, St. Mary's provided refuge and a safe space for witness statements and depositions to be recorded. The Celtic Trust meet regularly here. The An Gorta Mor committee meet here and indeed have chosen St. Mary's as the site for a Glasgow Irish community memorial to the Great Irish Hunger – which of course gave rise to re-emergence of Catholicism in this city and beyond, as well too, of course, to Celtic FC.

Five years passed after the funeral of Tommy Burns when, through the initiative of the Celtic Graves Society, and the green light from the Club, plans were afoot to celebrate a Mass in St. Mary's for the club's 125th Anniversary. Archbishop Tartaglia was invited to say the Mass, but literally having just assumed the presidency of the Bishops' Conference he was unable to be present. The lot fell to me to celebrate Mass, which turned out to be a packed to capacity. The scene was set by fantastic speakers before the Mass and the fans present were equally at home singing hymns of praise as they were singing football songs in the stadium. I remember it being a really prayerful, solemn and uplifting celebration. There was a tremendous feeling that it was right and good for us to be there!

The very next night I was invited as a guest of the club to witness the Bhoys rise up and defeat Barcelona. The icing on the cake! I remember feeling slightly sorry for the deflated Barcelona club officials after the match. They had attended Mass in Saint Mary's the previous night as our guests, and now it took all my might and discipline not to approach them and say 'Obviamente, Dios no habla espanol.' (Obviously, God doesn't speak Spanish!!} Since the 125th celebration Mass we have had a Mass every 6th November to commemorate the founding of Celtic by Brother Walfrid and others.

As well as being parish priest of St. Mary's, and more recently also St. Alphonsus', another job I love is my work with St. Margaret's Adoption Society. In this line of work the importance of knowing your family history and your origins cannot be treasured enough. In fact, the harm and devastation caused when people do not know their origins is almost immeasurable, and I would argue that the same is true for those who want to keep Celtic true to its roots. The Celtic way must always necessarily have a faith component, not a nebulous concept of faith, but a Catholic one. It is not by accident that Catholic comes from the Greek words 'Kata' and 'holos', colloquially translated as meaning universal, all welcoming, pertaining to the whole.

Celtic needs to be proud of not only its Catholic origins, but its Catholic identity, which needless to say, can also go hand in hand with its Irish cultural core. The last great prejudice in Scottish society is that of anti-Catholic hostility. We must make sure that we do not give in to the narrative that faith and football is a bad mix, as to do so robs us of our origins, our history, our nature, perspectives and values. Brother Walfrid and other founding fathers would mean nothing if this was allowed to happen. We were outsiders! And having awoken one Saturday morning in the Calton to see my car spray-painted with the words 'PROVOS GO HOME', I often think we still are!

Like many refugees in the modern world, we were hungry! And just as in Matthew chapter 25, 'When were you hungry, naked sick or in prison?' Walfrid and his compatriots saw the hungry and did something about it. He founded a great football club for feeding the poor and building community. For us who laud and walk the Celtic way we have been entrusted with a rich and valuable legacy.

It was in May 2017 that St. Mary's welcomed again the Celtic family. This time Archbishop Tartaglia led the Mass, to give thanks and to commemorate other giants of Celtic Football Club, 'the Lisbon Lions'. It's no secret the Archbishop is a die-hard Celtic fan, and he spoke with passion and warmth about his memories of Lisbon. In fact he was so enthused and animated that most of the congregation could have listened to him for an hour – an achievement for the Archbishop that is almost as rare as the European Victory itself!! Whilst the Stadium had echoed all season with '67, in the heat of Lisbon', it was time for a different kind of song. In the context of faith we gave thanks to God for His blessings, we prayed that the Lions who had passed on were at peace, and those Lions who were too infirm to be with us, found comfort and knew of our love and solidarity.

I reflect on the journey that I personally have made since arriving at St. Mary's. I think of the days leading up to Tommy Burns's funeral. The urbanely calm and pleasant man I met during that period, Peter Lawwell. The no nonsense straight talking, down to tacks, media man, I also met Tony Hamilton (now CEO Celtic Foundation). At this point these men were strangers, now today I call them friends. The same can be said of others that I have come to know that are associated with the club, the Foundation, the Celtic Graves Society, the Celtic Trust, and so the list goes on. Partly as a result of the dominant histories and cultures of the country we live in, and partly as a result of a secularizing, materialistic and rationalist 'West', I think there was a certain unease on all our parts to challenge the standard faith and football myth. We are now the better and richer for beginning to critically unravel it. I have enjoyed many engagements with the club, in matters football, charitable and spiritual, and I hope it is an alliance that goes from strength to strength.

The challenge ahead for me – and dare I say for us, the Celtic support, Celtic Football Club, the Celtic Foundation, and others – is that there are still poor children and families in the Calton and beyond, both materially poor, and alarmingly more than ever, spiritually poor. The St. Mary's Hall in which Celtic was founded has gone, the scores of priests and religious people who served the community have gone. As the last man standing I simply ask: what are we going to do about it? Walfrid's way, and therefore the Celtic way, is always one of action. Hail, Hail and (literally) KTF – Keep the Faith!

Born to be Celtic Minded

BRENDAN MCCARRON

So that everyone knows where I am coming from, I am a Socialist, Republican, Labour-voting, pro-European, pro-Scottish independence, son of Coatbridge, born in Scotland to parents from an Irish-Catholic background, who now lives in North East England. I don't believe in God, or Heaven or Hell, but I still mostly attend church on a Sunday as an hour of moral teaching from a source other than my own as it's always helpful and useful for my children to have some formal religious teaching which they can accept or reject in later life. I have had a lovely life and have been lucky in my family (my own and in-laws), country and cultural influences, and educational upbringing, which have moulded my views and outlook on life, which is generally (even pathologically) positive. My views have been long-held, some more than others, but most have been fairly stable throughout my fifty-seven years. Many of my beliefs have followed me from my childhood and teenage years, so perhaps this is a good place to start.

My father was born and grew up in Tyrone, Ireland, and my mother hailed from Coatbridge: her mother was born in Ireland and her paternal grandparents were also from Ireland. In modern terminology, my father was an economic refugee when he came to live in Coatbridge. His history resonates with Celtic and their Founding Fathers, who began the Club for people like him. In Coatbridge, he met and married my mother and had seven children, of which I was the sixth and the fifth son.

My early claim to fame was that I weighed in at twelve and

a half pounds at delivery, in the parental home on Christmas Eve, 1961. Despite being a hefty baby my mother claimed that she 'never made a sound during the birth, but said her rosary throughout' the delivery, and although it was a well-travelled pathway by the time of the sixth child, it was still quite a feat. However, my then fourteen year old brother Charles recollects banshee sounding howls and wails pervading his bedroom from downstairs during the birthing, which traumatised him for many years. I suspect my mother never lied, but her recollections from the past may not be completely accurate, as may be the case in recollections from my youth: but what is written here is as true as I can remember.

I had a joyous childhood which had large doses of fun, games, sports, religion and politics, of which politics became the major factor in the formation of my adult views. As a family we went to Sunday mass, my mother was in the Union of Catholic Mothers and my father was a member of the Society of St. Vincent de Paul. My mother, Margaret, was quite remarkable and although her culinary skills were not the greatest, she had a keen intellect, was a voracious reader and had strong views on justice, kindness and being fair-minded. She left school at the age of fourteen, worked in munitions factories during World War II, subsequently got married and raised seven children. When her last daughter, Helen, went to school, my mother was forty-seven and she re-started formal education at Night School gaining qualifications then called 'O' Grades and Highers, going on to work in the Civil Service.

My father Jimmy, was my hero! He was a hardworking man and for most of my childhood, worked nightshift in the Caterpillar Tractor Company and then during the day he helped support local people who had fallen on hard times and always in a non-judgmental way. He had all the time in the world for the living and didn't over indulge in commemorating the dead. He was not an obviously schooled man and was not highly politically driven, but was a committed Trade Unionist.

This was the house in which I grew up. It was a house full of fun and music ranging from Ray Charles through the years to ELO with the obligatory collection of Irish songs thrown in. I had large collection of traditional Irish music (particularly the Chieftains), Wolfe Tones, Christy Moore of course, and Teresa Duffy singing 'Songs of Ireland'. Perhaps unusually, my oldest brother Joseph had an LP of 'Songs of the Orange Hall'. It was an open house with everyone welcome, with no issues with creed, colour or beliefs, although in Coatbridge at that time it was very much a white working class area and distinctions and divisions were based on supporting Celtic or Rangers and which school attended: such things generally indicated ethnic and religious backgrounds and identities. Of which of course there is no harm, unless one wishes to use such information to harm: to be prejudicial and discriminatory against others?

Our family support Celtic and all the boys have been regular Parkhead attenders at some time in their lives. The first match I can remember was against Motherwell as a seven year old, and although I have no memories of the 1967 Lisbon final, I have strong memories of the 1970 European run and being tearful at the loss to Feyenoord in the final. God let me down in 1970, despite having a May Altar on my bedroom table, where I prayed every night for success. He wasn't listening or He liked Rotterdam boys' prayers better than mine. I was however at Seville in 2003. Boy, was that an experience! I went with my father-in-law, Frank, and we left Glasgow airport the day prior to the match. We were lucky! We flew and avoided the Herculean exploits of those travelling overland. In Seville I met so many people who I had not seen for many years; Paul Kennedy a primary school friend, Joe Clark a former patient and now friend, JJ Gilmour an old Coatbridge pal. I got my ticket from Joe McLaughlin who charged me under the face value for his spare ticket! This is what the Celtic fans I know do, they don't rip each other off. That feeling of sharing and not cheating fellow fans is precious.

I remember a cup final at Hamden in the late 1980s/early 1990s: a Cockney sounding ticket pundit was selling tickets at many times the face value. A number of Celtic fans surrounded him, took the tickets off him and gave him face value for the ten or so tickets he had and proceeded to sell them to fellow fans at face value. I have never seen such a ticket tout at Hampden since. My good friend Neil Patterson, a Celtic/Liverpool supporting Liverpudlian, bought his ticket from a Liverpool fan who purchased his ticket months earlier, so sure that Liverpool FC would be in the Seville final, before Celtic knocked them out. Neil paid hundreds of pounds for a ticket with the face value of thirty euros. On that day in May 2003, Seville was green and white, the Cathedral was dressed in a giant Celtic flag and the fans and locals were friends. I never saw an intoxicated person that day, as everyone was keeping their 'powder dry'. I arrived in the stadium about 6pm, almost 3 hours before the match was due to begin. A tannoy practice announcement was made wishing the crowd (before the crowd had arrived) welcome to the Europa Cup Final between Glasgow Celtic and Porto FC. I am not sure why, if it was the heat, the excitement or I was at something I never thought I would witness, but I started to cry with pride. Thirty minutes before the game was due to start, I made my last toilet visit before kick-off and on the concourse I met a dear old friend, James McDonald. We said hello and I said 'it was very emotional to be there' and within seconds we were both in tears. The match had not even started!

The football match was a roller coaster of emotions, was a fantastic occasion and although Celtic lost, I was left with great pride in my team and the beginning of an on-going dislike of then Porto coach Jose Mourinho, who plays football in a way football should not be played. That night when we returned to the hotel and most went to the bar; I went to bed and had one of the best sleeps of my life, tired, exhausted and content.

That is football and that is Celtic; dreams, hope and ambitions are tied up with the players on the park in whom you have an emotional investment. One is steeped in the history and legends of Charlie Tully, The Mighty Quinn, Jimmy McGrory, Patsy Gallagher, Jimmy Johnstone, and on that night in Seville, Henrik Larsson. Celtic lost to Porto, but I was very proud. To cap it all, Celtic supporters were awarded the Fair Play award by UEFA and FIFA, the first time it had been awarded to a club's fanbase.

I have fond memories of being a child of the 1960/70s and of 'tick' men visiting the house at the weekend collecting their dues from a number of 'penny policies' for life insurance from the Pearl, the Cooperative, the Rent and the Provident. The visiting adults provided stories and tales from their own pasts and joined in on our board games on many a wet Saturday afternoon to add to the recipe for a boy growing up in west central Scotland. I also loved and was influenced by the Saturday afternoon matinee on BBC2 at 3pm. The films (now called movies in the 21st century) on show were the great American movies of the thirties, forties and fifties and although I wished I was suave and sophisticated like Cary Grant, I felt more like James Stewart whose characters were flawed, but who tried to do the right thing and fight against injustice, cruelty and dishonesty. Then afterwards, the tele-printer would spring into action as I awaited the scores, hoping and usually getting a Celtic win.

One of the heroes of the McCarron house during the 1960s was Mr Breen, headmaster of St. Patrick's High School, where two of my brothers attended.'I never met Mr Breen, but stories of him'were legendary. He had ambitions that working class Catholic pupils attending his school would break the chains of discrimination and progress to university: both my brothers did. One story I recall hearing was that for many years banks in Coatbridge (and elsewhere) did not employ Catholics. Mr Breen wrote to all local bank managers to inform them that unless one of his pupils was employed by the bank in the following weeks, he would write to all parents with pupils in his school and advise that they withdraw their savings from those banks. Needless to say, the banks duly obliged with threat of this financial misfortune hanging over them. This occurred around the time of the assassination of the great Martin Luther King in the USA. On the day that the banks in Coatbridge (Airdrie Savings Bank, Clydesdale, Bank of Scotland and Royal Bank of Scotland) gave way and relented to Mr Breen's threat (in a town where the majority of people were Catholics of Irish descent) the pupils at St. Patricks were given a half day off school to celebrate the advancement of their human rights. My parents thought of him as their champion in promoting their rights as Catholics and challenging the established discriminatory and prejudicial status quo. Mr Breen reminds me of former Celtic Chairman John Reid saying 'there will be no more sitting at the back of the bus': that was only ten years or so ago. John Reid is also a former St. Patrick's School pupil from the time of Mr Breen.

The taking on of the footballing establishment in the era of

Neil Lennon as Celtic manager was welcomed by many, being driven by Reid and Celtic Lawyer Paul McBride, after an earlier 'victory' by Fergus McCann forcing the resignation of SFA Chairman Jim Farry for gross misconduct in delaying the registration of Jorge Cadette before a Scottish Cup semi-final against Rangers. Sadly, Farry walked away with a £200,000 pay-off for his misconduct and Celtic lost that semi-final. McBride did blot his copy book by joining the Scottish Conservatives, but redeemed himself by subsequently resigning and declaring them 'a bunch of unreconstructed morons'. I and many others were saddened by his premature death of a myocardial infarction in a hotel in Pakistan. One of our Celtic champions had gone.

I attended Columba High School in Coatbridge, which was influential in the formation of my values. Everybody I knew voted Labour although one family was suspected of voting Conservative, as they bought the Daily Express when everyone else bought the Daily Record (happily a paper I no longer purchase). I loved school, education and learning. Although I played in the school football team, I was never a great footballer resulting in ongoing ribbing by my brothers, but I did support Celtic, which gave me some kudos. Subsequent to school I went onto Glasgow University in 1980 to study medicine and qualified in 1985. University was probably the biggest influence in my life and supplied me with confidence as well as an excellent education: what a shame many other working class children, especially several generations of Scots-born Irish Catholics were not allowed such an opportunity. I fear the introduction of tuition fees will again prevent clever working class youths fulfilling their educational potential in the austerity driven early twenty-first century.

Overall my childhood was charmed and being one of the baby boomer generation I managed to get 'free' (not really free of course as they had been paid for by my parents' taxes) education at school and university and in the early 1980s a university grant. Bigotry and bias was never a large part of my pre-university upbringing, although I was aware of the Broons going to the Masonic Hall to see a 'braw' comedian in the DC Thomson's Christmas annual and The Corries singing 'Derry's Walls' on Scottish Television and passing it off as a folk song, which seemed a bit odd at the time. University was a cultural joy mixing with fellow students from all round the world and for the first time meeting people who openly declared they and their family voted Conservative!

The 1980s were a divisive time with Prime Minister Thatcher expressing contradictory views to mine on so many issues including the miners' strike, apartheid, Pol Pot and the killing fields of Cambodia, the football stadia murders in Chile and the hunger strikers in Ireland. Many supported the views of Thatcher and were critical of the Catholic Church for allowing the hunger strikers burial on 'sacred ground' and there was a general anti-Irish and Catholic feeling prevalent at the time in Scotland and across Britain generally. In Scotland, William Wolfe, leader of the SNP was a prominent figure in objecting to the Papal visit to Scotland in the early 1980s and also described Argentina as a priest-ridden country, a legacy that the SNP (particularly Alex Salmond who worked hard – in partnership with a certain Cardinal O'Brien – at attracting Catholic and Asian voters to his party) has taken years to shake off, though not yet completely.

The General Assembly of the Church of Scotland, often referred to the closest thing to a Scottish Parliament pre-devolution, was broadcast nightly on BBC1 during Assembly week into my living room. The Assembly often passed anti-Catholic motions and until 1986 voted in favour of the Westminster Confession, part of which declared the Pope as the anti-Christ. Some of the anti-Catholic sentiment I was exposed to was almost witty such as on Ash Wednesday when a number of dental students came to the lecture theatre with transfers of the Union flag on their forehead, rather than symbolic ashes, with t-shirts declaring that it was Sash Wednesday. There was also a debate at Glasgow University Union in the early 1980s, titled 'I'd rather be a Darkie than a Tim', which was and is so offensive on so many levels against so many people, yet was looked upon as being fair play by the Glasgow University Debating Club in the 1980s.

I was vocal and political and soon realised I was out of populist step on many of these issues. Unfortunately Celtic fans failed to come out of this period with their heads held high, as this was the time that Mark Walters became one of Rangers first ever black footballers and football was shamed by Celtic racists throwing bananas on his first visit to Parkhead. Gladly, the majority of Celtic fans reacted against this experience and in an era when such things characterised football clubs, Celtic supporters' moral code, symbolised by their anti-racist and anti-fascist credentials, shone through very quickly in the wake of this incident and have continued to do so ever since. On the political issues of the day I had an opinion but was frequently told by my colleagues that I would change my views once I started earning more money and joined the establishment, but I told them I wouldn't: I am pleased to say, I feel I haven't.

I qualified from university as a medical doctor in 1985 but almost missed my graduation when I was stopped by the police from crossing the road to get the Coatbridge to Glasgow bus – they wouldn't let me pass through an Orange Walk taking place during July. I had to stand and wait until the bigots passed, before being allowed to cross a public highway.

Most of my fellow graduates applied for junior doctor jobs in the local Glasgow hospitals, but I was advised by my colleagues not to bother applying for posts in the Victoria Infirmary as they didn't employ 'Catholic doctors'. I know fellow Catholics that faced similar apprehensions. Indeed one of my fellow students, also a kind, fair, good friend, was embarrassed to tell me their Consultant Surgeon relative who worked at the Victoria Infirmary never employed Catholics. I did work however, and had a great time and training in Stobhill Hospital. Later in my fledgling career, I returned to work at Monklands Hospital which was the local hospital for Coatbridge, a post I thoroughly enjoyed. However, some of the nursing staff found out that I was from Coatbridge and a Catholic and they would often 'humorously' refer to me as a 'Bead Rattler'. On one occasion when I asked my consultant if I could have the day off to attend the ordination of my cousin becoming a priest, he said 'oh dear that's not so good'. Anti-Catholicism and anti-Irishness, although sparse and not a daily event, was at times quite blatant and clearly at the root of much going on in society. However, I thought of myself as the local boy who had 'done good' and a catch for the ladies, despite my looks!

I dated one of the technicians in the hospital for some six month or so, but when visiting her sister's home, the sister's husband would talk about Masons' aprons and Lodge visits, and her sister would discuss how she found it repulsive that young girls were dressed up as brides in Holy Communion dresses. On one occasion I was fore-warned about a small rotund man, who resembled Barney Rubble from the Flintstones and was not pleased his daughter's friend was dating a Catholic. I met the 'Rubble' once when he approached me at a wedding reception and said 'so you're the Fenian?' I replied 'yes I am and are you the wee fat bastard': at which he turned and headed off, ironically feeling he was insulted? At the time I thought I was very funny, but I was also annoyed. I was being judged and disliked by people whom I had never met. This was because I was an Irish-descended Coatbridge Catholic. And this was similar to but less intense and critically, less public and unrecorded, than the disgraceful treatment Neil Lennon received when a Celtic player and manager.

Being disliked by people that I didn't know was still present after leaving the closeted existence of full time education. In 1999 I moved to live in England to work in Middlesbrough and one of my patients who I cared for regularly, again would chat, with the nurse in clinic in my presence, about Masons' aprons and about how glad they were they weren't Catholic. I would have to remind them that I was there and I could see them as well as hear them.

Living in England added many more miles to the McCarron week as my wife and I kept our season tickets (my wife Karen in the South Stand and I in the North Stand) and we were grateful for my children's maternal gran Margaret, being an ever-willing childminder. Initially we travelled up for every home game, but after one rainy Wednesday night when the wet road spray of lorries reduced the visibility to almost zero for parts of the trip, we restricted our mid-week evening journeys to European nights only. My colleagues in England always seemed impressed by this commitment to travel but feelings about Celtic are crystallised in the events of the UEFA Cup Final of 2003.

Living in England continues to surprise me. The working class support of the Conservative Party (and latterly UKIP), the aristocracy, the monarchy and Brexit is more open and common than appears the case in Scotland. There is also a greater tendency to blame their difficulties on others (who are often less fortunate) who are on benefits, immigrants, refugees, public sector workers with 'gold plated pensions' etc. A doctor colleague who was born in India and has lived and worked in Scotland and England puts it down to Scotland's philosophy of 'we are all Jock Tamson's bairns' compared to England's 'every man's home is his castle'. He might be correct although how applicable this is to Scotland's biggest number of incomers from Ireland is questionable. The Conservative Party's policies of austerity seem to have emboldened bitter judgmental attitudes in the masses and offer support to those who are willing to castigate the underprivileged such as Jacob Rees-Mogg and Ian Duncan Smith (both men so insecure that they cannot cope with having one surname) who describe themselves as staunch Catholics but appear to be terrible Christians with little humanity for those in need.

I blame the Conservative and Unionist Party who claim 'one nation conservatism' but often act as a major driver for societal divisions, and echo many of the views of UKIP, leading the charge against so called bogus asylum seekers and European citizens. The Conservative and Unionist Party have a long history of promoting divide-and-rule politics, typified by Randolph Churchill's playing of the Orange Card to halt rebellion and discontent from unified Presbyterian and Catholic workers in nineteenth century Ireland. In Scotland too the Conservative and Unionist Party played a large part in the racism and bigotry against Catholic-Irish immigrants who came to Scotland from the mid-nineteenth century onwards: a couple of centuries after Scottish colonists violently conquered much of Ulster during the British plantations. Irish immigration never really reached the Highlands or the Borders in substantial numbers, and both areas have remained fairly Conservative Party free, voting for Liberal or Independent MPs. I remember in my childhood, one of my friends who was not Catholic, gave me a Labour election flyer and him saying it was the Catholic Party and that his family voted Tory.

Glasgow Rangers is the natural fit of Scottish football with the Conservative and Unionist Party. We have seen Murdo Fraser, the leading Scottish Conservative Party figure criticising the police in Manchester and not Rangers fans, after the Rangers mass riot at the UEFA Cup Final there in 2008. Also, we've had the spectacle of a prospective Conservative MP leading the Orange Walk in Airdrie declaring that Orange tunes were beautiful.

Dara O'Brien refers to Glasgow as 'Belfast Lite' and anti-Catholicism continues in twenty-first century Scotland, and not just in Glasgow as some would like to claim. I joined the social media age in 2010 and was appalled at some posted comments especially around the time of Neil Lennon's first spell as Celtic manager. As well as unsavoury comments coming via social media, the popular press got involved with some journalists blaming Neil Lennon's on-field behaviour for attracting this abuse and that the threats directed at him were of his own making. It was a disgraceful time that allowed a football manager doing his job to receive repeated death threats, bullets sent through the post, threats to his family, having to leave his home, and to be punched in the face at a football ground on live television, only for the case to be dismissed in the Law Courts: without great establishment fuss. Threats were also delivered to other Celtic Irish players such as Niall McGinn – and we all know the abuse Aiden McGeady has disgracefully received in Scotland, for being a Scots-born football-playing Irishman. The media stoked this with sports pundits/commentators on BBC Saturday afternoon radio believing it witty to suggest that Aiden McGeady be forced to pay back his schooling fees when he elected to play for the Republic of Ireland and not Scotland: the first being his country or origin/ethnicity and the latter being his country of birth. It was reminiscent of Norman Tebbit's view that Asian immigrants should support England at cricket and not the country of their choosing, especially the one that they had originated from.

We all have a role to play in challenging these views and call out would-be jokes that are sectarian and racist. I have never liked the campaign Nil by Mouth as such issues are too great to be shut up, swept under any carpet, and whispered. Bigotry and racism should be discussed and not let those who hold such views to be left unchallenged. It is sad that although born in Scotland, there have been times in my life where I have felt that I was not really wanted by sections of Scotland because of my Irish Catholicism. However, I have always felt I belong with Celtic.

Certainly, like any section of society, it has its share of undesirables but Celtic is so much more than a football club. A club born out of supporting the poor, I am proud of the connections of Celtic Charities with the Refugee Council, Glasgow Night Shelter and many others, the welcoming of asylum seekers, the support given to Islam Feruz to remain in Glasgow (although he later made a mistake by joining Chelsea – in moral, historical, cultural and political terms, a much poorer club than Celtic), the Thai Tims. Celtic is a great Irish football club and Scottish institution. Celtic FC, from and of the diaspora, proud to come from Irish roots and not ashamed to say so, just like me!

Celtic through and through: a personal memoir

Joe O'Rourke

I remember a few years ago being asked by a Norwegian reporter I was doing a television interview for, 'when did I become a Celtic supporter'? The answer was easy, it was 4th February 1951, the day I was born. I was born in Port Glasgow, a well-known town on the lower Clyde. Port Glasgow was famous for really only one thing, shipbuilding. Some of the finest and largest ships to ever sail in the early part of the twentieth century were built in the Port's shipyards.

By the time I was born the Irish/Catholic/Celtic community was well established in the Port: attracted like many others to that part of Scotland by work. I was the youngest of six boys and we also had a sister. My early years were spent in a tenement building in George Street, and almost everyone lived in or near the town centre at that time. But, the town was expanding and families started to move to new housing: 'proper houses' with inside toilets and gardens. It was considered then by most around as a luxury to have your own liveable space.

My early days at St. John's Primary School were great, although it was a fair distance from our new house on Berwick Road. Usually after school I went to my Maw's (Granny) house in King Street: better known as 'the Fenian Alley'. You can probably guess that the vast majority of the people who lived in the Fenian Alley attended St. John the Baptist RC Church, which was no more than 250 yards away in the town centre.

The Alley was a big square set of tenement buildings (so I don't know how it got to be called 'an Alley'). There was about 100 houses in the Alley, most with large families of Irish immigrant origin. The Alley was a hub of activity every day, all day: there was always something going on. Sunday afternoon was football day. The big square in the middle of the tenements was tarmac, so it made for a good sized football park. The one Sunday when there was no football was Corpus Christi. For days before that Sunday all the men and women would whitewash the walls so everything looked spotlessly clean. Then on the Sunday itself, Mass would be held in St. John's and the procession with the priests and congregation would take the Blessed Sacrament over to the Alley for another Service in the square. In later years the AOH (Ancient Order of Hibernians: 'the Hibs') Accordion Band would play in the square when they returned from a parade in Glasgow, Coatbridge, Carfin, or over in Ireland.

St. John the Baptist Parish was founded in 1845, the actual church building was begun in 1853. The dates are significant as they coincide with An Gorta Mor, the 'Great Hunger' in Ireland and the mass emigration associated with that catastrophe. The parish was to serve the increasing number of Catholics in Port Glasgow, mostly people from Ireland, and a few from the Highlands as well. I served on the altar at St. John's in my young pre-teen days. I would walk down the hill from Berwick Road to serve 6am Mass. The Mass was for the Catholic men going to the shipyards, and both men and women going to the ropeworks. It was fine going down, but after Mass I had to walk up the hill then – not quite as pleasant.

In those days there were five priests in St. John's. Sometimes at 6am there would be two Masses going on simultaneously, one on the main altar, and one on the small Lady Altar at the side: that was so the priest could perform his daily duty. It was a lot different in those days, for instance you could only receive Holy Communion at High Mass, which was at 12 noon on Sunday, so it tended to be a very busy Mass.

Sundays were great for me and my family. Everyone went to Mass, including my older siblings who had been married and had their own houses by then. My brother-in-law Liam Duffy (originally from Derry) ran a pub at the bottom of Chapel Lane called The Huntly. After Mass he would open the pub and we would all go in: I was still young so it was lemonade and ice cream for me. Nonetheless, Liam would let in punters he knew who would be standing outside. He would give them a couple of halfs of whisky to 'sort' their hangover out, and off they would go. That was it, no pubs opened on a Sunday in those days. My sister Betty would work in the pub with Liam, when she wasn't a bus conductress that is. My older brother Tony also worked in the pub. Both of them had families to feed: Betty had ten children, and Tony had six. Tony worked in the ropeworks during the week beside my oldest brother John. John managed to escape though: he emigrated to Vancouver, Canada in June 1960 when I was only nine.

Also in Port Glasgow, in my early days there was an area known as the Glen, situated down the river where most of the shipyards operated: it was mainly native Scots Protestant. The houses down there were owned by the Lithgow family, who also owned the shipyards. To get a house you had to be recommended by a foreman or manager. Most of the foremen and managers weren't from Irish Catholic immigrant backgrounds and were 'Protestant', broadly speaking. They either lived at the Glen, or their families did. It was fine when work was plentiful, most people just got on with it, they were happy to have work to feed their families. There were occasions when it wasn't so economically cosy though and when there was a lack of work that often increased tensions between Catholics and Protestants: power, influence, bigotry, discrimination and prejudice all coming to the fore.

A big part of our family life was Celtic, our John was the first President of Port Glasgow Celtic Supporters Club: all my brothers were members. It was Tony that took me to the games in my younger days. My dad, also Joe, was a rivet heater in the shipyards: that didn't pay much so he ran bookies lines for Trainers in Glasgow on a Saturday. The local men were mostly hard working guys looking after their families. A Saturday was their only chance to relax, and also only chance to have a wee refreshment during the day. Apart from no pubs being opened on a Sunday, most men would work on a Sunday as overtime, and that probably paid for Saturday's enjoyment. My dad would come home from Glasgow on Saturday night. He would have a couple of haufs in Toner's across the street from our first house at 31b George Street. I think everyone lived in the town in the early fifties: we moved to Berwick Road around 1957.

The highlight of the week for me was definitely going to see the Celtic in Glasgow, I would sit on Tony's knee beside my mate John Dow who was sitting on his dad Jackie's knee. There was no motorway then, so it was a trek through Langbank, Bishopton, Renfrew, through Govan, and on to Celtic Park. I remember the bus would always stop at a small public toilet in Renfrew as coaches in those days never had a radio never mind a toilet: you'd be lucky if it had a heater on a cold day. About half the bus would get off, mostly the young team who couldn't hold their beer.

When it came time to go to high school I had a decision to make: if I passed my 11+ I got to go to St. Columba's Senior Secondary, away in darkest Greenock. Most of my mates were going to St. Stephen's Junior Secondary just down the road from my house. But my mam promised me a new racing bike if I passed, so pass I did. St. Columba's was fine, I was reasonably clever. Certainly no genius, but they had a cracking football team, and I wasn't a bad player back then. It was great for the ego as well, all the good looking girls liked the boys who made the football team. The downside of playing for the school team was if Celtic were away from home, it was a struggle to get back up from Greenock to make the bus for the match. So after first year the football team, and the girls, got dumped: Celtic was more important.

At that time you couldn't join the Port Celtic until you were sixteen, and you also weren't allowed onto the bus for games against Rangers unless you were the same age. So me and my mates started going on the train to games. In this day of millionaire footballers and mind-blowing sickening amounts of money in the game, believe it or not, we used to travel to Aberdeen on a Saturday morning on the same train as the soon to be Champions of Europe, the Lisbon Lions: well at least most of them. The games against Rangers were particularly enjoyable, especially when there was a main train station at Ibrox.

I could have stayed on at school and taken O levels and Highers, but I was desperate to start working to have a few bob in my pocket. So I left school and started working in the shipyards as a joiner's boy to start with. I was offered an apprenticeship with both the IBM and the Royal Ordinance Factory in Bishopton as an electrician, but that meant travelling and I wasn't really interested in doing that. So when I was sixteen I started my apprenticeship in the Kingston Yard as a plater. It was great at the start – all the apprentices would have a great old time of it.

In the shipyards it was different though and it was clear that dominance was the name of the game: Catholics of Irish descent were pure and simple dominated throughout the workplace. Right away it was clear to me that all the managers and foremen were 'not Catholic', quite the opposite: the vast majority were members of the Masons, and actively so. If often without broadcasting it. They certainly practised anti-Catholicism, broadcasting of which was usually left to those that were of an Orange hue (some were both of course). The shop stewards were the opposite again, the vast majority were Catholic, and Celtic supporters to boot.

I enjoyed my time there as an apprentice. An honest foreman called Hughie McColl gave us the opportunity to learn our trade, providing you wanted to learn. Sadly most of the apprentices wanted to treat the experience as a playground. I was actually lucky that I finished my apprenticeship. I was only in to about my sixth week when I threw a tiny bit of slag at another apprentice, unfortunately it hit a plater called Davy Baxter. Now Mr. Baxter was what some people refer to as a 'staunch protestant'. But it was much more than that really. He was in everything, the Masons, the Orange lodge, and the Protestant Athletic Club. He came charging up to me waving his fists and threatening to batter me, and calling me a wee Fenian bastard. I wonder how he knew? At sixteen I was pretty small, and this guy was a monster. There was a big scrap bucket next to us, so I picked a piece up and said go ahead and see how far you get. The journeyman I was working with was a Catholic named Tommy Moore, but he was really passive, so he said to Baxter, report him to the works manager, which he did. Just before the dinner break at 12 noon I was sent for by a senior manager called Stillie. He was a nasty wee guy and everyone was wary of him. Well, there was no messing around, he said to me 'your sacked, get out the yard'. I was sixteen and thinking my mam will kill me. But what happened was, all the apprentices had a meeting at dinner time and voted to go on strike. To cut a long story short, I ended up getting a two week suspension. Needless to say when I returned I didn't want to work with Mr Moore, and I just gave Baxter the daggers every time I saw him.

It probably turned out to be a good thing for me, because it let me see just how badly many workers (Catholics and Protestants) were treated in the big shipyards. However, most of the Catholics worked in what was known as the 'Black Squad' (rhyming with bad). The black squad were the platers, welders, caulker burners, and carpenters: those were the trades that were at the front line of building a ship, and thus the dirtiest jobs. I learned a lot under Hugh McColl, but I had made my mind up that as soon as my apprenticeship was completed I was leaving and going travelling. My big mate Hughie Corr was of the same mind. So I was approaching the end of my four year apprentice-ship and scanning the papers and job centre window for jobs down south. I noticed a few that looked interesting, but when it came down to it big Hughie wouldn't go, so I handed in my week's notice and left the following Friday. I was heartened that Hugh McColl tried to coax me to stay. That felt good because he was a good tradesman, and a good honest gaffer as well.

I was out a couple of weeks and not working, I was beginning to panic and was keen to go down south and learn about life away from the mollycoddling of my mam. But, I didn't want to go on my own. My luck turned. I played in a cup final on the Friday night, and came home to be told that I had a job to start on Monday morning in another shipyard called James Lamont and Co. Now that was a culture shock. Lamont's was an old small shipyard, with poor facilities, but the biggest difference was, the majority of the workforce was Catholic, including the gaffer plater Joe Duddy. The shop stewards convener was a guy called Wullie Lyall. Wullie was a cracking steward, I suppose you would call him a militant, but he was good, and very clever, especially as he was a welder. A couple of years after I started I was the platers' shop steward, Wullie got sacked for bad mouthing the managing director and we went on strike for three weeks. However, they were adamant they had a chance to get rid of a very good shop steward and they weren't going to give in as it turned out. I then became the yard convener at the age of twenty three. That was the start of my life trying to represent others.

Port Glasgow in the sixties and seventies was a good place to be, especially if you were a Celtic supporter – and by default for most people around, a Catholic of Irish descent. In the sixties Port Glasgow No 1 Branch was the biggest Celtic Supporters Branch in the world, with over 350 members. For a small town to have five and six buses leaving on a Saturday to travel to Glasgow to watch Celtic was phenomenal. We used to have two buses going to Aberdeen. One would return at 6pm after the match, but one would stay the night so the guys could go to the dancing. Going into the seventies that would be a return at midnight for the late bus, no more overnight stays. I think probably too many members were now married and the wives weren't happy with them staying the night.

And it wasn't just the Port No 1. At the same time there was a bus left the Hibs Hall, which was for members of the Ancient Order of Hibernians. There was also a bus left from a pub in the town run by a great wee guy called Paddy Folan: it was always an old double decker. For those of the right vintage, it was a half-crown on the bus, and since wee Paddy was a money lender, you got £2 going on the bus, payable back with a half-crown as interest. The only thing wee Paddy learned in school was that there were nine half-crown's in an old pound.

Port Glasgow is still a big Celtic supporting town, right now there are five different supporters' branches. Port Glasgow No 1 is still going, only with vastly reduced numbers in the era of the car. We also have the Port Harp which is made up mostly of members and friends of the Ancient Order of Hibernians (Hibs), Port Glasgow Emerald, (Brave) Tom Williams, and my own branch The Fenian Alley Bhoys: not bad from a population of about 15,000.

There have been great times as a Celtic supporter. 1967 was a brilliant year for every Celtic supporter. My first Cup Final was 1965, I was only six when we beat Rangers 7-1 in 1957. So in 1965 against Dunfermline I was really excited. I went with my brother Tony who unfortunately had lost an eye a couple of years earlier. For that game we were near the back at Hampden, and when Big Billy jumped to head the third and winning goal someone in front threw his hands up early and knocked Tony's false eye out. We were all jumping up and down while Tony was scrambling around in the black ash trying to find his eye: fortunately he succeeded, so we all could enjoy the celebrations.

Often you can identify eras by what a particular Celtic side achieved. For me it was firstly the Lisbon Lions, then it was the Nine in a Row team, then the Centenary Year team that won the double, then it was Martin's team which won the treble in his first year and went to the UEFA Cup Final in Seville. Strachan and Lenny did well and won a few trophies without breaking any records. So it is the 2017 'Invincibles' that have made history again, and more history by winning back-to-back trebles. Rodgers took the team not just to a new level, but up several levels. But, unless things change dramatically, it would be extremely difficult for Celtic to win the Champions League while playing domestically in Scotland. We just cannot compete with the money that teams in what is termed to be the big football countries get. Celtic got about £3 million for winning the league in 2018, Manchester City and Barcelona: probably in excess of £100 million. We're minnows, special, unique and original minnows, in a vast sea where money is king unfortunately.

I like to think I have lived in the best era to be an Irish-Catholic and Celtic supporter in Scotland. I have seen two Popes visit Scotland, the Lisbon Lions and the Invincibles, I have witnessed the Double Treble, I have seen Jimmy Johnstone, and been lucky enough to be able to say I was friends with the late great Tommy Burns. That's a bit of Heaven on earth for me.

Being Celtic Minded

Jim Craig

When I was a laddie, it did not take long for me to come across what is politely called, and regardless of how accurate or inaccurate a description, Glasgow's 'Religious Divide'. My own background was diverse. The Craigs were from Leith, Scots, all of them of the Protestant faith and Hibs fans to boot. My mum's family was from Ireland, on the paternal side by the name of Hughes from Westport, County Mayo and on the maternal side, Wisdoms from Portrush in County Antrim. My dad was a convert to Catholicism. That never caused a problem on either side and in fact, I could not have a better relationship with all the Craigs, Pop and Gran, uncles, aunts and cousins.

As a boy in the late 1940s, I spent a lot of time at my maternal grandparents' house in Govan, as my grandfather had been ill and then suffered from a stroke. My mum was there a lot helping out and after the evening meal, I can well recall the discussions at table, the main topic of which seemed to be the plight of Celtic Football Club. Naturally, I did not know the details at the time but the complaint from my uncles and grandfather was that the club was going nowhere and they needed to change things. Dad did not say much at these moments although when I read later about Scottish football at that time, he must have been feeling pretty good as in those years, his beloved Hibs were doing pretty well, at least in the league.

However, there was one aspect of these discussions which came across quite clearly, even to a boy under 10 years of age. Whatever team they supported, all my relations seemed to have no time for this other team called Rangers. As the years went by I became more aware of that club's'discriminatory and divisive signing policy. I also began to realise how much store was put on Celtic v. Rangers matches. These games only seemed to occur two or three times a year but for days beforehand, they were the dominant topic of the conversations in my grandparents' house. Everyone seemed to get so worked up about them, including my very sensible aunts!

My primary school, St. Anthony's, just along from Govan Cross, had a school team, which I started playing for at the age of about ten. St. Anthony's was the only Catholic school in Govan and, as we only played local schools, we were obviously up against what were then considered 'Protestant' schools. Today the term is non-denominational, but to us, as well as those that attended them then, they were 'Protestant', and whenever we played them, it was like a miniature Celtic v. Rangers encounter: majority v. minority on the field of play.

That carried on when I moved to St. Gerard's Senior Secondary. The matches that were a bit special were against Govan High and even in 1st, 2nd and 3rd year, these games attracted a crowd, many of which, I should imagine, were not drawn by the quality of the play but by the thought of another 'junior' Celtic v. Rangers clash. At that time, I was a tall, skinny boy but, in the centre-half role for these teams, facing the play all the time, I was in my element. The rougher it got, the more I liked it and I must now confess, after all these years, to have been undoubtedly influenced in my attitude, and not for the better, by the partisan nature of the encounter.

One's background always plays a part in one's character and behaviour and it certainly did seem to play a part in mine. Shortly after we met, my lovely Elisabeth, my wife now of 50 years, surprised me by saying 'you can be quite aggressive sometimes'! I was quite astonished, to be honest, but when I thought about, I came up with what I thought was a reasonable answer – well, darling, when I was at St. Gerard's, the people in charge did not make life easy for us, 'making' us wear a green blazer when the school lay about half-a-mile from Ibrox Park. Then, if you were chosen later on to become a prefect – as I was in my 4th, 5th and 6th years – they gave you gold braid to wear round the outside of the blazer. As you walked though Govan, you were like a target – no wonder I got aggressive!

In my last two years at school, I was chosen for the Scottish Schools Under-18 side, whose only fixture each year at that time was against England. There were trials every year for this team, as there had been for the Glasgow Schools XI, which I also played for between 1958 and 1961. And it was at one of these trial matches that a certain incident reminded me that religious discrimination could be not only disconcerting and upsetting, it could be career-changing – or perhaps 'career-hindering' might be a better expression. My experience was in football. God help, literally, others in various other employments who were held back because of ethnic and/or religious discrimination against them.

The Rangers scout who attended all these trial matches was a former star of the club from the 1930s and 1940s. I spoke to him regularly and found him a most pleasant and unassuming man. After one game, in which I thought I had played very well, I went across to see him. 'How did I do tonight, then,' I asked. He smiled and replied, 'You were very good, Jim.' I then came in with my well-rehearsed punch-line – 'Well, have you got the papers with you. I'm ready to sign any time.' He laughed and held up his hands. 'Ah! Jim. . . you know how it is, son.'

I knew how it was at the time and I don't think my views have changed in the intervening 50-odd years. Disgraceful! That's how it was. Would I have liked to be a Rangers player? No! But I still think that it was a disgrace that, even if I had wanted to, I would have been deprived of the chance at that time to play for Scotland's then most dominant football club, the biggest supported and wealthiest, just because I was a Catholic.

When I arrived at Celtic Park in the autumn of 1965, I was not expecting anything even resembling the religious discrimination that was well known in and around Glasgow's other big side and indeed beyond in wider society. As expected, I found none. Indeed, as had always been the case, the players and management came from differing ethnic and religious backgrounds.

Ronnie Simpson, for instance, was the son of Jimmy Simpson, who had been at centre-half for Rangers on the day that John Thomson received his fatal head injury at Ibrox on 5th September 1931. Ronnie was a master of the one-liner and also a dab hand at standing on tiptoe for group photos, as, at 5 feet 8 inches, he did not want to appear too small alongside the 6 feet 1 inch of McNeill, Gemmell and myself. Tam Gemmell was confidence personified. When abroad, he would be late for training, for meals etc and the Boss would berate me, as I was his room-mate, for not keeping an eye on him. Mind you, on one Holiday of Obligation, Big Tam – a Protestant – woke me early to tell me to go to Mass!

Bobby Murdoch controlled the play from the back and was great at it. After a match, he could very often be 'greeting'. He cried when we won, he bubbled when we lost, he even had tears in his eyes when we drew. The hard man exterior had a very soft side underneath. Bobby absolutely loved 'the Celtic'.

Billy McNeill had one moment I still treasure. The Catholic players were at Mass in Las Vegas and just after the collection had been taken up, Billy let out a groan, 'I've just put a 100 dollar bill in that plate!' The rest of us just dissolved. Unless you are careful, one American bank note can look very like another.

John Clark was a quiet bloke, very unflamboyant but also very effective. You could tell from his demeanor when a big occasion was looming. He would constantly re-arrange the fit of his jacket or adjust one of his seemingly unending supply of ties; and then go and hog one of the only two toilets in the Parkhead dressing-room at that time.

Jimmy Johnstone was an amazing player and also the friendliest guy you could ever come across. It is well known that he had a particular fear of flying. One day, when he was telling me about his plane coming back from America hitting an air pocket, he stared at me with those big eyes and declared, 'Honest to God, Cairney, we must have fallen for about five minutes!' Aye, right, wee man!

Willie Wallace had always been a thorn in the side of Celtic when at Hearts and thankfully, did the same to all our opponents when he came to Parkhead. Our relationship got off to an embarrassing start. Willie speaks with a rather hoarse voice and I asked if he had a sore throat? To my horror, he replied that he always spoke that way!

Steve Chalmers was a very friendly guy, good with newcomers and was particularly positive with me in my early days with the first team. On a plane trip to Tbilisi in 1966 I asked him why he always felt it necessary to sit on the outside seat – the one furthest away from the window? He replied, 'So that I can make a bolt for it if there is any trouble.' After a few minutes, I turned to him again to ask where exactly he was going to bolt to but he had fallen asleep.

Bertie Auld had a great confidence and was very good in the dressing room before a match, putting everyone at ease. In the tunnel at Lisbon, we must have looked quite an unprepossessing bunch alongside the bronzed and oiled Italians. Suddenly though, Bertie broke into the opening words of the Celtic Song, 'Hail, Hail, the Celts are here', and we all joined in. For that act alone, he deserves every Celt's thanks.

Bobby Lennox was a great presence wherever we were: noisy and effervescent. A few years ago, all of us attended a charity dinner in Dublin and Bobby announced from the reception desk that he and I had been paired together. 'Room 107,' he told me. We searched for it for some time on more than a few floors but could not find it. I then asked if I could see the card he was holding in one hand. It said that Messrs Craig and Lennox had booked in to the hotel at 1.07pm; I then also noticed that in his other hand, he had a block of wood attached to a key with the number 237 written on the wood. That's Bobby.

Those guys mentioned made up the team which won the European Cup in Lisbon in 1967 but there were also a few others involved at different stages, including one who was the only substitute for every match, yet never got on. That was John Fallon, who had a moment of glory some ten days later, when Celtic travelled to Spain and beat the Spanish champions Real Madrid by a single goal at the Bernabeu. John played and was superb that night.

Guys who just missed out on a place in Lisbon were Willie O'Neill, a quiet guy until he joined Johnstone and Lennox; Joe McBride, who, I suspect would have been one of the first names on the team sheet before a knee injury sustained against Aberdeen on Christmas Eve 1966 brought his season to a close; Charlie Gallagher, pleasant and unassuming but with a great touch in both feet; and John Hughes, Yogi or The Bear, another one whose size and strength on the pitch gave no indication of his quiet nature outside the game.

Training and playing with all these guys was not only good fun but also a great life experience. While we certainly were not in each other's houses all the time, we all got on well. We were Catholics and Protestants, of Irish and Scots descent, and big Billy was of course also part Lithuanian. There was no prejudice, discrimination or bias that encroached in our relationships: we were part of the Celtic family and all were or became, 'Celtic Minded' – through and through.

Occasionally, Glasgow's religious distinctions can throw up some unusual moments. In the late 1960s, I received a letter from the minister of a church on the south-side of Glasgow, asking if I would be the inspecting officer at the annual parade of the local branch of the Boy's Brigade. I phoned him up, explaining that I was a Catholic and I knew the Boy's Brigade was a Church of Scotland organisation. He replied that I might get a surprise if I attended. I duly did and as I walked along the rows of boys lined up, I noticed that more than a few of them had a line of white clothing showing above the normal blue shirt. At the nice tea and cakes provided after the inspection, I mentioned this to the minister who called across one of the boys mentioned and whispered in his ear. The laddie subsequently pulled down the front of his blue shirt and there underneath, was a Celtic strip. Apparently, the Boys' Brigade ran a football team and it was the only place in the neighbourhood for Celtic minded youths to get a game!

After my playing days were over and I had moved into broadcasting, visiting grounds round the country, it was very obvious that there was a bias against Celtic among more than one set of fans. Scotland's biggest club Rangers might have 'eventually' got all the attention on the prejudice issue but the practices there weren't unusual amongst some of Scotland's other football clubs. Of course, the antipathy against Celtic could have been for the club's recent years of success. However, that would be naive and would avoid much of Scotland's history over the past 400 odd years. Rangers v. Celtic games were still occasions that questioned the nature of football in Scotland. Then came major change.

I joined Celtic in the autumn of 1965 when I was still a dental student, so all my training was carried out in the evenings. Shortly afterwards, we were joined by a young man from Edinburgh. He was a nice laddie but a little too heavy on the weight side with a reluctance to run. He liked to get the ball to his feet. After training, I used to drive him to Queen Street station, during the whole trip encouraging him to work harder and especially get around the pitch a bit more. His name was Graeme Souness.

After playing all of his professional football life in England and Italy when he came into Ibrox as Rangers player/manager in 1986, desperate for personal as well as the club's success, Graeme Souness must have decided that the club's signing policy over the years was a hindrance, as players from all backgrounds suddenly came into Ibrox with their religious affiliations being much less of a factor than previously. It would be fair to say, though, that among the diehard supporters of the club, these innovations were not greeted quite so enthusiastically. It was not a decision needing the thinking power of a rocket scientist. By not signing players who were Catholic, Rangers had missed out on some good performers through the years, Di Stefano, Pele and Maradona springing to mind. Graeme deserves credit for his courage and perspicacity, regardless of any selfish reasons that might have been there.

In later years, when Rangers opened their new training centre at Auchenhowie in north-west Glasgow, a number of these incomers to Ibrox Stadium lived in Bearsden, a neighbouring suburb – and one where my family and I lived. Like the rest of the parishioners, I was in the unusual position, revolutionary even, of meeting Rangers players at Mass. I must say, they were nice guys and all of them were treated with some courtesy although, just before Celtic v. Rangers clashes, that politeness was naturally tinged with perhaps just a touch of asperity?

In the last two decades, while there certainly have been problems for Rangers off the field, there can be little doubt that their original signing policy has been discarded. Players are now signed for their ability and it is right and proper that this step has been taken. However, there is also little doubt that what is referred to as sectarianism is still a problem in Scotland, and such a public sport as football tends to suffer the consequences. In a recent survey, almost nine out of every ten people in Scotland believe that football is a cause of sectarianism in the country with 69% believing that it is only a problem in specific areas – mainly Glasgow and the West of Scotland.–I'll leave that bit to be debated by others.

When Celtic v. Rangers matches take place, they attract attention from not only the whole country but from the world outside Scotland, much of which is ready to condemn any drop in standards of behaviour – either on or off the field. These contests are difficult matches to play in, the players having to be aware of the intensive scrutiny they will all be under. I can clearly recall one of them from my own playing days, in the dressing-room pre-match, where, just after we had been given a short, sharp lecture from Jock Stein about challenging for every ball, winning every tackle and keeping the pressure on the opposition at all times, the Chairman, Sir Robert Kelly, came in and talked about how we must play the game in a sporting manner and not do anything that would harm the image of the sport. Conflicting advice from two club officials. . . and at a crucial time!

Has there been a lessening of the intensity of bigotry, prejudice and discrimination based on religious identity in Scotland in recent years? I do believe the answer is – yes! Will it ever die away completely? That is a more complex question. Any disease can become entrenched in a population. Hopefully, as the years go by and the current generation is succeeded by perhaps more enlightened ones, then there may be a lessening of any 'narrow-mindedness' that exists today. For the sake of our children and grandchildren, let's hope and pray that day arrives sooner rather than later.

George Galloway – a bhoy from Dundee's 'Little Ireland' –
pictured while campaigning in 2012 for election to the Westminster parliament
as a Respect candidate in Bradford West

An Irish story in Scotland: being Celtic Minded

GEORGE GALLOWAY

It's a long way to Tipperary. The Tipperary of my birth I mean. In the Irish ghetto of Lochee, Atholl Street and the attic one-room apartment, sloping roof and all – into which I was born in 1954. Atholl Street was in the slum heart of Lochee – then quite a separate place to Dundee – which was itself built around the teeming jute and flax mills underneath the tall and still standing Cox's Stack. Cox's Mill was king and both my grandfathers worked there as labourers. My maternal grandmother did too. It was hard work – as the Millworkers' Poet Mary Brooksbank put it: 'They fairly mak ye work for your 10/9d' (= 53 pence a week).

And my own family, indeed most of the families in Lochee, had to walk far to even get there. In their bare feet some of them from the cattle-boats in which they'd arrived from Ireland at Anderston Quay (which I would later ironically represent in Parliament). A glorious family it was too; O'Reillys (they later dropped the O' in case people tumbled they were too obviously Catholic) and Dougans, Floods, Feeneys and McInerneys: a veritable Celtic tree of Irishness.

There was absolutely no pretence that this family were Scottish, even those born in Dundee. We would have failed any 'cricket test' devised by any latter-day Norman Tebbit (or any of the other ethnic/nationality tests set for us by many others in Scotland since). 'If you're Irish come into the parlour' was their song, and anyone in their parlour (we of course had no parlour – I slept in a drawer as there was no room for a cot) almost certainly was Irish. In fact the main cleavage was between the old Irish who had arrived in Juteopolis in the nineteenth century and the 'newcomers' who had arrived in the decades before I was born.

In the parish of St. Mary's (Lochee) there was a Public Baths, a Public Library and a Public Park all bestowed upon the poverty-stricken millworkers in the ghetto as an act of charity. Some might describe it as 'reparations'. There was also the Lochee Boys Club where my great grandfather was an esteemed boxing coach and for which I would later both box and play football. Incidentally about a mile and a half way was St. Mary's Lane where for a brief time the great James Connolly lived.

Naturally support for the Irish Republican cause ran deep amongst the masses of Lochee – including in my own family some of whom were gun runners during the struggle for Irish independence in the early twentieth century.

As a youngster I learned through family narratives that the Scottish people didn't really want us there. That's a brutal truth attested to by the most cursory glance at the history books of the time, by the shame suffered by those like my father (who was not a Catholic but married my mother in a ceremony which all but one of his family refused to attend – a 'mixed marriage' in Scotland at that time was one between two white people who 'followed' Jesus in a different way). Even the local football teams were 'sectarianised' in the beginning. It was no accident that Dundee FC played in dark-blue and that Dundee United were originally called Dundee Hibernian. My father supported the latter and was further ostracised by many as a result. But my mother and all of her family supported a team a little further away but close to their hearts in the East End of Glasgow. Thus Celtic were always in my heart too.

Whilst Dundee was never as bad as west central Scotland so far as iniquity and bigotry was concerned, discrimination and prejudice against Irish-descended Catholics was never far away. I grew up assuming that no police officer (or for that matter fireman) would likely have been born in the likes of Atholl Street.

Equally I grew up (in a very Labour household) believing that in Labour circles we were disproportionately strong. The Irish, a marginalised minority in Scotland as in America too, sure knew how to do politics. And knew the importance of politics. They seemed to know that Irish Catholic life in Scotland needed political protection – that their way of life, in particular their schools – would not last long if left to the tender mercies of the majority of the Scottish population.

And the marching season every summer reminded them where power lay in Scottish society if they were in any danger of forgetting. In my memory there were no Orange Walks – demonstrations of ethno-religious supremacy to give them their Sunday name – in Dundee. Only on trips to Glasgow did we ever see them or hear about them at least. But my grandfather Tommy O'Reilly who managed to be a devout Catholic, a Communist and an Irish Republican all at the same time, would describe them to me in terms straight out of his Bolshevik playbook as 'The Black Hundreds', after the reactionary mobs of pogromists in pre-revolutionary Russia. He was in no doubt that if they could get away with it, their Scottish equivalents would surely pogrom us.

And brooding over all of this – 'Aye Ready' – was the famous Glasgow Rangers Football Club. We knew what they were 'ready' for. Neither did they keep it a secret. Long before the so-called 'Famine Song' we were aware they were forever telling us we didn't belong and asking 'why don't you go home?' They sang of how 'they' were the people (we knew what they thought we were) and of how they were the 'Billy Boys' and wading (in their dreams at least) 'up to their knees' in our 'Fenian blood'. Long before I knew that relatives of mine were actually 'Fenians' and had served prison sentences for being so. This too before I knew that a 'Fenian' was the standard term of abuse for people like me.

Glasgow Rangers was the Mecca for the religious, cultural and ethnic abusers even if they had auxiliary football teams in their own Scottish towns. It was 'the' football club par excellance (many others in Scotland had almost no Catholics or very few involved) which as a matter of company policy simply would not employ a Roman Catholic – even to cut their grass let alone play for their team. Even Sir Alex Ferguson – a former Rangers player – has talked of how we was ostracised just for being MARRIED to a Catholic – and he was a record £100,000 signing by the club. In later years – 1989 – when Glasgow was the European City of Culture, I was present when the first Roman Catholic ever to be allowed to get changed in the home dressing room at Rangers, played at Ibrox Park – his name was Francis Albert Sinatra!

In those days Rangers were a mighty institution for many of a type of Protestant that agreed with, supported, and if they could, practised anti-Catholic prejudice and discrimination. Glasgow Rangers FC was their totem pole: the very personification of Protestant supremacy in Scotland (there are other more religious and spiritual forms of Protestantism of course that focus on Jesus and being and doing good things in life). Thanks to the workings, schemes and despoiled aspirations of the club's erstwhile owner and still significant figure in parts of Scottish business and financial life, 'Sir' David Murray, Rangers went bankrupt – something inconceivable when I was a young man – and a trail of malfeasance and corruption now leads back to their door. In a real sense the Rangers I knew no longer exist but the conditions and the mind-set which attended them in their pomp, hasn't gone away. The power held in social, political, media, economic and cultural life in Scotland by that club and its fans has changed and has diminished. But, it is also still very much still there.

Related to such footballing bastions of anti-Catholic and anti-Irish prejudice and discrimination, added to some anti-working class ideologies, you could also experience and detect roadblocks against our progress in Scotland's political life. When I fought my first General Election campaign – in Glasgow Hillhead – in 1987, I like you perhaps imagined the Hillhead constituency to be a kind of Elysium, all West End and Kelvinside – maybe even 'above' basic and raw disdain and hatred for 'our kind'. That was true to a degree as educated and wealthy people not from an Irish Catholic background sometimes had many more things going on in their lives to be concerned with: but that's not the whole truth. I swiftly discovered that in some streets in Partick, some in Whiteinch and some in Scotstoun, people like me were far from welcome.

As was (and remains) my wont, I was campaigning on an open-topped bus on a busy Saturday afternoon in Byres Road, the heart of the West End of the City. We were stationary and I was giving it laldy into a microphone, my mother Sheila O'Reilly standing proudly beside me. I began to be conscious despite the din of a well-dressed Kelvinside-looking lady who was shouting something up at me from the street. Thinking she might be enquiring over the finer points of my stance on the Ethiopian famine which I'd recently become rather well-known for fighting, I stopped speaking and craned forward to hear more. . . 'We know what you are,' she said. 'Oh really,' I replied, 'and what am I?' 'You're nothing but a Fenian bastard,' she shouted, in the poshest Kelvinside accent you could imagine.

At which point, on the final Saturday of my first General Election campaign in the tumult of Byres Road shoppers, every one of them a swing voter in a marginal seat, my mother snatched the microphone and in a state of high dudgeon shouted back, 'He might be a Fenian but I can assure YOU – he is NO bastard!' Gee thanks, Ma. Anyway I won, and dumped the well-upholstered arse of Roy Jenkins, the leader of the breakaway SDP, at Central Station for the last time.

But in the next election in 1992, on the eve of poll I was woken up in the early hours by the breathless panic of my supporters. Sitting in my pyjamas I received the news that all over the (now Glasgow Kelvin) constituency thousands of green and white sticky backed posters had been plastered on every available surface bearing the legend 'Galloway=IRA' and that they were proving virtually impossible to cleanly remove. However, my hard work in my constituency, my honest endeavours to work for all equally and fairly regardless of their ethnic or religious background, and my representing of a Labour Party that often tried to do what it said on the tin, meant I doubled my majority. On that occasion well done the people of Glasgow Kelvin: good honest politics won the day.

When the late and great John Smith died on the eve of what I still believe would have been a great Labour Premiership, his obvious successor was the Scottish Secretary of the Labour Party Helen Liddell (nee Reilly, but no relation). Although I always respected her ability I was never a friend of Helen, we had way too many political differences for that. But she was a local woman, prominent in national politics, and easily capable of handling the rigours of a by-election which were then in media terms an ordeal by fire for political candidates. This I knew because between 1977 and 1983 when I first moved to London I had been a full-time Labour Organiser and Helen Liddell had been my boss. In by-elections all over the country I had been drafted in full-time as an election organiser helping the local members rise to the national challenge of a much reported by-election. Although we had some good local candidates in those by-elections some were not so, and Helen Liddell in most cases acted as if SHE were the candidate – and a good thing too.

So the Monklands by-election came along in 1994, Mrs Liddell was the candidate. I was already now myself an MP, and no longer required to relocate to Scottish towns and cities as an organiser. But old habits die hard, old loyalties too, and I duly pitched up with my clip-board and felt-tipped pen, my electoral register and my courage to the sticking post I set out onto the streets of Airdrie. I hadn't got far when some local men started shouting abuse of an indeterminate kind in my direction. 'Go home,' they were shouting. Go home? What, to Glasgow? Was this a 'Go home to Russia' type thing, which I had last heard before the collapse of the Soviet Union? How quaint, was the thought that flickered through my brain. And then the volley: 'You, Galloway, ya Fenian bastard, why don't you go home?' (One should be struck that this comment was being made to me almost twenty years before the well-known song in Scottish football arose towards Celtic supporters of Irish descent, 'The Famine is over, why don't you go home?')

And I was just a canvasser! Helen Liddell, 'happened' to come from neighbouring Coatbridge, a town with the highest percentage of Irish-descended Catholics of anywhere of similar or larger size in the whole of Britain. Her maiden name (uniquely in my experience) was Reilly, and this was uttered much during her by-election campaign, emphasising very much that her foes could identify 'what' she was. They didn't put an O' before her name, but they incanted it in a way which seemed to sing 'if you're Irish. . . don't come in to my [Airdrie] parlour'. I'd like to say that what happened on my first day in Airdrie was an isolated incident, but I'm writing this on a Sunday, and that would be a lie. I did have much worse experiences in Edinburgh, though – again, like Glasgow Hillhead, not often thought of as a rough-house.

One Saturday in particular I sat through the most prolonged and sustained sectarian abuse it has yet been my misfortune to experience – a full 90 minutes in the stand in Edinburgh's Tynecastle Park, home of Heart of Midlothian. The full-set of anti-Catholic and anti-Irish chants were ringing around the stadium from well before the kick-off. But when I was recognised as being in the building they didn't mistake me for Elvis! I swear hundreds of foaming at the mouth bigots didn't watch a minute of the match that day. They couldn't take their eyes, their hate, their pure black hearts, off me.

And so when I watched, many seasons later, the assault perpetrated upon the then Celtic manager Neil Lennon, on the touchline, in front of thousands in the stadium and on TV at the very same Tynecastle, I was moved to describe it as a day Scotland should have died of shame. And yet I knew that it would not. I knew that they would blame the victim: and so they did. It wasn't just that Neil Lennon was a 'taig' you see, it was that he was a proud one, who didn't lower his gaze before the 'peepul'. Who stood up straight, looked you in the eye and said: 'I am an Irishman and a Roman Catholic.'

I wrote a book about Neil Lennon called Open Season – Neil Lennon's year of living dangerously. Although it was a book about Lennon it was also a book about me and a book about people that share Irish ethnicity and Catholic heritage in Scotland. A book about how Celtic was our home, our hearth. About how we sheltered there, in the jungle, from the animals outside. About our pride in what Celtic has, and about what we have achieved. Despite the fact we were never really welcome here. Or maybe because of it.

With my decades in Glasgow politics now gone, I can reflect on being assaulted, my property damaged, been threatened with death and dismemberment, had the Orange Walk stop annually outside my Anderston home and been traduced maligned and smeared. I've even been allocated my own special branch and police protection – laterally by Joe Cahill QC. I can see, I can feel, I share experiences of being 'othered' by a host society that has never owned up to its sins – just like its (now probably slightly less) favourite football club. But we have survived, and many of us, despite the suffering and long term life-affecting social, economic, cultural, political and economic consequences, even acquiring the ability to hide or change their ethnicity and other relevant identities, have remained 'Celtic Minded'. Thank God. Oh! And welcome to the best wee country in the world.

Celtic minded?
You're damn right I am.
Couldn't help it really.
It was all pointing in the one
direction!

MATT LYNCH

'Uncle Matt' played for Celtic, brother Andy played for Celtic, nephew Simon played for Celtic, I also played for Celtic. Yip, in my dreams! Add the following into the mix and there you have it. Primary school: Our Lady of Lourdes, Cardonald, Secondary school: Our Lady of Lourdes, Cardonald, Parish: Our Lady of Lourdes, Cardonald.

I think Our Lady was trying to tell me something. But more of that later. I mean, how could it possibly go wrong? And to think it happened in the middle of Ibrox was a miracle in itself. You see I was born in St. Frances Nursing Home in Govan and the up-a-close was just down the road from the team that George Young and Willie Waddell used to play for. As a wee boy I was once given a pair of Willie's socks from Mr and Mrs Waddell, just two closes up. A lovely couple. Can't say the same for his son. After managing Rangers he joined the Daily Express as a sportswriter when I was the chief sub editor. I went to thank him for the socks but all I got was a grunt!

I had thirteen wonderful years growing up in Ibrox before

moving to Cardonald. Serving 7am Mass in St. Saviour's, Govan, was the beginning of my religious education – but certainly not the end. My boyhood pal was Mike Hawthorn, from across the landing. We were inseparable. We played football in the street together, we were in the same class together, we swam together for the school and we fought together. I won most of the time!

As altar boys our mums would wake us at 6am and we would make our way through the thick fog until we finally reached St. Saviours. When we discovered Celtic goalkeeper Frank Haffey's house was on route we didn't care whose chance it was to hit the gong at the consecration. It paled into insignificance as we daily sauntered past, hoping to catch a glimpse of him. Big Frank was our hero. He went on to the pitch immaculately dressed. Rumour had it he even took his comb with him. Boy, could he stylishly make a save. We were devastated when he let in nine goals against the English. 'What time is it?' was the joke of the day. 'It's nine passed Haffey,' was the reply.

We had some wonderful priests at St. Saviour's, none other than Father Cusack, the parish priest who was joined for a short spell by a young Thomas Winning, who in turn went on to be Cardinal, and who I was asked to investigate when I was with the Sunday Times. I am delighted to tell there was nothing negative to report. The other two members of that team were Catholic writer Gerard Warner and Mark Leishman, grandson of Lord Reith, the first Governor General of the BBC. Mark went in to become Prince Charles 'agent' in Scotland. Hey, nothing like a little name dropping. Christmas time meant 2 shillings and 6 pence as a reward for being 'good' altar boys. We were also taken to the circus in the Kelvin Hall.

Another Celtic icon came to light during this period. The great Jimmy McGrory was a fellow parishioner! My father knew him: then again my father seemed to know everyone in his role as Detective Sergeant George Lynch. Lots of consultations were going on between my father and Mr McGrory when Celtic showed an interest in brother Andrew, a winger with Hearts. I think he was filling my dad in about his knowledge of Jock Stein, who eventually signed my wee brother for £60 grand. We were friendly with another St. Savour's family who we would visit after Mass.

It's not everyone who can say they went out playing with Elish McPhilomy, former Lord Advocate of Scotland, now Dame Elish Frances Angiolini. More name dropping!

I had better explain the 'Uncle Matt' bit at this point. I am, of course, talking about Matt Lynch, sometimes right half, sometimes winger for Celtic. He signed in 1934 and gave 14 years' service. He was a distant relative of my dad and they both came from the Paisley area. When the families met in Girvan one year dad introduced me to the Celtic legend. I was seven years old. I was awestruck. I quickly concluded that he must be my Uncle Matt. He wasn't, but I got away with it for years. 'Yes, I was named after him,' I would proudly inform the inquisitor. The 'Uncle Matt' story doesn't end there.

Now a teenager and not the brightest of pupils – I was more interested in girls and football – I find myself in the mathematics class at Our Lady of Lourdes Secondary. Guess who the teacher was? Yip, you guessed right – 'Uncle Matt'. And guess who the dumbest pupil was. Yip, you guessed right – me! I met 'Uncle Matt' years later outside Parkhead and inquired if he was going to the Rangers v. Celtic game the following Saturday. 'I wouldn't give those . . . . . a penny,' was his reply.

As a 13-year old dad took me to Parkhead at every opportunity. Dad was certainly Celtic Minded. We would have the same routine on a Saturday, usually met by one of dad's colleagues on horseback. 'Morning George, taking the boy to the game?' was the remark. My dad would acknowledge him, knowing full well he was a mason and Rangers supporter. Talking of which my mother recalled the time they were invited to a policemans' do in the city. When it got out of hand and they started singing 'The Sash' my dad turned to his wife and said: 'That's it Jean. Get your coat, we're going home!' So many unwritten stories in this dear land.

Anyway, we would depart Parkhead, making our way down London Road, dodging the flying bottles if it was a Rangers-Celtic match, and head to the pub where I had my usual soft drink and dad had a hauf and a hauf! Dad was a story teller and he loved company. So, we move on.

Having sat nine 'O' Levels and got one, it was obvious I wasn't heading for an academic career. After a trial with St. Johnstone it was obvious I wasn't heading for a football career either. Two memories of that day at Muirton Park – Alec Ferguson was the left back and I was on the right; manager Bobby Brown handed me my wages in a brown packet. I think it was £3 something.

Back to my career path. Don't ask how or why but I started work as a copy boy with the Daily Record, then based in Hope Street. I was sweet 16. Six months later, after being apparently the best tea-maker in the office, a slightly inebriated night editor asked me if I would like to become a journalist. A year after that I was re-writing the stars column for the paper and was put in charge of the letters page. I sat next to the sports desk and mixed with some of the icons of the time – wee Jim Rodger, Ken Gallagher, Hugh Taylor and Arthur Montford senior, to name but a few. On my desk were Ruth Wishart, Rushworth Fogg, Ellen Graham, and Paul Foot, nephew of Michael Foot. There you go, name-dropping again.

During this period I took a weekend out to stay at Nunraw Abbey on the outskirts of Edinburgh. My first visit there was at the age of 10 when gran Lynch took me to stay with the monks. I really felt at home mixing and talking to these holy men. I've been several times since, although the main house has now been sold. On one occasion I was told journalist Malcolm Muggeridge was coming the week after I departed. I wondered if he would be sleeping in the same bed as me, so I left a note under the pillow welcoming him and wishing him well. I don't know if he ever got it, but I was heartened to discover years later that shortly after his visit he converted to Catholicism. I often wonder maybe he did get my note and was influenced by my remarks?

Back to my career. Two things stand out, writing a sports column for the Scottish Catholic Observer and launching Goal, Scotland's first ever football magazine. Still employed with the Record, a colleague of mine, Renee McOwan, left to edit the Catholic Observer, just around the corner in Waterloo Street. He invited me to write about football. So, every week I would pick a player, contact him and arrange to meet, usually at his house.

First up was Stevie Chambers. I made my way out to his house laden with fascinating questions: 'What school did you go to?' 'What was the best game you ever played?' Harry Hood, Joe McBride and a host of less well-known names got the same treatment. Yip, this was riveting, investigative reporting! When I was having tea with Mr and Mrs Chalmers there was a power cut so the interview was conducted in candlelight!

Now what was this 'Goal' thing all about, I hear you ask. It was a brave venture thought up by me and my pal Don MacQuarie who was a sub editor on the Daily Record sports desk. I was nineteen and Don was a few years older. We were passionate about football, and girls. I later introduced him to his wife. He also converted to Catholicism, being encouraged by then Father Thomas Winning no less. When we realised there was only one football magazine in the UK – Charles Buchan Football Monthly – we set about producing our own for Scotland. Don resigned from the Daily Record to go full time. I stayed on but was later reminded by a Record executive we apparently posed a threat to their circulation. 'Remember where your bread and butter comes from, son!' We had an office in St. Vincent Street, and as Torrisdale printing company, based in the south side, were at the forefront of 'new technology', we chose them as our printers. We were on our way! Where we were going we had no idea, but we were definitely on our way! First edition, 12 pages A4 glossy magazine. 10,000 copies. Price six old sixpence.

Some great articles included a memorable interview with Davie Wilson of Rangers and a picture of his wife Avril. Unfortunately, her father was 'furious' that we showed his daughter with her skirt up to her knees! Yip, times have certainly changed. We had a football cartoon section, a racing tipster, who was Ian Paul, a colleague at the Record, and who later joined the Glasgow Herald as chief sports writer, and pulling-no-punches Slater, a made-up name and depicted in caricature as someone who looked like Hugh Taylor. That didn't go down well with the Record. We were always attacking the SFA. What do the initials really stand for was our mantra. We also fell out with one club (can't remember which one) who banned us from the Press Box. However, we paid our way in and reported the game from the terracing.

It may have been a professionally-produced magazine, but the distribution was another ball game! We relied on our friends to take bundles to grounds throughout Scotland and stand outside the turnstiles shouting: 'Get your Goal magazine here!' I opted for Ibrox. I had a good response and a lot of sixpences in my pocket. The games over, we all made our way to the office laden with sixpences.

Goal lasted ten editions as the lack of business acumen proved to be our downfall. Don got a job as a writer with the Daily Mail and I was poised to leave the Record for pastures new, but not before Schoenstatt came into my life! I was now 20. Mum came home one night excited at a Union of Catholic Mothers meeting she had attended. I was half listening, but my interest picked up when she said the speaker was a German nun who didn't wear a habit and stayed in a council house in Simshill in Glasgow. I could feel a story coming on and I was given the go-ahead to write it for the Catholic Observer. I telephoned: 'Hello sister, I was wondering if I could come to see you to find out why you are in Scotland?' When I rang the doorbell I was greeted by a bubbly woman who had prepared a meal for me. Sister Xavera, then known as Sister Deininger, explained she had been employed by Bonn to look after the German-speaking Catholics who had stayed in Scotland after the war. Her 'parish' was wide, travelling to the northernmost tip of Scotland down as far south as Manchester. But sister's real mission was Schoenstatt, a village which means 'a beautiful place', nestled a few miles from Koblenz. The movement was founded by Father Joseph Kentenich who had spent time in Dachau and exiled by the church to the USA. After writing the article for the Observer, I was hooked on Schoenstatt. From Simshill, sister took up residence in Ardmore, former home of Bishop Scanlan in Langside Drive, before moving to Campsie Glen. I visited Schoenstatt in Germany twice: once to meet Father Kentenich, the other to record the early history of Schoenstatt in Scotland.

The year 1962 was good for me but a bad one for Celtic who ended up fourth in Division 1 as well as losing to Rangers in the Scottish Cup final replay. It also saw the departure of my boyhood idol Pat Crerand: but there were first-team debuts for

Ian Young and Frank McCarron, two players I knew. Frank played for Our Lady of Lourdes' first team. Other players from the school who had professional careers included Paul Breslin (Queens Park), Tony Taylor (Celtic, Kilmarnock, Crystal Palace), Gerry McQueen (St. Mirren, Kilmarnock, Crystal Palace and Manchester United), and Tommy Craig, Celtic assistant manager.

I was to follow Ian Young as right back at Neilston Waverley, the team his father managed. It was also time for me to move on. With talk of 'new technology', I joined Lord Thomson's Echo, a new, modern paper in Hemel Hempstead. A year later, and with marriage on the cards, I returned to Glasgow to join the Daily Express as a news sub editor. Editor Ian McColl, who later replaced Alistair Burnett in Fleet Street, promoted me to chief sub editor, the youngest ever I may add.

At the same time my brother Andy signed for Celtic and was a regular first-team player, albeit at left back and not the winger he was signed as. Well, there was no way Bobby Lennox was giving up that position. 'Don't worry, I got him off,' as wee Jim Rodger, who had also left the Record for the Express, informed me as I was planning the edition for that night. Andy had been sent off in a friendly in Ireland and put doubt on whether he would play in the opening game of the season. But the wee pit boy from Shotts was known as 'Mr Fixit', and so it came to pass that the 'charge' was dropped.'Legend had it that Jim Rodger couldn't even write his name and had his copy re-written, but his contacts made up for that. I recall standing outside Glasgow Central Station with the press gang waiting for the new Prime Minister, Ted Heath, to arrive. When he did he spotted Jim in the crowd: 'Good to see you Jim,' he bellowed!'

Disaster strikes. A new editor arrives and we have a clash of personalities. One of us had to go. I picked the short straw. I joined the Glasgow Herald, and some months later the Express folded its operation in Albion Street. I then took up my first editorship by relaunching the Paisley Daily Express and was later offered the position of editor of the Ayrshire Post, which suited me as I stayed in Saltcoats at the time.

I found myself sitting next to Danny McGrain's dad at

Hampden. It's 1977 and I'm there with my old man. It's the Scottish Cup final against Rangers. It's a penalty and my brother scores the only goal of the game! It's party time in the Lynch household. Well, it's not every day your son plays for Celtic and scores the winner against Rangers. My father's ambition had been fulfilled!

But my ambition was to become a Rupert Murdoch, and so for the next six years I was a director and half owner of the Free Press group of newspapers in Ayrshire. We had a weekly circulation of 100,000, but, partly because of pressure from the unions, I had to put the company into liquidation. I didn't become a Murdoch but I joined his newspaper, the Sunday Times, as chief sub editor in Scotland. He made me redundant seven years later. I ventured to the Middle East as editorial director of The Peninsula, an Arab-owned newspaper based in Qatar. I team up with a fellow Celtic supporter who is employed by the embassy and we keep up-to-date with the results and exchange memories of the team we cherish. Two years later I return to Glasgow and buy the much loved Govan Press title through Companies House for the extravagant sum of £14 something. The previous owners had omitted to keep it in the family! It's almost a one-man show and I eventually sold the newspaper. I retire from working life, I'm in my 74th year on this earth: with Celtic by my side.

Celtic Minded? You're damn right I am. Irish is my DNA. The Lynchs and the Shearins go deep into the heart of Ireland, where St. Patrick brought the faith to the people. Faith? Well, what about the faith of Saint Patrick, of Brother Walfrid? Legacy? Keep the Faith? How meaningful might these people and slogans be in the-oh so 'advanced' twenty first century? Well, contrary often to the ways of this world and dominant definitions of so-called success, the charity work of many thousands of individual Celtic fans, groups and organisations of fans, of a number of people at the club itself, of the Kano Foundation, the Celtic Foundation, of individuals like Tommy Burns and many more: all inspired by the same faith that drove Brother Walfrid to do what he did in and with his life. Walfrid, a keystone in our club's history. It is people like Walfrid that offer our club, our supporters an opportunity: an opportunity to be different, be distinguishable, to strive to be better on, and more importantly off, the field.

One thing I'm sure about Brother Walfrid is that he would be horrified at the ideologically driven culture of disrespect for human life that has evolved in Scotland, Britain and elsewhere in the western world in particular. Not only in the seemingly eternal wars engaged in by the same countries century after century, decade after decade, and the scourges of greed and material and financial accumulation that create and sustain great depths of poverty across the globe, but also with regards numerous modern iniquities regarding life itself. People like Walfrid were 'for life', regardless of its stage or condition. For those that share Walfrid's faith and vision, all humanity has an inherent equality and quality. Respect and dignity for human life was one of his driving forces and motivations: why else would he be motivated to do what he did? Requisite morals, emotions and actions are part of the DNA of Brother Walfrid and his ilk. It is in this light that five wonderful children and sixteen magnificent grand-children later I can now devote myself to the things that really matter – becoming a better version of myself. Even Celtic can play a part in this. There I go, name dropping again.

Dunfermline Celtic 1960s – Denis Canavan is 2nd from left, back row

'Never forget from whence ye came'

DENIS CANAVAN

At the outset, I should declare several interests. I am a shareholder in Falkirk FC and East Stirlingshire FC, as well as Celtic FC, and I keep a friendly eye on Cowdenbeath FC: the latter because that is where I was born and brought up. I still retain an interest in the fortunes of Ballingry Rovers FC, Spartans FC and Edinburgh University FC for whom I used to play. I am also very proud to have been Honorary President of Milton Amateurs FC for over 40 years. I also support the team my 15 year-old son plays for, Dunipace Juniors, who were founded in 1888. Unlike some die-hard football fans, I have always believed it possible to have some form of allegiance to or connection with more than one club.

My Celtic connections though are in my DNA. I was born and brought up in Fife but three of my four grandparents were born in Ireland, my paternal grandfather in Carrickmore, County Tyrone. His family came to Scotland as economic migrants in the 1880s. Grandad left school aged 10 and went to work down a coal mine at the age of 12. Some years ago, I was told by the Irish Embassy in London that my close ancestry made me eligible for an Irish passport. So far I have not taken up the offer, although the outcome of Brexit might persuade me otherwise.

I was also told by a reliable source that I was eligible to play international football for Northern Ireland and the Republic of Ireland as well as for Scotland. If I had the choice, I would have chosen Scotland, the land of my birth, but I fully respect and understand those who, in similar circumstances, would make a different choice. As things turned out, in my case, I had no choice because I soon realised that I was not good enough to play at international level. However, I did play in the green and white hoops for a team called Dunfermline Celtic which could have got me into trouble with the Scottish football authorities. In the 1960s Dunfermline Celtic played Sunday football which at that time was officially banned in 'Calvinist' Scotland. If the Sabbatarian zealots at the SFA had ever found out that I played for Edinburgh University (a full member of the SFA) on a Saturday and also played for Dunfermline Celtic (outlawed by the SFA) on a Sunday, I would probably have got the Willie Woodburn treatment: suspended sine die!

In my childhood, my first love affair with a football club was with Cowdenbeath FC, long before they came to be known as the Blue Brazil. My grandfather used to be President of the club and his brother, Barney, was a legendary player. Just before the outbreak of World War II, Cowdenbeath were champions of the second division at a time when it really was the second top division. If it had not been for the war, they would have won promotion but, following league reconstruction in 1945, they were denied a place in the top flight by the Scottish Football League. Nevertheless, they had a relatively big fan base at that time but not all of them were paying customers. There was at most football grounds a practice of boys getting in free by being lifted over the turnstile: but, in Cowdenbeath, it was different. In good mining tradition, we tunnelled under the perimeter fence. However, when the team was doing badly, there was sometimes a rush to the tunnel before the final whistle: something akin to 'the Great Escape'!

During my early childhood, Celtic's achievements were not much to boast about, although there were many tales of pre-war Celtic legends, especially those with local connections like Chic Geatons from Lochgelly and John Thomson from Bowhill, who had tragically lost his life in a Rangers-Celtic match in 1931. The heroic goalkeeper's grave in Bowhill Cemetey became a place of pilgrimage for many Celtic fans. During the 1940s and early

1950s, Hibs and Rangers dominated the A Division of the Scottish League. The first major Celtic success which I recall was in 1951, when the Hoops beat Motherwell 1-0 in the final of the Scottish Cup. But two years later, Celtic rocked the British football establishment by winning the Coronation Cup. According to some critics, Celtic had no right to be in the competition because, apart from that Scottish Cup victory in 1951, they had won virtually nothing since the end of World War II. In retrospect, it almost beggars belief that Celtic beat both Arsenal and Manchester United and that Hibs beat both Spurs and Newcastle United, thus setting the scene for a final at Hampden involving two clubs from Scotland: which Celtic won 2-0.

The Celtic stars that day included Willie Fernie, a Fifer from Kinglassie, Neil Mochan, a Falkirk bairn, Mike Haughney, who hailed from Dalkeith, and Bertie Peacock from Coleraine, County Derry. That helped to spread the message that Celtic were more than a Glasgow club and their appeal stretched much wider than the West of Scotland. In some school playgrounds throughout Scotland and further afield, there was probably more excitement about the Coronation Cup than there was about the Coronation itself.

I shall always remember the first time I saw a top league match. My big brother, Raymond, took me to Bayview Stadium in Methil to see East Fife against Celtic. East Fife was a very strong club in the 1940s and 1950s, more than holding their own in the top division of the Scottish League. They were Scottish Cup winners in 1938 and won the League Cup three times in the immediate post-war decade. Jock Stein was playing centre-half in that first ever Celtic team I saw and I have a vivid memory of his performance. Jock would be the first to admit that he was not the most cultured player in the world nor the most energetic. He hardly broke sweat that day but he did not need to, because his reading of the game, his positional sense and timing were so superb that he seemed to stroll effortlessly through the match. I was therefore rather bemused when Jock suddenly broke into a sprint for the dressing room as soon as the ref blew the final whistle. It was almost a decade later that I discovered why. I was playing at Bayview for Ballingry Rovers in a Cup final against a team called Novar Star. Ballingry must have drawn the short straw because we had the visitors' dressing room. When I entered the room, I could hardly believe my eyes. There were no showers and the only bathing facility for the entire team was a small one-man bath about the same size as what you would see in a council house bathroom. I then realised why Stein had sprinted off the park at the final whistle. The big man, being an ex-miner, was making sure he would be first in the bath!

Stein was a revolutionary force in Scottish football. I recall hearing him speak at a meeting in Cowdenbeath Miners' Welfare Institute shortly after his appointment as manager of Dunfermline. He was determined to take his message out to the mining communities of West Fife with whom he had a natural rapport. He was a visionary who transformed Dunfermline from a struggling outfit to become one of the best clubs in Scotland. I was not present at the 1961 Scottish Cup Final when Jock Stein's Dunfermline beat Celtic, but I well remember my first ever attendance at a Scottish Cup Final four years later when Jock Stein's Celtic gained an historic victory. Billy McNeill's winning goal heralded the start of the greatest era in Celtic's history.

I never made it to Lisbon in 1967 because I was an impoverished student with important exams ahead, but I did manage the European Cup Semi- Final in 1970, when Celtic beat Leeds United 2-1 at Hampden. I was one of the crowd of 136,505, which is still to this day a record attendance for any match between two clubs in Europe. When wee Billy Bremner scored the opening goal for Leeds, I thought the writing was on the wall, but Celtic fought back to win a deserved victory. A few years later, Bremner got a rousing reception from pupils at St. Modan's High School, Stirling, where I was teaching at the time. Many of the pupils were Celtic supporters but Billy was their hero because he was the most famous former pupil of the school and a native of Raploch, which everyone knows is the footballing capital of Scotland.

During my school days, I always preferred playing football rather than spectating. I used to play for my school team on a Saturday morning and for the Scouts on a Saturday afternoon. Two of my team-mates were the Callaghan brothers, Willie who went on to play for Dunfermline and Scotland, and Tommy, who also went on to play for Dunfermline before Jock Stein signed him for Celtic. I remember coming home with my fellow Scouts from a match on a Saturday afternoon when we heard an unconfirmed report that Celtic had beaten Rangers 7 – 1 in the League Cup Final. 'Aye, right!' was the initial response. There were no iphones or even transistor radios in those days and it was only when we got home to check the football results on 'the wireless', that we fully appreciated that historic event: a world record for a national cup final.

Bobby Collins was a member of that famous team. Known as 'the wee barra', Collins became one of my boyhood heroes when I accidentally overheard my PE teacher claiming that I was far too small to be a footballer. I immediately thought of Bobby Collins who was not much taller than five feet but was a colossus on the football field. When I was still at school, I had a brief encounter with Bobby at Central Park, home of Cowdenbeath FC. Bobby was a Bevin boy who had chosen, or perhaps been conscripted, to work as a coal miner rather than do national service in the armed forces. At that time, many of the Bevin boys did their underground training in Cowdenbeath, where they stayed in a miners' hostel. After a hard shift down the pit, there would not have been time for Bobby to commute to Glasgow for his football training. Celtic therefore made arrangements for Bobby to train with Cowdenbeath FC at Central Park. When I read about it in the paper, I was determined to get Bobby's autograph but I did not have enough money to buy an autograph book. So I cut one of my school jotters in half and, armed with a pencil, I headed for Central Park shortly before the evening training session was due to start.

I waited a long time and had almost given up hope when I saw a diminutive helmeted figure approaching the stadium wearing pit clothes and covered in coal dust from head to foot. It might have been any miner just walking home from his work but something convinced me it was the wee man himself. I plucked up the courage to ask: 'Hey, Mister! Are you Bobby Collins?' 'Aye, son, but how did ye ken it wis me?' I explained that I'd seen his photo in the paper and he duly obliged by giving me not only his autograph but also his fingerprints because he had obviously not even had time to wash his hands after his work. I wish now that I had kept that coal-stained jotter to this day. What a souvenir! Now, there are no working miners left in Cowdenbeath or anywhere else in Scotland (nor any professional footballers that are also miners!) and, as for 'the wee barra', we'll never see his likes again.

Celtic had not been favourites to win the Derby League Cup Final in 1957 but they certainly were odds-on favourites to win that same trophy in 1971. Jock Stein was manager, several of his Lisbon Lions were still in the squad and Celtic had again reached the European Cup Final in the previous year. The opposition was newly promoted Partick Thistle, famously deemed by the BBC Grandstand presenter to have 'no chance'. I went to Hampden to see that match or at least with that intention. At that time, I was the Head of Mathematics at St. Modan's High School, Stirling. I was accompanied by Peter Conlan, Head of Technical Education, and Father Jim Thomson, the school chaplain. As a result of the logistical capability which has become the hallmark of the Scottish football authorities throughout the years, the gates at Hampden Park were closed a few minutes after the kick-off, despite the fact that there were thousands still queuing to get in and there were only about 60,000 spectators in the stadium which at that time had the capacity to hold twice that number. The St. Modan's trio turned up a few minutes before the kick-off but we were astonished to find ourselves locked out of the stadium when the turnstiles were closed. Not to be out-done, we did a recce and, using a combination of technical, mathematical and theological initiative, we somehow managed to scale the wall of the National Stadium. It was like a military operation but, by the time the mission was accomplished, we discovered that the mighty Partick Thistle were hammering Jock Stein's men by four goals to nil. Celtic managed to pull one back in the second half but it was still a historic humiliation. As every football supporter knows, you can't win them all but I've never quite believed those who sing, 'We don't care if we win, lose or draw'.

I always played to win, even in amateur football. I never

played professional but I very much enjoyed playing senior football in the East of Scotland League for Edinburgh University and then Spartans. When my playing days were over, I went to see Celtic more than occasionally but, when I was elected MP for Falkirk West, I went to most of Falkirk's home matches. The club used to invite me as a boardroom guest, when I sometimes had the opportunity of meeting directors from visiting clubs, including Celtic, when they were in the same league. I met Fergus McCann at Brockville not long after he became Chairman of Celtic. His late father, Alan McCann, had been a previous Rector of St. Modan's High School, Stirling. In general I was impressed by Fergus's business acumen, his integrity and his vision for Celtic, including his efforts to give the fans a stake in the ownership of the club. Before Fergus took over, Celtic were on the brink of extinction because of gross mismanagement by the previous board. Fergus came to the rescue and put the club on a firm financial footing. McCann may have made some mistakes during his tenure, and he was in many senses, as he said himself, there to make money, but no-one can deny that he was a major player in saving the club and laying the foundations for a secure future. However, on that particular occasion at Brockville, Fergus came away a disappointed man. The Celts could only manage a 1-1 draw with the Bairns and I well remember being chided by a fellow MP, a Celtic supporter, when I rose to cheer Falkirk's goal. My retort? 'Like a good socialist, I usually support the under-dog!' Celtic of course, may have traditionally been the underdog in Scottish society but not usually when on the football field against Falkirk.

After I retired, I accepted an invitation to become the first ever chairperson of Falkirk Football Community Foundation, a registered charity set up with the aim of strengthening links between the football club and the community. I did not require much persuasion because I had a strong affinity with Falkirk FC and, as parliamentary representative for Falkirk, I had the privilege of serving the local community for a third of a century. Unfortunately, after about four years chairing the Foundation, I felt I had no option but to resign because of a fundamental disagreement with certain board members of the club who did not share my views on the need for a transparent, accountable relationship between the club and the foundation. However, I still strongly believe that football as a sport is of huge potential benefit to the wider community and I am pleased to see that some clubs, including Celtic, have established charitable foundations with that aim. After all, that was the main reason why Brother Walfrid founded the club and he would strongly agree with the biblical maxim, 'Never forget from whence ye came.'

As well as being a community club, Celtic also has a great family tradition. As a result often of ties and links with heritage, ethnicity, religion and community, children inherit a love of the club from their parents and grandparents and many families have enjoyed memorable occasions together in and around Celtic and teh club has also given huge support to families at times of need. In 1989, I lost my then youngest son, Paul, at the age of 16. He was an avid Celtic fan and I well remember some of the Celtic players taking time out to visit him at Strathcarron Hospice a few days before he died. Nineteen years later, in a cruel twist of fate, one of those players himself died of the same illness, a malignant melanoma. His name was Tommy Burns.

I have since lost three other children. Life can be very cruel at times but life also goes on. I have one remaining son Adam, now aged 16, a proud Celtic season ticket holder, who has already witnessed some of the magnificent achievements of 'The Invincibles' era. I am sure that we shall share many more happy times together at Celtic Park but I would like to end with one of my favourite stories about the only time I had the privilege of actually playing there.

Shortly after the Scottish Parliament was founded in 1999, I took part in a charity match between a cross-party team of MSPs and an ecumenical team of ministers and priests. Both teams had the privilege of being welcomed at the official stadium entrance and Celtic had official team-sheets specially printed for the occasion. The MSPs got the use of the home dressing room, complete with a massive communal bath for our use after the match but which I think has since been outlawed by the Health and Safety experts. After changing into our playing gear, we marched in awesome wonder through the famous tunnel and on to the hallowed turf. There were probably less than a hundred spectators but I dreamed that we were being cheered on by a multitude. We were following in the footsteps of legends like Willie Maley, Patsy Gallacher, Jimmy Quinn, John Thomson, Jimmy McGrory, Bobby Collins, Jock Stein, Henrik Larsson, Billy McNeill, Jimmy Johnstone and the other Lisbon Lions. What an unforgettable occasion. The only thing that went wrong for us that day was the result. The clergy beat the politicians but we put that down to divine intervention and the belief that the clerics were anointed. Brother Walfrid probably looked down and smiled. He knew what side he was on. We should always follow his light in similar matters.

'No more Catholics left': the acceptable form of racism in Scottish society

AIDAN DONALDSON

In a hilarious, but more seriously politically/culturally revealing scene in the Danny Boyle film, T2: Trainspotting, the central character, Renton (Ewan McGregor) and his accomplice. Simon (aka) Sick Boy (Johnny Lee Miller) travel to an Orange Hall in west central Scotland with the intention of relieving the patrons of their bank cards. Before entering Renton explains to Simon and his Bulgarian girlfriend, Veronika, that 'these are people who've been abandoned by their political class. But at least they have a sense of identity which is summed up in four digits.' He then rolls his sleeve up and uses markers to inscribe the four numbers that he trusts will help him overcome all suspicion – '1690' He then enters the premises musing that those inside 'now feel estranged from the modern, secular United Kingdom. Some of their anti-Catholic and anti-Irish songs have been banned, but they still gather and remain loyal to the victory of 1690 and to a simpler, less tolerant time.'

Everything seems to be going according to plan until the pair attempt to leave the premises. It seems that their 'outsider' presence has been noticed and a rather large and intimidating doorman suggests that they might give the people a song. And so Renton and Simon make the long walk to the stage where everyone (apart from the by now petrified duo) is staring with suspicion at them awaiting confirmation of their otherness.

Thinking on his feet, Renton gets Simon to play the only two chords that he knows on the piano while he frantically makes a song up on the spot which he hopes will ingratiate themselves with the patrons and help them escape unscathed. Fortunately for the two lads on stage the 'song' works a treat and is instantly appreciated and embraced by the former suspicious gathering who now join in joyously with Renton's anthem that choruses with 'no more Catholics left'. The lads beat it and jump into the car driven away at speed by Veronika. They then hit every ATM they can and to their delight Renton's cunning plan worked as in almost all cases, the four digit pin number of the unsuspecting brethren who were no doubt still celebrating that there were 'no more Catholics left', was precisely as he had predicted – 1690.

This scene in particular was singled out for praise for its humour and Frankie Boyle's sharp political commentary. It was seen by commentators as an example of the small and vanishing dark underbelly that exists in some parts of society, especially, but certainly not solely, west central Scotland. It certainly could not be represented as in any way mainstream and might only be found (if at all) if one searched very deeply into secret extremist loyalist gatherings. It certainly would not be something that anyone could reasonably expect to witness being openly espoused by people in public? That's one reading of it.

Death threats, physical attacks and sectarian abuse: the cost of playing for Celtic

Neil Francis Lennon is a much acclaimed former footballer from Lurgan in Co Armagh. A summary of his football career might state that he first played senior football for the Irish League club Glenavon before moving to Manchester City as a trainee at the age of 17. After three years on Manchester City's books Neil Lennon moved to Crewe Alexandra and then to Leicester City. In 2002 Martin O'Neill brought him to Celtic where he made over 200 appearances in the hoops and was appointed captain in 2005. In 2007 he ended his illustrious career at Celtic (as a player at least) and went back to England where his playing career finished with a season at Nottingham Forrest and one at

Wycombe Wanders. We might also be told that Neil Lennon also made 40 appearances for the Northern Ireland team. In 2008 he was brought back to Celtic Park by Gordon Strachan on the coaching staff to replace the legendary Tommy Burns who had fallen ill (terminally as it turned out).

When Tony Mowbray's ill-fated managerial career at Celtic ended in March 2010 Lennon was appointed caretaker manager for the rest of the season. He was appointed manager of Celtic on a full-time basis for the start of the 2010-11 season and remained there for four years, guiding the club to three successive SPL titles, domestic cup successes and continuing to re-build the club's reputation in Europe. In October 2014 Neil Lennon left Celtic to become manager of Bolton Wanders where he stayed for two seasons before going back to Scotland in 2016 to take up the manager's reins at Hibernian. He led the club to the Scottish Championship title at the first time of asking and ended a three year absence from the SPL. In February 2019 he again returned to Celtic as manager and to some success again of course.

Interesting as it is, this synopsis of Neil Lennon's career in football does not tell even half the story of his career in Scotland: even for those historians who only deal in 'facts'. Despite being a combative footballer Neil Lennon attracted little attention in the English or Scottish press during his playing days in England. The only notable incident of any controversy that involved the man from Lurgan was during a league match in 1998 against Newcastle United when the England international captain Alan Shearer kicked Lennon (playing for Leicester at the time) in the face. Shearer apologised afterwards but was charged by the football authorities with misconduct. He was acquitted of the charge in somewhat controversial circumstances with some commentators believing that Shearer's position as England captain may have been of some benefit to him. Neil Lennon himself gave evidence in Shearer's defence: possibly indicative of his natural inclination to avoid conflict and controversy? This all changed in 2002 when Neil Lennon joined Celtic.

When Neil Lennon came to Celtic in 2000 he was already an established member of the Northern Ireland international football team having made his debut some six years earlier. He had no problems of note up to then and was just seen by most Northern Ireland supporters for what he was – a key member of the team. Northern Ireland plays at Windsor Park and the support tends to be from the Protestant/Unionist/Loyalist community – but not exclusively, as some Catholics in Northern Ireland do follow that side although many others from the Catholic community support the Republic of Ireland.

A previous Northern Ireland footballer who found himself victim of serious sectarian abuse from many in the home crowd at Windsor Park was another Celtic player, Belfast native Anton Rogan. In related fashion, it seemed that so long as Neil Francis Lennon played for any team other than Celtic, Northern Ireland supporters were prepared to accept him as representing 'their wee country'. In an interview in 2006[1] Neil Lennon revealed how he had discussed with his 'mentor and manager' Martin O'Neill what the reaction of Northern Ireland supporters might be following his signing for Celtic. They concurred that while hard-core of fans might be annoyed, neither of them anticipated the degree of hostility or the lack of support from the Northern Ireland football authorities when things did indeed get extremely nasty. Almost immediately following his signing for Celtic graffiti expressing 'Neil Lennon – RIP' begun to appear on walls in loyalist areas.

His first game at Windsor Park following his move to Celtic was a friendly against Norway on 28th February 2001. Lennon expected some reaction from a section of the Northern Ireland support. After all, as he states in his interview with the Guardian, 'I had heard anti-Catholic songs being sung at Windsor Park internationals before but, like most Catholic players, played on and ignored them.' What Neil Lennon experienced this time was something he had not encountered before:

> 'From the moment I went on to that pitch to play against Norway I was the target of an unremitting chorus of boos, jeers, catcalls and insults. . . and at times it seemed as though it was the only sound to be heard. Deep down, it was the sheer scale of things which upset me.'

[1] Guardian, 29 August 2006

The man from Lurgan is very clear what had changed:

'I had played 35 times for my country before that night and had a good relationship with most fans, who knew I gave my all for Northern Ireland. So what had happened to make things so different? Answer: I now played for Celtic.'

Lennon also expressed great disappointment at how his situation was handled by the Northern Ireland Football authorities, the media and society in general. After all, here was an established international footballer suddenly finding himself the target of racial and religious abuse by his own supporters (incidentally, such things were common too with regards numerous Celtic players playing for Scotland until the early 1990s). Yet there was no major outcry or call for examination of conscience about a society which witnessed one of its finest footballers being subject to such vile abuse and hatred. There was worse to come.

Neil Lennon is a brave man who refuses to bow down before bigots and haters. He continued to play for Northern Ireland despite the vitriol and abuse hurled at him from many within the ranks of the Northern Ireland support. If his own football association refused to face up to the problem that was, well, its problem. Until one day in August 2002. Lennon had been selected to play for Northern Ireland against Cyprus in a friendly at Windsor Park. He was delighted to be told that he would captain the team for the first time in his international career. However, it seems that for some, a Catholic Celtic player wearing the armband of captain at Windsor Park was a step too far.

Neil Lennon's international career came to an abrupt end shortly before he had been supposed to lead out Northern Ireland at Windsor Park. A death threat from the Loyalist Volunteer Force had been phoned to a Belfast media source and Lennon decided that it simply wasn't worth the risk. He announced his decision and flew to Glasgow to join his team mates at Celtic. If he thought that by leaving Northern Ireland behind this was the end of the bigotry and hatred he had suffered he was sadly mistaken. Those who demonstrated vitriol towards the Celtic footballer were not restricted to the stands at Windsor Park.

Neil Lennon returned to Scotland to play his football for his club. The anti-Catholic and anti-Irish abuse he received in the green and white hoops of Celtic was quite shocking. And it wasn't just limited to clubs whose supporters traditionally demonstrated an antipathy towards those deemed to be of an Irish/Catholic/Celtic background. Neil Lennon was booed at almost every ground he played and the volume was now turned up several decibels. Perhaps one of the worst displays of this hatred occurred on 21st November 2004 at Ibrox. It was an ill-tempered game which Celtic lost 2-0 and in which two Celtic players (Alan Thompson and Chris Sutton) were sent off. Yet, the attention of the press was not on the game itself but on the Celtic manager, Martin O'Neill, who walked to the Celtic support at the end of the game with his arm around Lennon who had been the victim of constant abuse throughout the game by huge numbers of the Rangers support. In the post-match interview it was suggested to the Celtic manager that he might have been 'provocative' in leading Lennon to the travelling supporters. O'Neill would have none of it, complaining instead about the treatment his player had received throughout the 90 minutes from the vast majority of Rangers supporters and pointedly compared it to the racial abuse given by Spanish supporters who targeted England's black players in a friendly international game the previous Wednesday in Madrid. The Celtic manager gave his answer to the press:

> I applauded the crowd because the support was fantastic – and because Neil Lennon was abused from start to finish I think I had a right to show some support. He was verbally abused in a racial and sectarian manner.

One might have thought that this would have led to some deep soul-searching by the Scottish media and in wider society: maybe even the SNP would call a summit? Labour even? Might the Daily Record begin to self-reflect and look at how it 'addressed' and represented such issues? The Herald? Would the judiciary have something to say? 'Show racism the red card'? Nil By Mouth?

After all, Martin O'Neill, an articulate, thoughtful and generally well-respected individual, had stated that one of his players had been subjected to racial and sectarian abuse akin to the racial abuse black players from England had suffered in Spain. And it could not be denied as the game had been seen on television by millions of people. Yet no Scottish introspection took place.

The response of the media and Scottish society in general was that Neil Lennon somehow brought it on himself, that he was responsible for attracting such hatred, that he was the guilty party. Well, he certainly was 'guilty' – of being an Irish-born Catholic playing for Celtic – and for many this became the 'green light' to hurl racist and sectarian abuse at him without fear of censure or question. This has been the accepted and perceived wisdom ever since. Throughout his playing days at Celtic Neil Lennon was the victim of sectarian and racial abuse because of his ethnic, national and religious identities and culture. His time as Celtic manager (2011 – 2014) were as successful as his time as a Celtic player – but even more hate-filled. The bigots most certainly upped their game and Scottish society accepted this as the norm, didn't say anything of substance, or was mildly embarrassed if others outside Scotland saw it, or/and, more often than not, blamed Lennon himself for 'attracting' bigotry.

It was truly shocking. The young manager of Celtic Football Club not only suffered sectarian abuse the length and breadth of Scotland. He was physically attacked on the streets of Glasgow while socialising. He received death threats and bullets and a suspect device through the post. At one stage he had to have a 24-hour armed police guard outside his family home which had to be refitted with new security alarms and systems. He was not even safe in the dugout.

In 'perhaps' one of the most recent shameful nights in Scottish football history, on 11th May 2011 Celtic were playing Hearts at a packed Tynecastle. Four minutes into the second half Gary Hooper put Celtic 2-0 in the lead. As Hearts re-started the game all eyes were on the action on the pitch. . . except those of one Hearts supporter. The Hearts fan ran into the Celtic technical area and commenced to physically attack the Celtic manager. The police and stewards quickly responded and Hearts fan John Wilson was arrested and taken away. Four months later he appeared before Edinburgh Sheriff Court charged with a breach of the peace aggravated by religious prejudice. Wilson admitted in open court that he had lunged at the Celtic manager, struck him in the head, assaulted him and called him a 'Fenian w*****.' He also had attempted to plead guilty to the assault at an earlier stage in the court proceedings, if the allegation that the incident was aggravated by religious prejudice was removed. After three days of trial the jury found Wilson guilty of conducting himself in a disorderly manner, running on to the pitch, running at the away team dugout, shouting, swearing, causing disturbance to the crowd and breaching the peace. However, the jury concluded that the charge of assault on Neil Lennon by aggravated religious prejudice was 'not proven'.

The game had been transmitted live on television to a huge audience throughout the world. The incident became a major global news item and was watched by countless millions across the planet. It was discussed in numerous newspapers, radio shows and on television. The accused even admitted that he assaulted Neil Lennon. Yet this was still not enough evidence for the jury of 8 men and 7 women to convict him in modern, tolerant and inclusive Scotland.

Throughout the campaign of racist and sectarian abuse that has been visited on Neil Lennon, the media and Scottish society in general has tended to go to the 'default position': that he brings it on himself; that he is somehow to blame; that it is his fault. (see Celtic Minded 2, Irene Reid's contribution) It never had happened before. Perhaps his statement when he received the death-threat that finished his international career in 2001 should make many journalists and in Scottish society hang their heads in shame? So what had happened to make things so different? Answer: 'I now played for Celtic.'

> If Neil Francis Lennon were black it is safe to say that in this day and age in Scotland/Britain, the racial, ethnic and religious prejudice visited upon Celtic's Neil Lennon would have been treated very differently.

If Neil Francis Lennon were black it is safe to say that in this day and age in Scotland/Britain, the racial, ethnic and religious prejudice visited upon Celtic's Neil Lennon would have been treated very differently. But Alabama has changed too – hasn't it?

Aiden McGeady

Aiden McGeady is a talented and gifted footballer. Born just outside Glasgow he began his senior football career at Celtic in 2004 before moving to Spartak Moscow in 2010. He played for Everton (and Sheffield Wednesday and Preston North End on loan). In 2017-19 he played with Sunderland. He has also more than 90 international appearances for the Republic of Ireland. Hence the problem. McGeady was seen by many as one of the most promising players of his generation and it is only natural that many Scottish football supporters might have been disappointed when he declared his allegiance to the Republic of Ireland team in 2004 – for McGeady and many others of the Irish diaspora (and a common enough practice in international sport more generally), his country of origin. His proclamation for the Republic should not have come as a great surprise as he already played for Ireland at U17, U19 and U21 level. Furthermore, clips on social media of McGeady demonstrating his skills as a schoolboy might hint at his national preference: he was usually wearing a Republic of Ireland top. Photographs of family holidays show the McGeady family visiting grandparents in Donegal and meeting up with cousins, aunts, uncles and other members of the extended family. Scottish-born indeed, and no less Irish for it.

Disappointment is one thing, hatred another. Aiden McGeady became the target of sectarian and racial abuse at football grounds throughout Scotland – though it was rarely 'called out' as such. This was not limited to elements on the terraces and stands. The media and many football pundits joined in – indeed, it could be argued, even led – the campaign against the young Irishman. The constant narrative was that McGeady (and by extension the Celtic fandom) had rejected the country of his birth and could expect nothing but justified anger and condemnation from Scottish society. They must be told to 'get over their Irishness' and accept that they are really Scottish, as BBC radio sports presenter James Traynor and others in the Scottish media and in Scottish football have suggested.

However, I imagine the outrage there would be if a journalist declared that the Pakistani community in the UK should get over their allegiance to the country of their forefathers and stop supporting the Pakistani cricket team? Or the Polish, Italian, West Indian or Chinese communities for that matter? Quickly, casual racism crept into the language of some journalists with comments such as the need 'to Scottify' (BBC Scotland Chick Young) the footballer as if he needed cleansed after declaring for Ireland.

The hostility spread as sections of the Tartan Army joined in. This was particularly evident in 2014 when Scotland played the Republic of Ireland in a European Championship Qualifying Round at Celtic Park. Both Aiden McGeady and Glasgow-born James McCarthy (not a Celtic player) were selected to play for Ireland. Again voices in the media raised the temperature. Former Scottish international footballer Gordon McQueen stated that 'I hope they get a horrible reception because they deserve it. I've got no time for these players. . . I hope it's hard for them coming back here with Ireland.'[2] McQueen continued that he 'played alongside Bob Wilson and Bruce Rioch, who were born in England but they always considered themselves Scottish.' It seems that the former Scotland centre-half doesn't do irony. Or, might there be more to be said about his comments? Well, certainly not by any particular critique carried out within the Scottish popular media, that in fact, generally reproduced the comments of the old Scottish football warrior and who utilised them to support their own case against McGeady.

Aidan McGeady left Celtic for Spartak Moscow in 2010. In a candid interview with the Irish News McGeady reported the reason for his departure from Glasgow was not driven by a need to 'improve his game', nor for a lucrative contract. He stated that he had been driven away from Scottish football (and his family in Scotland) by the naked sectarian racism he faced week in and week out in many stadia in Scotland. According to McGeady:

> There are a lot of horrible places in Scotland for that sort of thing. . . Some fans hate everything Celtic stands for and everything I stand for as an Irish Catholic playing for Celtic. . . It begins during warm-ups before games with all sorts of stuff being shouted at you, even from little kids.[3]

In another interview with the Daily Record he explained the reason that he left the club he adored was simple: the death threats and abuse had got too much for him.[4] Once again the bigots had won. Once again no significant soul-searching or introspection on the part of football, politicians, social and cultural commentators etc in Scotland. Scottish society was again silent on this. Or, was it? Had it already in fact had its say through the many people that had degraded and abused McGeady's ethnicity

Imagine the outrage there would be if a journalist declared that the Pakistani community in the UK should get over their allegiance to the country of their forefathers and stop supporting the Pakistani cricket team?

[2] 'Daily Record, 9/10/2014

[3] Irish News, 18/8/2010

[4] Daily Record, 20/8/2010

over several years in and around the Scottish mainstream media and throughout Scottish football?

'We hate Catholics, everyone hates Roman Catholics'

Towards the end of the 2016-2017 football season, it had become clear to all that the fortunes of Celtic, inspired by new manager Brendan Rodgers, were on the cusp of something truly remarkable as they ran out Treble-winners and undefeated in all domestic competitions (repeated of course in 2017/18). Celtic's traditional rivals Rangers ended up 39 points adrift of the title-winners. Nonetheless, we still hear the infamous 'Famine Song' in and around Orange and Rangers type events, 'The Bouncy' remains as popular as ever with the Rangers faithful – with its allusions to the murder of Robert Hamill in Armagh in the 1980s. 'The Billy Boys' – the signature song of the 1930s sectarian razor gang led by fascist Billy Fullerton – with its chilling line 'up to our knees in Fenian blood', is belted out with gusto at many Rangers events. In 2016-17 numerous Rangers fans took up the American song-writer and pop star Tiffney's 1987 hit 'I think we're alone now', changing the words to 'We hate Catholics, everyone hates Roman Catholics.' Substitute the word 'Catholic' for 'blacks', 'Muslims', 'Jews', or any other group and maybe this song would be perceived and addressed differently in Scotland? Well. . . maybe?

Which brings us back to the Orange Hall scene in T2: Trainspotting. In it Renton suggests that it is only in such private places where these sentiments can be heard (and only 'among their own'). He is wrong. These songs and attitudes can be openly expressed by massive crowds in football stadia in Scotland. It is now twenty years since the world-renowned Scottish composer, James MacMillan, stunned Scotland with his famous address at the Edinburgh Festival in 1999 by calling anti-Catholic sleep-walking bigotry 'Scotland's shame'. It would seem that little has changed since. Many in Scotland are reluctant, afraid even, of opening up 'sectarianism' for what it really has been in Scotland: 150 years of popular and deeply embedded anti-Catholic and anti-Irish bigotry and prejudice.

No other soccer club but Celtic

Alan Milton

So there we were. Trooping around in the 1991 Clondalkin St. Patrick's Day parade in seasonal drizzle embarrassed for fear we'd be seen by our peers. Knowledgeable even then – at 13 years of age – that occupying the role of banner bearer at the front of the team group meant scant chance of being missed by the merry onlookers and festive celebrants. O'Connell Street it wasn't but as far as west Dublin went, this was major league. All the while a pair of orange sponge-muff earphones covered my ears connected to a brick-like walkman (like a radio for our very younger readers) buried deep beneath the layers of clothing deployed against the weather.

That Celtic were playing Rangers in a city I'd never been to let alone in a fixture I'd never attended, was beside the point, but my attention lay far from the bad attempts at timely marching and the straight lines we had set off with in mind. As Celtic v. Rangers game goes this was a fixture that lived on in the imagination long after the 2-0 Celtic Park home win that was etched on the credit side of the home ledger. Terry Hurlock, Mark Walters and Mark Hateley all walked that day – as did Peter Grant – as Graeme Souness' English-charged Rangers team imploded in spectacular fashion in one of the more robust clashes involving the cross-city rivals – an assertion in itself: a St. Patrick's Day massacre right enough.

At that age I couldn't explain the desire to battle with the unpredictable and sometimes deafening but always frustrating Medium Wave frequencies in an effort to keep abreast of proceedings in Glasgow's east end. BBC Five Live and/or Radio Clyde were not broadcast with the good citizens of West Dublin in mind. Cheap, primitive transistors complemented the deficiencies. Long before the days of round-the-clock live satellite soccer the dash home to try and catch an extremely scarce glimpse of the action at 20 past the hour courtesy of Sky News' hourly sports bulletin, was a common if often forlorn experience. Having the story brought to life in pictures was always a result but one that was never guaranteed: following the fortunes of Celtic in Ireland was tricky at that time to say the least. Nonetheless the connection and fascination with Celtic was there from an early stage.

Many boys in Ireland, in addition to their interest in Irish sporting teams – in my instance Gaelic games and Gaelic football in particular – tended to adopt an English team for the purposes of Match of the Day on a Saturday night and the resulting playground banter and jibes. As part of this unusual dalliance with a team from Grand Britannia, a country whose post and ongoing colonial influence in Ireland was still often resented, an allegiance to Celtic on that same island is certainly of a different quality. In many ways it was 'Celtic plus one' reflecting the widespread apathy to domestic soccer in Ireland.

Another manifestation of the links to Celtic on Irish shores was of course the explosion in the purchase and wearing of replica sports jerseys/shirts from the 1980s in particular. Previously a passion for a given club – in any code or league – was left undetected thanks to corduroy trousers and denim or checked shirts or whatever the chosen attire. However, the huge growth in the wearing of sporting apparel – not least the playing colours of a club – provided a visual presence not just at games but on street corners and on estates everywhere that a certain team or club had a following.

In this regard the penny most certainly dropped on a trip to Germany with my Dad to see Ireland compete at Euro '88 when my father's redundancy payout took a hammering not only to get us there, but to keep us on the banks of the Neckar and

Rhine even long after Jack Charlton's men had taken stage exit left. Ray Houghton's 8th minute looping header beyond Peter Shilton in Stuttgart on June 10th meant little else mattered thereafter but the hordes of Irish-accented hooped jersey wearers everywhere Ireland went – further underlined an attachment to the club that was evident to me even then that ran across generations (I have since heard that a small number of the Scots-born Irish diaspora from Scotland were in attendance that day – including the editor of the Celtic Minded series).

When you scraped beneath the surface it wasn't hard to see why. During these impressionable years the circle was completed. From seeing Irish tricolours on Scottish football terraces the curiosity was sated. Once the ability to look into this under my own steam re-affirmed what was handed down from Dad about the special nature of Celtic, it was open season on a rooted interest. The history was nothing less than intoxicating.

Downtrodden, marginalised people forced to flee their homes in a desperate attempt to carve out a better existence faced further degradation and oft times humiliation because of their faith and ethnicity in a hostile land. A Ballymote Marist Brother steps forward not knowing the feat he was about to oversee in creating a sporting and social outlet with the intention of assisting the poorest of the poor through Christian, charitable relief. What follows is in essence a global movement but one that remains true to its origins and roots. This in the face of more than a century's long 'deny your Irishness' subservience or 'The Famine is over why don't you go home' onslaught. This too in an age when history, tradition and culture are becoming less relevant too, or more artificially constructed by other clubs.

While the story has trod the boards with no little success the only wonder is that it hasn't been committed to celluloid for Hollywood consumption. That's without mention of the feats of the Lisbon Lions and Jock Stein's teams of that era and so much more besides. Of course to those of a younger generation the following admission will seem quaint at best. The Celtic View was not only of its time, it was ahead of its time. Crucially, it was also stocked in one of my local newsagents, Mannions on Monastery Road, and the almost weekly pilgrimage to secure a copy didn't really surprise those around me given my penchant for devouring the written word made even more appealing when the subject was sport.

These of course had to be kept long after their relevance diminished and piles of the View lay under my bed in my parents' house long after I left simply because I couldn't bear to see them dumped. Impressively persistent colour pictures of Gerry Creaney, Paul McStay and Dariusz 'Jackie' Dziekanowski and other such luminaries adorned random copies outlining the feats and shortcomings of the latest performances and resulting sagas. While memorable moments such as Joe Miller's 1989 Hampden glory strike had helped fuel the early fascination, it was through The View that 'aspects' of some of Celtic's more challenging times were chronicled. The 'Sack the Board' campaign and the dwindling attendances. The plans for Cambuslang complete with stadium model and of course the momentum generated by 'big-spending' Rangers with each passing title – even if a different and more truth seeking light has been 'partly' cast on that passage of time in more recent years.

Staying in touch with a club was one thing. Getting to see them in the flesh, another entirely. Being regular visitors to Ireland for friendly games offered an opportunity to see the movement roll into town and the local battalions of supporters mobilised. However, it was never the same. How could it be? Friendly games in what passes for a balmy Irish summer – short sleeves in the rain – against domestic opposition nearly always hopelessly outclassed, did not make for the sort of offering I imagined the trip to Govan or Gorgie to be. Of course the right of passage that is the conferring of pub-going status represented another phase of maturity and the construct of another layer in the relationship with a club and how it was engaged with. The male bonding, the machismo and of course the whiff of cordite – testosterone induced and produced en masse in the laboratories that constitute the terraces.

A burning desire to make 'The Jungle' had gnawed away at me subconsciously: but it's not easy to pull off such a feat when still in your teens. The scale of Celtic Park, even in its undeveloped state, and the mass of humanity on the vast terraces always registered with me and provided a reference point to sporting experiences elsewhere, not least Hill 16 at Croke Park by which stage had become the domestic comparison. In all of this it is hard to overestimate the fascination with the Celtic-Rangers rivalry.

The shared sponsors, the Mo Johnston episode, the societal spill-over and the enduring allure of the fixture that placed it right up there beside Boca Juniors and River Plate and Barcelona and Real Madrid when in reality Scotland should not be trading at that level. The cross-generational dominance and jousting and the ability of the rivalry to remain relevant and potent despite or perhaps because of the passing of time. When you come from a country where the same type of sporting edginess does not exist, it's alluring and fascinating in equal measure.

For a young Dubliner it's hard not to get caught up with what the Dublin Gaelic football team means to the city. For one – like so many others – who played for many years, it's virtually impossible. The big championship days out at Croke Park which often attract crowds of 70-80,000 are without rival on this island in terms of scale and reach. The games – not least those against Kerry when they come – are the litmus test in what the GAA has to offer in terms of rivalry. But, despite the deep reach and legacy, it's simply not comparable to Glasgow.

There is no segregation and the community ethos comparable with Celtic is shared by both teams and indeed all of those who make the GAA the community volunteer movement that it is. Of course these are not the only overlapping virtues of the GAA and Celtic. The proliferation of county and club shirts visible at Celtic at every single fixture – home and away – serves a reminder of the crossover in interest and allegiances. The dual interest of so many of those who cross the Irish Sea week-in, week-out to lend their support to Celtic, twinned with their passion for Gaelic games is extremely common, not least in Ireland's Ulster counties where often the relationship with Celtic is much more widespread. Indeed, a part of the explanation for the small numbers of Irish-descended who play Gaelic games in Scotland comparable to other countries (Australia, England and North America) that attracted such large scale Irish immigration, is clearly to do with the existence of Celtic there. This meant they had a powerful ready-made cultural touchpoint on arrival, thus negating the need to create the GAA club units from scratch that occurred elsewhere.

Of course no self-respecting supporter can fail to scratch the itch of making the pilgrimage and at 19 years of age that was finally addressed. In the mid-nineties the supporters' clubs of various teams had notes carried in the Evening Herald and of course those of the Naomh Padraig branch were regularly digested by us. The frequency of the trips and the dedication of the supporters given the expense involved was something that was difficult to ignore. A mixture of college and home buddies signed up to travel with them to make the overnight trip via bus from O'Connell Street at some ungodly hour to Larne via Drogheda, where groups of young men in similar states of merriment were collected. If the old tape of rebel songs wasn't worn out by the time we boarded the ferry it had to be by the time the crossing was complete. Being deposited in Glasgow's east end finally cemented many years of ardent interest and proved a stamp of authentication.

A non-descript home win over Hearts (courtesy of Craig Burley) viewed from the upper echelons of the Lisbon Lions Stand, at a time when the stadium redevelopment was not yet complete, ensured a personal winning start to the record of games attended before the return journey was embarked upon. It was to be the start of something. Many of the same wanderers would return time and time again scratching the Celtic-Rangers itch home and away – more often than not ticketless going and sometimes remaining that way. That fixture, more than any other, was the one that lifted a lid on an underbelly of Scottish life that probably has to be seen to be fully understood.

European season passes followed including some of the most memorable nights of recent times at the great stadium. AC Milan, Manchester United (home and away), Juventus (less memorable for obvious reasons), Barcelona, Copenhagen and countless other league, cup and league cup games in between. There is no doubting the importance of the Irish heritage of the club to followers from Ireland and stories including the provision of the national flag by then Taoiseach (Prime Minister) Eamon de Valera and of course the battle to keep it flying drove enquiry and interest. Of equal importance is the enduring link that remains buoyant to this day.

The presence of so many other Irish-born players (and hundreds of others of Irish decent of course) down through the years helps sustain the Irish in Ireland connections; from Packie Bonner, Anton Rogan, Chris Morris, Mick McCarthy, Paul Byrne, Neil Lennon, Aidan McGeady, Robbie and Roy Keane not to mention Martin O'Neill and the current owner Dermot Desmond. A number of these too have been former GAA players in Ireland. That list of names – by no means complete – is a tangible manifestation of the live link in a playing and managerial sense between the club and the island that did so much to influence its emergence.

Of course the more things change in Ireland the more they stay the same. From a political standpoint there is no denying the emergence of a different Ireland since the mid to late 1990s. How these changes have rested with the Celtic support base – or those of them interested in the affairs of Ireland – could be the subject of a paper all of its own and this remains topical to this very day. The fortunes of Rangers have been scrutinised by followers of Celtic here in Ireland, just like anywhere else, and for many the saga of recent years has been a bittersweet experience. Although what Rangers have 'done' to Scottish football since the 1990s has been particularly detrimental to Celtic, the absence of the Celtic v. Rangers clashes during the worst years of self-inflicted decline on the part of Rangers, also robbed Celtic of media attention and exposure and of course huge days out. If truth be told it has also deprived the club of traction similar to that which prevailed in my younger days. It has also ensured that the resulting dominance means the question of Celtic playing in a league other than Scotland remains topical as followers speculate about any such move allowing the club to harness the full potential of its global fan-base while at the same time addressing the ridiculous imbalance in television money. It's not a new topic of discussion and it's one that is unlikely to end anytime soon.

In more recent times my job as an employee of the GAA, following many years covering Gaelic games as a journalist, has provided me with a first-hand view of how the club organises itself and maximises its assets. Of equal interest, it also allowed me to see first-hand the work of the Celtic Foundation and the special strand that still runs through the club from top to bottom and back again. It serves as a reminder that a club does not have to forget its roots, its original raison d'etre and indeed in this instance it would not be allowed to do so. Tony Hamilton, Chief Executive of the Foundation, has become a friend as part of that process and I look forward to my visits to Glasgow whenever possible in all probability with the next generation next time around.

The presence of successful Gaelic football and hurling teams – sometimes parading coveted GAA silverware at Celtic Park – also reminds us of the ties and connections. If they are going to Scotland to be shown off they are not going to any other club ground. However it's the planes, trains and automobiles feat week after week that helps feed the live and unique connection between the club and Ireland – at least from the perspective of those supporters living on the island of Ireland. The fortunes of a football club or indeed any sporting entity tend to ebb and flow and if truth be told over a lifetime, ebb more than flow in most instances. However, the attraction that plants the initial seed runs deep and remains regardless of short term gains and losses. And so it goes. Celtic of Glasgow. A club but so much more.

Celtic FC: The Mix, Influences and Birth

BRENDAN SWEENEY

It was truly fitting that when we celebrated Celtic's 125th anniversary, the club worked with the Celtic Graves Society to arrange a Mass at St. Mary's in Calton: our birthplace. It was from that same chapel that Brother Walfrid and the Founding Fathers that came out after midday mass on Sunday 6th November 1887 to walk 100 yards behind the chapel building to number 67 East Rose St. There, they took a left along an alleyway prophetically called 'Irish Wynd' to enter St. Mary's small League of the Cross Hall, which had only been in use for the previous year. They met to formally constitute Celtic Football Club, a ghetto club that would rise to become one of the biggest football institutions on the planet.

But when you look at the history of Celtic, you must go back much further than 1887 in Glasgow's dark east end for the defining moments that led to the circumstances being right for our foundation. As noted in the Celtic Minded series of books, in 1790 there were 60 anti-Catholic societies in Glasgow at a time when there were only 39 Catholics living in the city. In other words, every Catholic in the city could have their own anti-Catholic society named after them – and some could have had two!

So how did we arrive at the circumstances less than a century later, which provided the platform for a group of Catholic Irishmen to form a football club with its humble aims clearly stated:

> The main objective of the club is to supply the east end
> conferences of the St. Vincent De Paul Society with funds for the

maintenance of the Dinner Tables of our needy children in the missions of St. Mary's, Sacred Heart and St. Michael's.

In fact, we have to go back to the 1840s to understand the first two things that started a chain of events which intertwined in a very complex manner to create the conditions for Celtic to evolve.

The first was the construction of St. Mary's chapel in Calton in Glasgow's east end in 1842: this as a result of the heavy influx of Irish workers into the city as well as much smaller numbers that came from the highlands of Scotland. It was only the second Catholic chapel to be built in Glasgow and so its boundaries covered the whole of the east end within a radius of 5 miles north, south and east. As a result of Irish immigration, by 1873 the Catholic population had grown so much in the east end that missions were built in Bridgeton at Sacred Heart and then, just three years later, in Parkhead at St. Michael's. Despite these missions being detached from the mother parish, St. Mary's continued to grow until its population was estimated to be around 10,000 at the time of Celtic's foundation – in just one parish! Appropriately, the size of St. Mary's Parish resembles those of many in modern day Africa – which today we often recognise as 'mission territory'.

The parish was central to the growth and the education of the Catholic presence in the city and many religious as well as political organisations flourished from within – the League of the Cross, the St. Vincent De Paul Society, the Catholic Union and the Irish National Foresters to name a few. The St. Mary's branch of the Irish National League in fact had the largest membership outside of Ireland and was named 'The Home Government Branch', so huge was its membership.

In prominent positions amongst many of these groups were the Founding Fathers of Celtic, the sharpest minds of the parish who honed their debating and organisational skills and brought these together to form Celtic. It was one of the reasons why Celtic hit the ground running in 1888. The Founding Fathers had already worked together in the close-knit organisations already mentioned and they knew each other's strengths.

In 1878, when Celtic's first Patron Charles Eyre became the first Catholic Archbishop of Glasgow in the three centuries since the Reformation, it was the Englishman who was chosen deliberately to bring together Scotland's Catholic population; minority native Scots and majority immigrant Irish. Thus, he united his flock, built chapels and schools. He began a process of giving Catholics back their pride. Without this, the Founding Fathers would not have been given the tools to reflect something about the diaspora in the sporting arena.

Amidst small but significant Irish immigration to the Glasgow and Lanarkshire areas and the subsequent development of St. Mary's, just three years after the parish was built the Great Hunger took place in Ireland: a cataclysmic event that meant that within twenty years half the population of Ireland had either died or fled the island through emigration. Over 100,000 came to Scotland and settled mainly in the Glasgow and Lanarkshire areas, with thousands also in Dundee and Edinburgh. In terms of the development of sport/football in Scotland, it's a fact that in every area where the Irish settled in large numbers, a generation or so later they formed football clubs – Dundee Harp, Hibernian and Celtic being three that rose to the top of the game in Scotland.

It should never be forgotten that it was the offspring of the Great Hunger that were solely and directly responsible for the foundation of Celtic Football Club. A century and a half after the Famine, the Celtic support rightly remember that tragic event in song as we join Mary in sad lament at the cruel exile of her husband Michael to foreign lands for the heinous crime of stealing cheap scraps of Indian corn to feed his starving family. If ever a song summed up our club there is none better than 'The Fields of Athenry'.

It is essential that whilst we sing the words of this beautiful ballad, that we pause to reflect on the lyrics and the emotion and meaning behind them. Today also, it is essential too, that we act to support, and appreciate and construct, an everlasting memorial to An Gorta Mor, in the very city that benefitted so much from the arrival of the Irish.

The next vital ingredient in the birth of Celtic came about

almost by coincidence when two Marist brothers travelled from France to Tipperary after being invited to set up a Marist boarding school there in 1855 by a French linen merchant, Mr Charles Thiebaut. On deciding that the time was not yet right, they travelled back to Lille via Glasgow where they met with Bishop Murdoch and Fr. Chisholm, who had just set up St. Mungo's school in the north of the city. The Bishop promptly requested that three Marist Brothers be transferred from London to Glasgow to teach at the new school.

Remarkably, in the very same year, 15 year-old Andrew Kerins escaped the immediate after effects of the Great Hunger by sailing on a coal ship from Sligo to his new life in Glasgow: after funding the trip by selling a young foal at Ballymote market. He settled in the parish of St. Mungo's and it was there at night school where he became fascinated by the work of the Marist Brothers, whilst working by day at the growing iron works or on the construction of the railway.

Andrew Kerins greatly appreciated the opportunity – amongst the despair and poverty of Glasgow in the 1850s and 60s – that the teaching of the Marist Brothers had given him. Age 24, motivated by his Catholic beliefs and principles and a decision to increase substantially his Christian activism, he decided to devote his life to serving others by joining the Marist Brothers' teaching order.

The Marist Order was founded in France and so Andrew Kerins travelled to Beauchamp in the north of the country where he spent five years learning at the Marist novitiate. On 12th April, 1869 he returned to Glasgow to teach at his first school, St. Mungo's, where it is stated in the school log book for that day: 'Andrew Kerins and Hugh O'Neill were entered as assistants'. Andrew Kerins of course became known as Brother Walfrid and ironically he was put in charge of the same night classes where he had gained his first education in Glasgow.

A year later, in another crucial step towards the formation of Celtic, he moved to the larger school at St. Mary's where shortly afterwards he introduced a football into the playground as an incentive to get the schoolkids to arrive early at school and not to fight with the kids from the other schools en route. The initiative took off and by March 1871, Brother Walfrid was already aware of the growing influence of football amongst the working class.

In 1873, when the chapel and school of Sacred Heart were built in nearby Bridgeton as a satellite parish to St. Mary's, there was only one candidate that Limerick man Fr. Noonan, also from St. Mary's, wanted to take with him as headmaster – Brother Walfrid. He may only have worked at St. Mary's for just over three years, but the contacts he made in that time would prove vital to the foundation of Celtic fourteen years later.

The next vital ingredient that Brother Walfrid faced at Sacred Heart was the Poor Children's Dinners Tables, which he established in the freezing winter of 1884 with the assistance of the St. Vincent De Paul Society. In 1871, he had introduced a ball into the playground at St. Mary's: thirteen years later he had to put food on the table to encourage the kids to attend school (think 2019 and Mary's Meals in numerous countries and Project Gambia in Africa) – it was probably the only meal the kids would get that day.

In Brother Walfrid's own words – the one and only time ever recorded in the Catholic Observer in 1895 – he said:

> In 1884, the good Brothers of the St. Vincent De Paul opened the penny dinners for the school children, by which means the children were provided with a good warm meal for a penny. Should parents prefer, they could send the bread and the children could get a large bowl of broth or soup for a halfpenny and those who were not able to pay got a substantial meal free. This has been a great blessing to the poor children. The expenses for some time were met by subscriptions and collections, sermons etc, until the Celtic FC was started, the committee of which gave the good Brothers 33 shillings a week up to a short time since.

In its first year, the Poor Children's Dinner Tables at Sacred Heart provided over 48,500 dinners and 1150 breakfasts. St. Mary's, St. Michael's and St. Andrews on the Clyde quickly followed suit, but funding this initiative soon became a major concern. A year later a 'Breakfast Table' was set up on Savoy

Street, behind Sacred Heart, where schoolkids were fed a large bowl of porridge and milk. Priests and Bishops gave Charity Sermons to raise much needed funds, but it was a hand-to-mouth existence as every penny that came in quickly went straight back out again to put food on the table.

The situation was desperate by February 1886 when the school roll rose from 300 in 1874 to 1200 twelve years later. The congregation also rose from 2000 to 6000. Clearly funding had to found to meet the spiralling costs of the Poor Children's Dinner Tables. The seriousness of the situation was evident when no less a man than Archbishop Charles Eyre took to the pulpit at Sacred Heart with a Charity Sermon as he spelled out the increased costs being incurred, the crisis in funding it and the dangers of proselytism: whereby children were forced to 'take the soup' at a soup kitchen arranged by other faiths, in return for their religious allegiance.

Thankfully, no less than Brother Walfrid, a man well aware of the plight of the children, was in the audience that night, and he made it his personal crusade to ensure that the Poor Children's Dinner Tables would be maintained. He had witnessed the severity of the problem first hand and he had a plan. He had noticed how the game of football had increased hugely in popularity amongst the working class and he had already founded two local junior teams – Columba and Eastern Rovers – in an effort to keep the young men of his parish off the street corners. Now the time was right to use his contacts and his influence in the city to arrange a charity football match, with all funds raised towards the Poor Children's Dinner Tables at Sacred Heart.

Brother Walfrid immediately called on Clyde Football Club, who were based in the parish of Sacred Heart in Bridgeton and they agreed to host a charity match between themselves and a club of the St. Vincent De Paul's choosing. Obviously, an Irish club would prove a bigger attraction and so Brother Walfrid contacted both Hibernian and Dundee Harp. Hibs already had a fixture on 8th May 1886 and so it was Dundee Harp who took on Clyde at Barrowfield with adverts placed in the Catholic Observer as well as on every lamp post in the area.

The rain stayed away and a decent crowd turned out paying sixpence a head as both teams played their strongest elevens. Brother Walfrid probably couldn't have written a better script for the match itself, as Clyde took a first half lead before Dundee Harp stormed back in the second half to win 2-1: naturally, the enthusiastic crowd showed their appreciation. After the game, Brother Walfrid presided over the lunch at the post-match social as both teams returned to Sacred Heart School House where toasts were read out and replied to with great gusto.

Three months later, and with the funds raised at the Clyde match having dwindled away, Brother Walfrid decided to organise another charity match, and this time he managed to get the biggest Irish club in Scotland to take part, as Hibernian agreed to take on St. Peter's (from the parish of that name) in Partick. September 18th 1886 was the date for the match, with the funds raised going to the Poor Children's Dinner Tables at St. Mary's, where the headmaster was Brother Dorotheus, who would assist Brother Walfrid in founding Celtic little over a year later. Indeed, it was Dorotheus who carried out Celtic's early audits.

On the day, Hibs had to play Stoke at Hibernian Park in a return match and with no other date available, they were forced to send a Reserve Team to Glengarry Park in Bridgeton to face St. Peter's. Despite the disappointment, 1000 spectators turned out – paying sixpence each – and again the script couldn't have been better written as St. Peter's caused a huge shock, beating Hibs Reserve team 5-0, as the locals lapped it up.

In November 1886, Brother Walfrid attended the St. Vincent De Paul's 33rd annual concert and he listened intently as Archbishop Charles Eyre once again focussed on the two main topics of the day: the maintenance of the Dinner Tables and the threat of proselytism. A lot of good work had been done in the nine months since Brother Walfrid was so moved when the desperation of the situation had been spelled out in Sacred Heart by the Archbishop: but he realised there was still a lot more to be done to help manage the problem. Walfrid had recently been promoted to Brother Superior with overall charge of all Marist activity in the city. Added to his carrying out relevant duties as headmaster of Sacred Heart, he now began to feel a greater sense of responsibility as well as a capacity to act on this. He wouldn't let anyone down. To fund the Poor Children's Dinner Tables, football was now central in his mind.

The final influencing factor in the formation of Celtic arrived just three months later as Hibernian reached the final of the Scottish Cup for the first time on 12th February 1887. Brother Walfrid again used all his contacts at St. Mary's as 'a committee of Glasgow Irishmen' feted Hibernian to an after-match dinner in St. Mary's Hall. The very fact that Hibernian, on beating Dumbarton 2-1, brought the Scottish Cup back to St. Mary's Hall before they returned to show it off in Edinburgh underlined Brother Walfrid's influence and importance.

Tom Maley claimed years later that in the Hibernian Secretary John McFadden's speech, he urged those present in Glasgow to 'go and do likewise': in other words, to form an Irish club in Glasgow. However, his speech and that of Dr. John Conway who became the first Honorary President of Celtic nine months later are available in full and if he did say these words, it wasn't in his speech. It may have been in private conversation which Tom Maley was privy to. The words which were to herald the formation of Celtic Football Club came from Dr. John Conway when he stated;

> Now we all desire to give the Hibernian that high commendation which they have so well earned, and as it has become proverbial that imitation is the sincerest flattery, I think we could not please them better than by following their example each in our own department.

A steering committee were given the task of looking at the feasibility of an Irish football club in Glasgow and that question was soon answered as the Glasgow Irish were awoken by the success of Hibernian winning the Scottish Cup. If Hibernian could achieve this with the backing of 25,000 Irishmen in the east – what could Celtic do with ten times that level of support in the west of Scotland?

Once celebrations died down, Brother Walfrid had the maintenance of the Poor Children's Dinner Tables to focus on and so he organised another charity match at Clyde's ground on 26th May 1887 between two of the biggest clubs in Scotland – Hibernian, winners of the Scottish Cup and Renton, recent winners of the Charity Cup. To add competition to the occasion a trophy was donated and named the East End Catholic Charity Cup. Better still there was bad blood between Hibs and Renton because the latter had scored a controversial winner in their last encounter just a month previously. It was a masterstroke – it had all the hallmarks of an embryonic Celtic Committee at work – and an incredible crowd of 12,000 turned up: more than had attended the Scottish Cup final!

If there was ever a doubt between 12th February and 26th May 1887 that Glasgow could sustain an Irish club, any remnants of that doubt disappeared on that day. Discussions immediately began between the three largest parishes of St. Mary's, St. Alphonsus and St. Andrew's with the aim of starting an Irish club in Glasgow. As is often the case – with such an emotional debate – discussions became heated and St. Alphonsus and St. Andrew's felt sidelined by the more prominent parishioners of the mother parish: both withdrew, although many of their parishioners remained. Instead, they were replaced by Sacred Heart and St. Michael's.

The East End Charity Cup Final was an incredible success but better still, the match had finished a 1-1 draw and a replay was required. For Brother Walfrid, this was 'an opportunity'. It was only fair to get both teams back to Barrowfield at the start of the next season with every penny raised going to the Poor Children's Dinner Tables again. The date was set for 6th August and although Brother Walfrid was praying for yet another draw, Hibs were trounced 6-0 in the pouring rain which had limited the crowd to a very respectable 4000. Neil McCallum scored five of Renton's goals and before the end of that same season, he would become the first player to score a goal for Celtic on 28th May 1888.

You would be forgiven for picturing Brother Walfrid and Archbishop Charles Eyre doing cartwheels as they counted the takings from both matches and the formation of Celtic Football Club was only three months away. Life without Celtic was coming to an end for evermore and all the main facets were finally coming together; the emergence of the parish of St. Mary's in the Calton, the Great Hunger causing the emigration of 100,000 men, women and children to Scotland, the revival of Catholicism there, the arrival of the Marist Order, and Brother Walfrid in particular, in the aftermath of that same Great Hunger, the need to maintain the Poor Children's Dinner Tables in the three parishes in the east end of Glasgow, and the rise in the popularity of football and in particular Hibernian (showing what an Irish club could achieve). From the combination of all these influencing factors arose Celtic. Celtic was/is unique in a number of ways from any other football club in Scotland and Britain. Firstly, the club had a committee, a built-in support and a ground leased for five years – the last thing was actually a ball and some players.

Almost 130 years later, Celtic remains a vehicle for good and amongst the biggest names in world football. The Club and even more importantly, its support, should never ever forget the humble beginnings of an Irish Football Club, later to become a Scottish institution, formed to fund the Poor Children's Dinner tables in the back streets of three Catholic parishes in Glasgow's poverty-drenched east end.

The team comes first

PAUL QUIGLEY

As a Celtic fan born at the beginning of the 1990s, I was raised on the stories of the old Jungle and the Celtic End. My dad and my uncle would regale me with tales of their youth; of the busses they ran, the pubs that they drank in, and of their own spot in Paradise from which they would watch Celtic's legends; Hay, Dalglish, McGrain, McStay and many more. My earliest memories of Celtic are almost all focused on stories from before I was born, no doubt at least partly a result of the on and off-field difficulties the club was going through coinciding with my earliest years of childhood. I heard all about the heady days of Johnny Doyle's header against Real Madrid, the mythic status of the 10 men that won the league, of the vile Rapid Vienna, whose goalkeeper's cowardice was only matched by that of our own board in agreeing to replay that infamous match in Manchester.

I don't doubt for a second that some of my dad's, and certainly most of my uncle's, stories, were drastically watered down versions fit for the ears of a young child. However, I was still able to understand even from that age that supporting Celtic was about much more than heading along to a stadium, taking your seat and watching the match unfold. Being a Celtic supporter to many meant much more than that, and this was epitomised by the camaraderie of the Jungle. My favourite picture from my youth was taken in the old stadium to the backdrop of these terraces, with me a little over a year old looking resplendent in a green and white striped tracksuit, held in my dad's arms as we posed next to Packie Bonner and Gordon Marshall. This was as close as I would get to these terraces as the old made way for the new, for better or for worse.

My formative years as an active Celtic fan came as Martin O'Neill transformed our club, and the ferocious European nights as we took on the continent's biggest and best, typified that period. I instantly became captivated watching Larsson under the Parkhead lights. We had a team that was afraid of nobody, and when that crowd got going, even the very biggest stars would so often wilt under the pressure. The noise was deafening, the sense of occasion palpable. I was absolutely hooked as I roared on my heroes.

As I grew a bit older though and started to go to games with my younger brother or my friends from school I began to feel somewhat short-changed. The all-seater stadium, the 'family atmosphere', the exorbitant ticket prices, and the ever-increasing sanitisation of the entire football experience stood in stark contrast to the tales I had heard in my youth of the raucousness of the old Celtic Park. I could hear the noise when we played in the Champions League, or feel the camaraderie on occasion in the right company, but it was fewer and further between than I had longed for.

The Gordon Strachan years brought success in terms of trophies, but like many others of my generation, the truth is that I wanted more from supporting Celtic. I wanted to rival the stories of my dad and my uncle. I wanted to support the team rather than to simply sit and watch them. Then in 2006, the movement was founded which would enable me to do all of that in the Green Brigade, following in the same traditions that have always been a part of our club. First from the brake clubs right up to 'The Jungle'. Then came the ultras. The majority of the founding members of what was to become the Green Brigade were first members of the JungleBhoys, a club-sanctioned group of Celtic fans who wanted to add a bit of colour and noise. It was clear from early on that different members within this well-intentioned group had different ideas and attitudes, but in hindsight, a split of some sort was inevitable.

The JungleBhoys planned an anti-sectarian display for a home

Celtic and Scotland star Kieran Tierney connects with the fans evoking the Spirit of the Jungle

The roots, resistance and identities of part of Celtic's core support

game against Rangers. However, once the operational staff at Ibrox got wind of this they ordered that their own club-sanctioned group proceed with a similar display. Unfortunately, an action which was intended to be a strike against the bigoted traditions of Rangers and to highlight the fundamental differences between our club and theirs, became for Celtic fans a hollow act of tokenism which merely perpetuated the eternal myth in Scottish society that 'one side is as bad as the other'. Many members of the JungleBhoys railed and voted against proceeding with this action, but the hierarchy overruled the dissenters and the two banners were flown in the respective home and away ends of Celtic Park and the truth is that this was a decision that the group would not recover from. Many of those that disagreed opted to leave, and three of these young guys, along with another budding ultra, met shortly thereafter in an east end pub to form what became the Green Brigade. I doubt that any of them had any real idea as to what it would become and all four remain hugely influential members within the group today.

From the outset, this new group was to have a different modus operandi to that of its predecessor, operating entirely independently from the club, asserting a more politicised identity and proclaiming an ultras mentality, which would inevitably court greater controversy and with it, evoke deeper degrees of both admiration and scorn. The truth: it is the ultra approach that makes the Green Brigade so different in Scottish football.

I joined the Green Brigade in the 2008/09 season, approximately two years after its foundation and there were several motivating factors leading to such a decision. The group had really made their name at this point off the back of the iconic 'Scotland's Shame' banner targeted at the away end on the night that Jan Vennegoor of Hesselink's late header just about kept us alive in that year's title race. The efforts made to bring back the noise and the colour peaked my interest, even if admittedly it would be a while before the noise aspect in particular would properly take off.

However, in November of 2008, Celtic wore the Earl Haig poppy on our strip, a symbol that for so many fans (many of them having past relations that participated in both World Wars) is synonymous with British military imperialism. For many it did not represent the fallen of the great wars, but rather seemed to be a justification for past wars and a propaganda tool for further wars: especially those seen by many as immoral conflicts. For many Celtic Minded people Celtic wearing that symbol was a tacit agreement with such things, an official validation and sanction. Celtic is more than a football club, but the very things that ensure that status were under threat and I wanted to be part of the fight against that.

I rallied against new Celtic chair John Reid. I walked out of Celtic Park rather than watch the sacrosanct green and white hoops be sullied by the red poppy and all that it symbolises: a fact more than evident by how it is used by those that care little for life or limb or who have mentalities linked to British militarism, imperialism and colonialism – past and present.

In the early days, the group presence inside Celtic Park was not much to write home about. For most of us, we had grown up watching 'Gazzeta Football Italia', with James Richardson's soothing voice talking the audience through the goals of Batistuta, Baggio and Inzaghi. The scenes on the terraces however were the real attraction here. The romanticism of Italian football was all about the colour, the huge flags, the chanting in unison, the artistic banners, the pyrotechnics and the unassailable Italian style. It was a bewitching spectacle for a young football fan to watch on a Sunday afternoon.

This was what we aspired to in the darkened corner of 111 within Celtic Park: though in hindsight we could not have been much further from those scenes. We would be crammed in to the back three rows of 111, usually 3 people to a seat, trying mostly in vain to enthuse those around us to join in. On a good day there would be 25 of us, singing and jumping for 90 minutes, leaving the stadium with hoarse voices, bruised shins and very little else to show for our efforts. The banners that the group began to produce though started to catch the imagination of the support, with some noticeably edgier displays. 'Blow Them Away' versus Man United, 'Some Men Fight For Silver' in the derby and the 'Graffiti On The Wall' action against Aberdeen were displays which helped to establish a clear visual distinction between the Green Brigade and the similar groups who'd come before. This too attracted the attention of the police even from very early on, and arrests made around this time set the tone for a tumultuous relationship with the powers that be.

Some games were turning points not only for the group, but also for the collective mentality of the wider Celtic support. One such game came in the 2008/09 season at Ibrox when Scott McDonald fired a half volley flying over and beyond the despairing arms of a flailing Allan McGregor, sending us 7 points clear at the top of the table going into the new year. Prior to the match there was a confetti display organised but the small banner prepared for halftime stole all the plaudits. The same Rangers supporters group who had participated in the so-called anti-sectarian display with the JungleBhoys were singing an entirely different, and indeed contrary, tune this time. They flew a banner depicting a Celtic fan hopping upon the 'offended bus' whilst a nearby signpost urged us all to return to Ireland by way of the Stranraer ferry.

What an outcry in Scotland if these words said; Pakistanis go home, Chinese go home, Poles go home – anyone else? Maybe, 'The Famine is over why don't you go home'? Our mole was thrilled to uncover this work prior to its unveiling, and the effort to usurp it began in earnest. A new banner was made in the exact same style, but with the Celtic fan leading the bus to another title win, the title across the banner reading 'BUS-TED'.

When the bigoted hordes unveiled their banner, the Green Brigade dropped theirs, and dropped some mouths simultan-eously in the Govan Rear. The Celtic support went wild: as if Paddy McCourt himself had just came on to score a last minute winner. The game was poised at 0-0 on the pitch but the away fans had taken the lead in the stands, and when the game restarted, the Celtic fans were in clear ascendancy. This was foot-balling one-upmanship at its most pure. McDonald's winner soon came and we brought the bells in with smiles on our faces.

Another was in March of 2009 when we faced our old rivals again, this time at Hampden in the League Cup Final. The Green Brigade had prepared the group's first ever display of note at the national stadium, preparing a sea of green and white flags to be flown in the Celtic end, broken in to blocks of solid colour. The plan with any display is for it to go when the teams emerge from the tunnel, to give the players and the fans that last minute jolt before the action begins to go out there and dominate our opponents, whoever they may be. On this particular occasion, Hampden was a sea of green and white half an hour before a ball was kicked in anger. The Celtic support waved their flags and cheered the players throughout their warm up, as the support in the opposite end stood in silence, waiting to hold up their card to make up the mosaic that their supporters groups had laid out. Nonetheless, from the minute the flags went up until Stephen McManus lofted that trophy above his head, the Celtic fans unequivocally dominated the battle in the stands. Clips of the fans singing Amhran na bhFiann at this game can still be found online: this day belonged to us.[1]

As the Green Brigade increasingly became a substantially important bedrock and feature of the Celtic match day experience, Neil Lennon took charge of the team: coinciding with the group being given our own official area within 111. He immediately roused the troops as he swore to bring back the thunder. This was music to our ears and the displaying of a banner, which demanded that he lead us to war – football war of course – marked his first match: the whole club was crying out for an injection of ardour. The timing was perfect and the stage was set.

With each passing home match, we were proving what we could bring to the occasion, and while we were not quite the famed AC Milan ultras of the Fossa Dei Leoni, we were improving week on week in terms of the noise and colour we brought. Our actions outside of the stadium were also capturing the wider imagination, as our annual anti-discrimination football tournament grew with each passing year. Our charitable efforts increased and we would later go on to hold large food-bank collections to help the poorest in society and to uphold the legacy of Brother Walfrid with the backing of the unique generosity of the Celtic support.

1. https://www.youtube.com/watch?v=ZmWbfkHbt9Q

Nevertheless, just as it looked like the upward trajectory might never end, the group's first major controversy lurked around the corner. Celtic again adorned the red poppy, and as the club dismissed the concerns of supporters who viewed this as a political symbol of brutality and imperialism: the group felt inclined to act and to take a principled stand.

We expected backlash but perhaps not of the magnitude that unfolded. The reaction was initially muted, before the press went in to a state of apoplexy as we released a statement proclaiming that the only thing we regretted was our spelling error. This story was broadcast across the globe and the press across Britain was united in condemning us. Jackie Bird read out our statement on BBC Reporting Scotland as a digitalised image of our group skull slowly rotated onscreen. It was frankly surreal, and was our first taste of notoriety on that scale.

My feeling at the time was that the support's reaction to the entire situation was mixed, there were many who disagreed with the poppy on the strip but also with our approach, whilst others fell more strongly to the for or against category. However, soon the hypocrisy of those who had enforced the poppy on our strip taking such an anti-Green Brigade position was too much for most to bear. Football and politics have, and always will be, inextricably linked, however hard or soft. Nonetheless, this incident perfectly captured the insincerity of those who would claim otherwise but who seek to use this very mantra to attack us. The poppy itself is a military and political symbol and if it was to be 'weaponised' and forced upon our club and supporters then the supporters have a civic right to oppose that with which they politically disagree. To their eternal credit, the fan organisations, lead initially by the unwavering vanguards in the Celtic Trust, condemned our attackers. We would live to fight another day, and the poppy has not adorned our strip since. This I believe is the will and morality of the vast majority of the support.

The 2010/11 season was unlike any other, leading to incredible sagas from referee strikes to bullets and bombs sent to Irish/Catholic individuals through the post. This season was to bring us the infamously so-called shame game, a match which resulted in 3 red cards, several touchline brawls and more

Rangers players being shown yellow cards than the number of Celtic fans arrested on the night (with most of these arrests being for the heinous crime of smoking in the toilet).

In response to the 'sensationalist' match reporting of the mainstream media, then First Minister, Hearts supporter Alex Salmond, called an emergency summit. The result of this meeting was eventually the Offensive Behaviour at Football and Threatening Communications (Scotland) Act 2012. Football fans no longer had the same rights as everyone else and could now face up to 5 years in prison if they did something which someone, somewhere, might find offensive. Soon to follow was an unrivalled period of unrest as Scotland once again struggled to come to terms with the question posed by the Irish self-identification of the Irish diaspora, over a century and a half after the major wave of immigration from the Emerald Isle caused by An Gorta Mor.

The natives were restless and the results were abhorrent. Bombs and bullets were sent to a number of those associated with Catholicism, Celtic and Irishness in Scotland – to make the croppies lie down. The SNP often refer back to this period in defence of their shambolic policy of criminalising football fans. Something had to be done they claimed. What they choose to overlook however is that sending a homemade bomb was already a criminal offence and that what they proposed would have had no impact during this period whatsoever, even if they felt it made them look honest and sincere.

Fans Against Criminalisation were formed to oppose this soon-to-be law, and the campaign group consisted of the Green Brigade, the Celtic Trust, the Celtic Supporters' Association, the Affiliation of Registered Celtic Supporters' Clubs and the Association of Irish Celtic Supporters' Clubs. The Justice Committee then heard evidence from across Scottish civil society. It was informed repeatedly by such as Professor Tom Devine to reverse course, the act was illiberal, dangerous and not fit for purpose: but the SNP persevered. The period between the Act going through Parliament and the first few months of its enacting, October 2011 to May 2012, was particularly turbulent for the group. The police have since admitted that their approach throughout this period was to pursue a tactic of 'shock & awe'. During this time, there were flashpoints at almost every game.

Several months later, scenes of disorder on the Gallowgate stemming from an extraordinary overreaction from Police Scotland to a peaceful march shocked many. For what was intended to be a small march of solidarity with the mounting number of fans facing bans from football matches, the police summoned in excess of 200 officers, 20 horses, 20 vans and a helicopter in a blatant show of force as orchestrated by the soon-to-be Chief Constable of newly created Police Scotland, Stephen House. An independent witness, who acted as such during poll tax and miners' protests in the 1980s and anti-war demonstrations in the early 2000s, said that it was the worst example of police brutality she had witnessed. The police wielded their batons and literally lashed out at men, women and children and the SNP Scottish Government faced questions over our treatment.

Stephen House came out fighting, as he wrote to every elected representative who had spoken to him and denounced all those who dared to stand up for us. He claimed that of the 14 arrested, all would be convicted, and, that following this victory for the Procurator Fiscal, the police would release footage, which would shame the Green Brigade and anyone who came to our defence. Nobody else was charged in the end however, not a single person was convicted for anything prior to the police wading in to the crowd, and, the police released no footage afterwards. This incident though in particular served to do nothing more than strengthen our resolve as it also in turn blackened the reputation of these particular members of Scotland's police.

Rather than be deterred by the violence of the state, the group and FAC opted to respond the next week by marching up the very same route. We held our second massive demonstration at George Square, which drew thousands of fans, and then marched the highway up to Celtic Park. The feeling of turning left on the Gallowgate, preparing for the possibility of more confrontation with the police will live with me forever. As always, I was most proud of the group when we have just disregarded the possible adverse consequences and stood up for ourselves and for what was right. There were however, no mounted officers on this day charged with stopping us.

Fortunately, this period was not all confrontation with the police and government, and the group continued to grow in our section for the purposes it was founded: creating improved displays and helping to generate increasing levels of noise with new songs that the Celtic support would take to their hearts. 'Just Can't Get Enough', a song previously the subject of ridicule and contempt, became a firm fan favourite. The back and forth of 'Come On You Bhoys in Green' was quickly perfected by the entire stadium, and the huddle as 60,000 people turned their back on the game to embrace and jump in unison was a sight to behold.

We faced the old Rangers for the last ever time at Celtic Park in April of 2012. With the group now famed for our banners and displays, there was pressure on us to help deliver one final blow to our archrivals: this before they were killed off by the taxman because of their cheating, greed, and self-serving dealings over many years. It was initially suggested we might seek to do a tifo similar to that of Real Madrid's group Ultras Sur. In a match against Atletico Madrid, this fan group displayed a banner depicting a young Atleti fan lying in bed, hiding under the covers and surrounded by various intimidating characters, from classic scary movies, with Freddy Krueger and Michael Myers dawning the Real colours to haunt their rival's sleep.

It was suggested we perhaps do something similar, but with Hector the Taxman and Craig Whyte the scary figures in this drama. One member however had a sudden eureka moment and the idea of a banner depicting the four horseman of the apocalypse was born. The stadium roared as the banner was unfurled and the entire home support were unrelenting in their derision of the travelling fans. We all sang of Craig Whyte (though the true arch culprit, culprits and others that colluded were probably missed in such chanting) and the looming reality of liquidation as a coffin was passed from stand to stand. The rebels had won and no amount of delusion in Govan and beyond can alter that. Rangers were gone but we had our eyes on bigger things once again.[2]

2. https:// www.youtube.com/ watch?v=vrUpq4PQ8_M

As the club made its long awaited return to the group stages of the Champions League, we were drawn against Barcelona, due to face them at home almost 125 years to the day since Celtic were formed in St. Mary's in Glasgow's east end. Billy McNeill once famously quipped that there is often a fairy-tale about this club, and on the evidence of how this match was to unfold, you would find such an argument difficult to dispute. Understanding the mammoth sense of occasion, the group took the decision to do something that we had never done before and turned to the support to back us financially to help fund a full stadium display, befitting of this moment in our history. The response was humbling, as thousands of pounds were raised: we were acutely aware that we owed it to those who had donated to ensure that our efforts were worthy.

The whole build-up to this game was quite simply special. The Mass held in St. Mary's set the tone even prior to the match, and the sense of occasion was palpable from the second one entered the footprint of the ground. The team entered our arena with their heads held high and their chests puffed out, glancing around them at the tribute to 125 years of the famous Glasgow Celtic. As they soaked in the atmosphere that the Parkhead cauldron was creating, they exuded the confidence that they would require to take on and beat arguably the greatest club side there has ever been: Celtic ran out 2-1 winners against the might of Messi, Xavi and Iniesta. The team went on to reach the last 16 of the Champions League, and the European nights we'd all been longing for and the thunder that Neil Lennon had promised had indeed returned.

By the time of the 2013/14 season however, the Offensive Behaviour at Football Act meant that arrest cases were piling up week on week over the song, Roll of Honour. Shortly prior to the home tie against Ajax in October 2013, 7 members were arrested and charged under the OBA for allegedly singing this song. At this point, the group and the FAC campaign were doing all that we could to engage with Celtic on the issue, to find some common ground and to work together. There was early talk within the group of doing an edgy action against Ajax, like the Bobby Sands/William Wallace one we eventually went on to do against AC Milan. Soon, the group went on to produce arguably one of our best ever home displays, commemorating the Lions and Jock Stein as the forefathers of relentless, expressive attacking football and a fantastic night was had by all as the team won 2-1.

Nevertheless, with seven members and friends facing convictions under the terms of the Act, with the club refusing to help, with a Government going unchallenged, and a police force gone mad, I still to this day do not think we had much of a choice but to do something special. Clearly, a banner of Bobby Sands and William Wallace off the top tier of the Lisbon Lions stand was dramatic, highlighting as it did the hypocrisy (particularly on the part of the SNP) inherent within the Offensive Behaviour Act and spectacularly making the point we intended. Why should Scottish society diminish and shame our legends and outstanding historical and political figures (Sands) while lauding its own (Wallace)?

By the time of the Ronny Deila era discussions had begun to take place about the prospect of a safe-standing section being created. Over the course of the next two years, our members liaised with the club, who to its credit pursued this much more than expected. As the Deila era wore on, the group produced some great displays and helped create impressive atmospheres. After two years of Ronny, Brendan Rodgers was announced as our new manager and a wave of optimism washed over everyone connected to the club. In addition, Celtic had officially revealed that Celtic Park would be home to the first ever safe-standing section in the UK: which we would be charged with leading down the front of our spiritual home in section 111. Political change was afoot as well as the Scottish National Party lost their absolute majority in the Scottish Parliamentary elections, paving the way for repeal of the Offensive Behaviour at Football Act. Our spirits lifted by recent developments, 70 of us jetted off to Santa Ponsa to celebrate the 10-year anniversary of our group, to sing of Brendan Rodgers and let off some flares down by the beach. A new dawn was on the horizon, but nobody could have predicted the kind of season that lay ahead.

We opened the new section with a large banner paying

homage to the generations that came before us, from the spirit of The Jungle to the ultras block of 111. There was little time to settle in however before our next big controversy, as Celtic were drawn against Hapoel Be'er Sheva, the Israeli champions, in the third round of qualification for the holy grail of the Champions League group stages. As a group, we have always been proud to support the anti-colonial cause of the Palestinian people. However, given that UEFA had previously fined the club as a result of supporters displaying the flag of Palestine, our mettle was about to be tested.

The truth is that we felt that we had a moral obligation to do what little we could and to use what platform we had to make it clear that we condemn the occupation of Palestine and subjugation of her people. To allow the match to pass without some form of protest against the Israeli government would have been to allow their crimes to be normalised and accepted. Naturally, we knew there might be consequences but we were more than prepared for them. We flew the Palestinian flag proudly in our section. In the aftermath of our action, this story was to become international news, broadcast by every media outlet from Russia Today to Fox News. One common argument trotted out by those condemning us was that football is no place for such gestures, and that ultimately some flags at a match would have no impact on the people we proclaimed to be speaking for. What was to happen next however would confound the naysayers.

As UEFA announced its intention to open disciplinary proceedings, the group and the Celtic fans in general were swept in a deluge of support from all over the globe. The pictures emanating from Palestine of young children, breaking open their piggy banks to donate what little pocket money they had collected towards paying the inevitable fine demanded by UEFA, will live with me forever. The impact that our action had on them was clear, and the criticism from various other quarters mattered not a jot in comparison. The Celtic badge was projected on the walls of Ramallah and the club gained thousands of new supporters, almost overnight. When we launched a JustGiving project to 'Match the Fine for Palestine', the reaction was overwhelming and we eventually were able to donate £176k to

Palestinian charities of our choosing. This stands as demonstrable proof of the positive impact that football fans can have, and, we will maintain our close links with the recipients, the Lajee Centre, to support them in the coming years in any way we can.

As the 2016-17 season kicked in to gear, it quickly became apparent that something very special was happening on the field and in the stands. Our new section was everything we had dreamed it would be and more and every single game at Celtic Park became a joy to attend. North Curve Celtic was founded and thousands were now able to make a fortnightly pilgrimage to watch Celtic play, knowing that they could stand with their mates and support the team in the way that past generations had taken for granted. On the park, a new team was being moulded capable of playing fast, expressive, relentlessly attacking football. It was a season that will live long in the memory. The bond between the fans and the team made it all the more special, personified by Kieran Tierney, one of our own out there on the pitch playing for us.

Everything we had longed for seemed to be here. We had our equivalent of The Jungle in our own paradise, we had managed to create the scenes that we had merely dreamt of and we now had a team that played with the kind of passion the fans demanded. In the season that would mark the fiftieth anniversary of the club's greatest achievement, we paid homage to the Lisbon Lions, with thanks to the incredibly generous backing of the Celtic support, with another full stadium tifo in their honour. The current team cemented its own place in history by completing a domestic treble without losing a single match along the way. By 2017-18 the Double Treble was achieved and in 2018-19 the Treble Treble is due to be completed by time of the launch of this book.

We have come a long way from the early meetings and crammed days in the back of 111. There are now young fans who go to games who have simply always known the Green Brigade to be there in some shape or form. It remains our duty to the traditions of the club to build on what we have achieved so far and to ensure that spirit of The Jungle lives on.

An open heart and an open spirit: links with Europe

Ròisín Coll & Bob Davis

From its origins, Celtic Football Club has had a close connection with Europe. The Marist brothers, an order founded in France in 1816 by Fr Jean-Claude Colin, afforded the club from its foundation a sense of belonging to the wider international networks of the Catholic Church and especially to its charitable presence in the great and growing European cities. The club's founder, Brother Walfrid, intended that Celtic from its outset would address the plight of Glasgow's Irish Catholic poor whilst maintaining the population within the orbit of the wider Church and its spiritual life.

From this rich genealogy there arose among the club's supporters a natural sense of attachment to wider European traditions and institutions that predated the emergence of a European platform for football competition itself. Important work by Raymond McCluskey (2006) has overturned earlier simplistic stereotypes of a working class Irish Catholic community of narrowed cultural horizons by highlighting the presence across the community of broader European expressions of Catholic identity – such as parish support of and participation in pilgrimages to Lourdes, Rome and Fatima; the establishment of and involvement in prayer groups and other organisations centred on the patronage and charisma of a range of European saints and spiritual leaders (eg. St. Vincent De Paul); and the continuing presence at the heart of the community of apostolic orders and congregations with deep continental roots (eg. Jesuits,

Redemptorists, Sisters of Mercy). All of these features were of course set in the context of a Church with a common language of liturgy and ideas spanning those same European nations that would soon prove to be the crucible of twentieth century European football played at the highest levels of international excellence.

Hence the daily fabric of working class Irish Catholic life in Scotland was routinely, even unconsciously, imprinted with 'the idea of Europe', even where the population's actual geographical mobility and opportunity might be limited. Celtic Football Club was the beneficiary of all of these influences. The concept of 'following' the club in Europe fitted naturally with the experience of 'following' other trends and movements integral to the life of the Irish Catholic community from which the club had emerged.

The resultant, detailed record of Celtic's fortunes in European football competition has been well documented elsewhere in soccer literature, club memoirs and sports journalism. Nevertheless, there are key highlights from this experience that remain integral to understanding Celtic's relationship with Europe as the club's fortunes advanced.

Obviously, foremost among these is Lisbon 1967 (Bradley and Kelly address marginalised critical aspects of this historic victory in the international academic journal, Soccer & Society 2019). As several commentators observed in the jubilee year, the winning of the European Cup entered Celtic folklore as much for cultural and social reasons as sporting ones. The late 1960s was a golden age of (relative) Scottish working class prosperity and a degree of progress also in Irish-descended Catholic social mobility. While the trip to Lisbon was indeed for many fans their first excursion to continental Europe, for many others it sat alongside the increase in family holidays to Spain, the growing popularity of Mallorca and even the expansion of employment opportunities for skilled tradesmen in places like West Germany.

The legendary triumph of a group of football players passionately attached to the club and locally sourced coexisted with a steady increase in community confidence and cosmopolitan expectation of which Europe, and travel to Europe, was often the focus. Lisbon not only reflected this trend, it represented a major milestone within it. In securing the sport's most prestigious trophy, against quite overwhelming odds, Celtic's achievement symbolised a wider demand for domestic and international recognition on the part of a disadvantaged community that had always seen the European stage as a setting commensurate with its cultural and religious pedigree as well as its reasserted ambitions and talents. Unsurprisingly, these sentiments echoed movements and events centred in this period on the island of Ireland itself.

while 30,000 tickets were sold to Celtic fans for the match against Porto, more than 50,000 additional supporters joined the sporting pilgrimage to Seville

Moving on a generation to Seville 2003, the profile of the Celtic support base had of course changed and evolved considerably. An iconic moment in one of the official DVD recordings of Seville shows a map illustrating the points of origin of the Celtic travelling support. It highlights the fact that by the turn of the millennium the diaspora had put down roots both globally and continentally, moving beyond the anglosphere to bases including most of the major European capitals. The ease of travel, the technology-assisted networking, the generally more diverse and layered nature of the fan base underpinning the movement of supporters to Seville also pointed to greater levels of prosperity, mobility and cultural self-confidence across the original community and its descendants. An important folk statistic from the time indicated that while 30,000 tickets were sold to Celtic fans for the match against Porto, more than 50,000 additional supporters joined the sporting pilgrimage to Seville.

Between these two undoubted pinnacles of the Celtic experience of European football, lies a catalogue of 'European nights' stretching across the multiple campaigns and trophies in which the club has competed over a number of decades. Inclusion in this catalogue is often the basis of heated discussion and competing memories, as supporters vie with each other in recalling last-minute victories, titanic two-leg contests, wins snatched from the jaws of defeat, stellar individual performances, and goals worthy of the finest that football can produce.

Who can forget the September-October 1992 3-0 victory at Celtic Park over Cologne – after Celtic had lost the first leg 0-2? A late and brilliant John Collins clincher. Or a young, transitional Celtic team triumph over a formidable Ujpest Dozsa side in 1972, with Celtic showing great mettle and nous to win 2-1 away in Budapest (thanks to a mesmeric Lou Macari) – in what Jock Stein described as the club's best European performance since Lisbon. Or Celtic overcoming Real Madrid 2-0 in 1980 with performances of true brilliance from Alan Sneddon and George McCluskey? Or Shunsuke Nakamura's iconic 81st minute free-kick winner against the seemingly invincible Manchester United in November 2006?

It is hence small wonder to Celtic fans that soccer giants such as Gianluigi Buffon and Lionel Messi, and commentators like Clyde Tyldesley, have acclaimed Celtic Park for the best sporting atmosphere in European footballing competition. Andres Iniesta observed that, 'The Celtic fans are very special and the Club and players can be very proud of them. They are the very best I have ever heard'. Michael Owen declared that, 'The best atmosphere I have ever played in was at Celtic Park in the UEFA Cup for Liverpool'. Paolo Maldini went so far as to recommend that, 'every professional footballer should seek to play at least one game at Celtic Park. I have never felt anything like it' (Lynch, YouTube, 2018). There might be similar numbers elsewhere, sometimes even better stadiums, but there is something in the Celtic supporter psycho-social, cultural, historical and religious experience and DNA, as a largely diasporic marginalised people, that connects Celtic supporters with each other in a very unique way. This clearly gets expressed vocally and visually during major domestic and European nights.

> With some obvious exceptions, Celtic fans have a European, even a global, reputation for their welcome, their camaraderie and for generally 'spreading the sunshine'

Several common themes arise from these experiences that are central to understanding Celtic's relationship with Europe. One of these might be called fraternity. The welcome, the rapport with and hospitality of Celtic fans towards fans of competing teams whether home or away – and often amidst the acknow-ledgement of fierce rivalry – this is part of what it means to be Celtic. With some obvious exceptions, Celtic fans have a European, even a global, reputation for their welcome, their camaraderie and for generally 'spreading the sunshine' wherever they go. Numerous articles appeared after Seville with accolades for the Celtic fans' behaviour, merriment and positivity, commenting on how they can be 'trusted' (See eg 'Celtic Fans so civil in Seville',

https://m.youtube.com/watch?v=x4dt4XzjJoo&feature=youtu.be

Daily Telegraph, 25 May 2003). This clearly stands in stark contrast with fans of some other football teams, where we hear routinely of some European cities having to issue storm warnings before their arrival!

Many locations hosting Celtic in other European fixtures echo similar sentiments to those recorded after Seville. City mayors, police forces, football authorities, football managers, referees and indeed players have all been quick to commend and praise the atmosphere created by the fans. This pattern, which has existed throughout the Celtic story, recently culminated in the accolade of a 'FIFA Best' award in 2017 in recognition of the fiftieth anniversary tribute to the 1967 winners. In being true to our roots Celtic fans must always seek to uphold and maintain such outstanding behaviour and positive attitudes.

Another theme might be connection: the historic affinity that has been struck up with teams like St. Pauli, Celta Vigo, Barcelona, and now perhaps PSG. This is often with clubs with similar or parallel pedigrees, with deep roots in working class, diasporic, or culturally and politically marginalised communities.

A third obvious theme related to this is what might be termed the sense of destiny: that we belong here; that this is our stage; that we can and ought to perform and entertain naturally on the European platform, with the best and most charismatic clubs and football players that the sport can supply. Lisbon and Seville crystallised this, but it is a drive deep in the sociological and community soul of the fans and the institution – not only for the bottom line (though that is increasingly critical too), but for the spectacle of association football expressed at the level of an art.

A fourth and maybe less obvious theme is learning: that these international nights, and the overall experience of participating in the world's most prized footballing trophies, is one of the sites where we learn to be European (rather than learning to trash or lord over things European). This starts with the club's philosophy: we welcome inclusion on the European stage because it will teach us something – something akin to some previous manager's emphasis on fitness, on youth development, tactics, the mentoring of younger players by older, on achieving by hard work and experience a level of the highest athletic and sporting excellence to be found in the game. These principles radiate through travelling fans too in the form of a kind of cultural and recreational respect. Scotland may be internationally perceived as an infamously monoglot country, and Celtic fans show no more appetite than any other people in Scotland to speak European languages, but at least in this spirit of enquiry and curiosity we travel across the continent with an openness of mind to culture, to place, to street life, to food, to community and entertainment; to what makes other people and other countries tick. To the beating heart of Europe in all its difference and diversity. Travelling Celtic fans must ensure this positivity is maintained in years to come.

Despite the advance of secularism, it seems quite clear that the cultural roots of these inclinations are fundamentally religious in origin. They stem from the undoubted imprint of the Catholic faith and its forms of life on the community and its cultural practices over many generations. Central to this is a shared life-affirming language of faith, devotion, reverence, solidarity, effort and goodwill, sustaining fans on their travels to locations familiar and unfamiliar on the pilgrim routes of Europe.

There are many conclusions we can draw from reflecting on Celtic's 'idea' of Europe in this fashion. Some of them are enduring truths; others mirror the particular historical moment through which we are living. We ought to observe, of course, that the team and the support's corridor to Europe starts from its Irish origins. Hence, we have no problem in recognising that Ireland is in Europe too. So far from provincialising and marginalising us, as a long history of commentary and prejudice has done (and still does amongst certain types of minds), our ethnic, cultural and religious attachments to Ireland 'Europeanise' and internationalise us. Celtic hence participates not simply in a European competition, but as part of a European vision. One which Europeanises 'these islands' as the Good Friday Agreement calls them, affording us an alternative anti-imperial understanding of this Atlantic archipelago and the peoples ancient and new which inhabit it. Yes, this is a vision in which we can recognise an Irish diaspora of holy figures, state-builders and poets, affirming together a migrant Irishness that kept ideas and education and culture moving and breathing in places like Rome,

Paris, Vienna and Glasgow. This is a Europe of mutual recognition, where we see ourselves in the eyes of others: where our team has satellite colonies of supporters and friends filling Irish pubs across the Continent, from Dublin to Warsaw, from Singapore to North America and Australasia.

If it seems likely this understanding in Britain of Europe and Europeaness appears to be faltering in the face of more confrontational and regressive particularisms, we should caution ourselves as walls rise and borders close that football in general has a tarnished history in these movements of feeling. We might then take hold of the memories, the sentiments and the values highlighted in this essay in order to show that the Celtic way implies a different and more expansive idea of Europe – and one which perhaps more than ever we must strive to keep alive.

Memories of
a Celtic-Minded Par

ALAN BAIRNER

In 2001, I wrote, 'My hometown soccer team was Dunfermline Athletic and, in a sense, the world famous 'Glasgow' rivalry need not have concerned me at all. Yet I was conscious from an early age that this rivalry was about more than soccer. . . it seemed as if everyone in Scotland had to take a side even if they usually supported another, smaller club. In this regard, I chose, not for the last time in my life it has to be said, to be perverse'.[1] How was it that a young Pars fan, brought up in the Church of Scotland, was attracted to Celtic rather than to what was at the time still the pride and joy of the Scottish Protestant establishment, the club(s) known as Rangers? What follows is my attempt to answer that question, at least to my own satisfaction if not to anyone else's.

Part of the explanation is that Celtic were not Rangers.[2] My maternal grandfather was a long-serving elder in the Church of Scotland. He took me regularly to watch Raith Rovers in the late 1950s and through the 1960s. Rangers, he left me in no doubt, was not the team for us. My father had won the King's Medal in the Boys' Brigade, served in the submarine service in World War Two and became a Freemason shortly after he was demobbed. As far as he too was concerned, however, we were Dunfermline Athletic supporters and should have no truck with the Gers, regardless of our religion. What did the Battle of the Boyne really matter to those of us brought up in the Kirk? During the eighteenth century, notable Presbyterian clerics, such as Francis

[1] Bairner, A. (2001). Sport, Nationalism and Globalization. European and North American Perspectives. Albany, NY, State University of New York Press, p. xiii.

[2] Bairner, A. (2012). 'The Sash We Never Sang'. Rangers Standard: Debating Our Club, July (http://www.therangersstandard.co.uk/index.php/articles/rfc-politics/139-the-sash-we-never-sang).

183

Hutcheson who had left behind the narrow ground of Ulster Unionist politics to study and teach at the universities of Edinburgh and Glasgow, helped to fuel the Scottish Enlightenment. Meanwhile some of their co-religionists back home, such as Henry Joy McCracken, had joined the United Irishmen and fought alongside Catholics against British imperialism in the quest for social justice in Ireland and in opposition to the landed, Episcopalian ruling class. This was 'our' Presbyterianism – fighting oppression, in accord with the prevailing ethos of the New Testament, rather than demonising Catholics.

Parades were another factor in my reasoning that Catholics were not the bad people that some in our community would have had us believe.[3] When I was growing up, from our second floor High Street window, we had a perfect view of radically contrasting processions. Along came the bishops, then the monsignors, after them the parish priests and nuns. Following on were ordinary Catholic pilgrims from all over Scotland on their way from St. Margaret's grave to East End Park, home of Dunfermline Athletic, where Mass would be celebrated (coincidentally the editor of this volume remembers attending one of these occasions as a child). The procession was quiet and dignified and my father, mother and I, once followed the pilgrims until we reached the town cemetery from where we could watch the service taking place inside the football ground. Around the same time, from that same High Street window, we also saw a parade of the Royal Black Preceptory, accompanied by 'Protestant' flute and accordion bands. It was loud, aggressive and not at all dignified. Who were the real Christians, I wondered?

In the 1950s, in addition to that of Andrew Carnegie, St. Margaret was the other name that most Dunfermline children knew from an early age. Taking visitors to Dunfermline to see St. Margaret's grave, and also the cave where she went for private prayer, was a regular family ritual when I was a child. Born in Hungary of English descent, Queen Margaret of Scotland (later St. Margaret) had married Malcolm III (Malcolm Canmore) in 1069 and quickly set about bringing refinement and piety to the Scottish court. Nagy tells us that she is remembered in the chapel of Edinburgh Castle, in the empty sarcophagus at Dunfermline, and by the holy relics kept in the Ursuline convent of St. Margaret

[3] Bairner, A. (2011). 'Urban walking and the pedagogies of the street', Sport, Education and Society, 16 (3), pp. 371-384.

in Edinburgh.[4] Sir Noel Paton, a local man, was responsible for
the painting of 'Queen Margaret and King Malcolm Canmore'
which hangs in Dunfermline Town Hall. Margaret died in 1093
at Edinburgh Castle and her body was taken to the Church of
the Holy Trinity at Dunfermline (subsequently replaced by
Dunfermline Abbey) and buried opposite the Altar and the Cross.[5]

Her grave is now located outside the Abbey. Subsequently,
according to one historian, 'Dunfermline played a key part in
raising the status of the kingship of the Scots during the mid-
thirteenth century, first, by negotiating Margaret's canonization
and, second, by appearing to be the venue for the kings of Scots
to receive the rites of coronation and unction'.[6]

Despite this religious digression, I do not want to give the
impression here that I am making a simplistic equation between
Celtic Football Club and Catholicism in Scotland. I am well aware
that many non-Catholics support the club and indeed fans who
were born and brought up as Catholics have long since given lie
to the claim almost certainly mistakenly, perhaps mischievously,
attributed to the founder of the Society of Jesus (the Jesuits),
St. Ignatius Loyola, 'Give me the child for the first seven years
and I will give you the man'. The only point I wish to make here
is simply that when I was growing up, the Catholic Church was
frequently represented as a mysterious, distrustful, authoritarian
and powerful institution as purportedly evidenced by the well-
established belief that priests got into Celtic Park free (in actual
fact so also were Church of Scotland ministers) and were given
the best grandstand seats.

My observation of the St. Margaret's pilgrimage led me, as
a boy attending Church of Scotland Sunday School where the
teacher told us dirty jokes, to take a rather different view of the
Catholic Church such that, if hating Catholicism meant having to
hate Celtic and vice versa, then I was out.

There was always much more to my Celtic-mindedness than
an atavistic dislike of Rangers. In the beginning, perhaps it had
something to do with the green and white hoops or, even more
so, the white shirts with green sleeves and a large shamrock
emblazoned on the chest. The fact that the shorts were unnum-
bered was idiosyncratically attractive. Such superficialities can

[4] Nagy, K. (1973). Saint Margaret of Scotland and Hungary, Glasgow, John S. Burns.

[6] Taylor, A. 2009). 'Historical writing in twelfth- and thirteenth- century Scotland: the Dunfermline compilation', Historical Research, 83 (220), pp 228-252, p. 251.

[6] Ratcliffe Barnett, T. (1926). Margaret of Scotland. Queen and Saint. Edinburgh, Oliver and Boyd. See also Turgot. Bishop of St. Andrews (1980). The Life of St. Margaret. Queen of Scotland. Dunfermline. St. Margaret's Catholic Church.

perhaps best be categorised under the heading of banal Celtic-mindedness. Now that I am in my mid-sixties, however, I am able to reflect more seriously on the significant events, people and places that have influenced my positive attitude towards Celtic over the years.

The story must start with one man – Jock Stein – a Celtic man, of course, 'Celtic Minded', but also the man who turned Dunfermline Athletic from a struggling provincial outfit into a club that temporarily graced the European football stage and gave Pars fans such 'a guid conceit o' oorselves': which, I believe, most of us who lived through the sixties still possess. This is one reason why such an effort was made by supporters to save the club from extinction and to accept our recent financial troubles with grace and humility.

Stein had captained Celtic to victory in the Coronation Cup in 1953 and to a league and cup double the following year. When he arrived at East End Park on 14th March 1960 as the new Dunfermline manager, however, he was a relatively unknown quantity to most Pars fans. Yet, as Bob Crampsey wrote, 'It is fascinating if ultimately profitless to speculate on the subsequent history of Dunfermline Athletic had the club's directors not appointed Jock Stein'.[7] Of further note, Stein waited to be told if he had got the job in the Carousel Restaurant, adjoining the Regal Cinema and two doors away from the tenement where I grew up.

When Stein took up his new position, Dunfermline lay third from bottom of the First Division with only six matches to play: the first match under his leadership was to be against his old club. On 19th March, Dunfermline beat Celtic 3-2 at East End Park and went on to win all of their remaining five games, finishing 6th bottom, only four places behind Celtic.

The Stein revolution had begun and for me it was to become personal. At the beginning of the following season, Mr Stein visited my cub pack, the 2nd Fife YMCA, to talk to us about the previous season's European Cup Final at Hampden Park in which Real Madrid had beaten Eintracht Frankfurt by seven goals to three. A flickering cine film showed highlights of the game which

[7] Crampsey, B. (1986). Mr Stein. A Biography of Jock Stein C.B.E. 1922-1985. Edinburgh, Mainstream, p. 47.

Stein described as the greatest he had ever seen. But there'was more to come. For half an hour he spoke to this group of boys as if we were grown-ups about football strategies and tactics. We knew then, if we did not know it already, that our team was in safe hands. After we had been given the chance to ask the manager some questions, we ate bags of chips which had been lathered with so much salt and vinegar that they had turned into a congealed mess but were they good! And so were our young lives, and, they were about to get even better.

On 22nd April 1961, Dunfermline met Celtic in the Scottish Cup Final watched by 113,328 spectators and, as Welsh troubadour Max Boyce used to say, I know 'cos I was there'. Stein had prepared for the game by taking his team to the Seamill Hydro Hotel, using his Celtic connections to outwit his former club which had often used the hotel as a base in the past.[8] My father and I sat high up in the stand surrounded by Celtic supporters who gave me sweets and my dad regular swigs from their bottles. At the end of the game, which ended in a 0-0 draw, they shook our hands and wished us good luck in the replay. Did they mean it? Probably not but it was kind of them to say it and good fortune was certainly with us when on 26th April, in a game which kicked off at 6.15 pm because Hampden had no floodlights, the Pars won the Scottish Cup for the first time in the club's history, beating Celtic by two goals to nil in front of 87,660 people.'

Bob Kelly, a Celtic man through and through, and at the time, President of the Scottish Football Association, looked on as his wife presented the cup to Dunfermline captain, Ronnie Mailer. His feelings must have been mixed as he absorbed what the man whom he had brought as a player from Llanelly to Celtic Park had just achieved. But, as he told the Scottish Daily Express, 'It's no loss what a friend gets'.[9] After the game, as Bob Crampsey recalled, 'All the way back to Fife ribbons of people stood in the rain, most to applaud the triumph of Dunfermline, not a few to celebrate the downfall of Celtic'.[10] As an idealistic ten-year-old, I did not even consider the latter explanation at the time.

The European games that followed opened up a new world to local schoolchildren sated as they were by a diet of stories

[8] See Macpherson, A. (2007). Jock Stein. A Definitive Biography. Newbury, Berkshire, Highdown, p. 84.

[9] Quoted in Macpherson, Jock Stein, p. 87.

[10] Crampsey, Mr Stein, p. 53.

about Carnegie, Dunfermline-born capitalist robber baron turned philanthropist. It was a world which was unknown to supporters of most provincial clubs in Scotland and which saw the arrival in the Auld Grey Toon throughout the 1960s of players from Hungary, the former Yugoslavia, Sweden, France, Spain, the Basque Country and many others. Arguably the climax came on the night of 19th December, 1962 while Jock Stein was still manager. Having lost 0-4 away to Valencia in the first leg of an Inter-Cities Fairs Cup tie, the Pars won the return leg 6-2 on an icy pitch with two teenage wingers in the side. Away goals did not count in those days so a third game was played in Portugal which Valencia won. Nevertheless, that second leg, together with the Scottish Cup triumph of 1961, must go down as one of Jock Stein's miracles, surpassed of course, a few years later, by the European Cup triumph by the Lisbon Lions.

Stein left Dunfermline in April 1964, disappointingly initially to Hibernian and not Celtic, a move that most Dunfermline fans would have found easier to accept. As Crampsey observed, 'he left a remarkable inheritance'.[11] The club he had taken over in 1960, of small achievement, of minimal ambition, would remain in the forefront of Scottish football for five years after his departure, a long time in football terms.

After Stein's departure, notable games have helped to keep the competitive relationship between Celtic and Dunfermline alive – a Scottish Cup Final win for Celtic on 24th April 1965, followed by a 5-1 home win for the Pars four days later, a 5-4 victory for Celtic in a league match at East End Park on 19th November 1966 and a 2-0 away win for Dunfermline on 27th January 1968 in the first round of the Scottish Cup. There was also the remarkable encounter a few months later on 30th April 1968 between league champions Celtic and cup winners Dunfermline played in front of the biggest crowd ever seen at East End Park, officially recorded as 27,816: although my impression was that there were many more than that inside the ground (and on the floodlight pylons and the roofs of the covered enclosures). A game, in which according to some, there was nothing at stake, although those of us who were there knew differently, was won 2-1 by Celtic.

[11] Crampsey, Mr Stein, p. 62.

Of more recent memory, the Scottish Cup Final of 2004 ended with Celtic winning 3-1 with goals from Henrik Larsson (2) and Stilian Petrov. However, a half time lead courtesy of a goal scored by Andrius Skerla allowed the Pars supporters to celebrate during the interval as though it was 1961 all over again.

The European Cup Final of 1967 was another important landmark in my personal relationship with Celtic. The unexpected victory over Inter Milan was celebrated by my father and me, in large part, I suspect, because it had been achieved under the astute leadership of Jock Stein who had been so instrumental in the recent history of our own small club. We were also enthused, however, by the fact that a team from Scotland had taken on the best in Europe and won. I must still have been rather naive in thinking that football fans all over Scotland would have been feeling the same way. My naivety would be shattered, however, when I watched the 1970 European Cup Final on a television in Edinburgh University's Men's (yes, Men's!) Union and realised that many fellow Scottish students were 'supporting' Feyenoord. Fights broke out at the final whistle and I was left to ponder on how twenty-two year old, George Connelly, a fellow Fifer, educated at St. Margaret's School in Dunfermline, must have been feeling.[12] Little did I know at the time that one of the greatest prodigies in Scottish football was already almost halfway through his professional career, a tragedy arguably only surpassed in the annals of Celtic's history by the early death of another Fifer, John Thomson, who passed away after suffering a fatal injury at the age of 22 in a Rangers v. Celtic game played on 5th September 1931, and is buried in Bowhill, the small West Fife village through which I travelled every weekday morning in the first half of 1974 to teach at Auchterderran Junior High School.[13]

Finally as far as significant games between the two clubs are concerned, on 7th May 1988, already relegated Dunfermline went to Celtic Park to play against a Celtic team celebrating the club's centenary. The large travelling support unfurled a banner informing their manager Jim Leishman that they would be back, adding in a postscript, 'Happy Birthday Celtic'.[14] Perhaps I was not alone in my Celtic-mindedness. The Pars fans' gesture was acknowledged in the Celtic Fanzine, Not The View, at the start of the following season.

[12] See Connelly G. with Cooney, B. (2008). Celtic's Lost Legend. The George Connelly Story. Edinburgh, Black and White Publishing.

[13] See Greig, T. (2003). My Search for Celtic's John. Glasgow, Ogilivie Writings.

[14] I am grateful to John Kelly (contributor to this volume of Celtic Minded) for reminding me of this particular episode in the history of relations between our two clubs. I am also gratified by the fact that John has seen fit to grace the East End Park main stand with his presence on two occasions in the past three seasons.

Their sporting attitude on the day the Celts were presented with the League trophy, the banner which read 'JIM WE'LL BE BACK, PS HAPPY BIRTHDAY CELTIC', and the way they supported their team despite the fact that they had already, sadly, been relegated, won them a lot of friends that day, and made the match a real pleasure to be at.

NTV added, 'Well done the Pars fans, and you'll be back!'[15]

The fact that I lived and worked for twenty five years in Belfast, from 1978-2013, could perhaps have turned my Celtic-mindedness into something more full blown. Certainly I got to know many Celtic supporters as good friends, and watching Cliftonville regularly with some of them meant that, by the time I left for England in 2003, my local team was the one member of the Irish League that could most easily be compared with Celtic.

I was not, of course, oblivious to the inter-communal conflict of those years. When a game to be played on 14th August 1984 was first arranged, it was to be an occasion for celebration. Cliftonville would play host to Celtic Football Club with most people in the ground being supporters of both teams. But a few days before the game was scheduled to take place, a young Catholic man, Sean Downes, who had been attending a republican rally in west Belfast, had been killed by a plastic bullet fired by a Royal Ulster Constabulary (RUC) reservist who was later charged with manslaughter, although he was subsequently acquitted. Tensions were running high and yet there was no immediate cause for alarm about a game to be played in front of a sizeable crowd of like-minded people. Nevertheless, a large RUC contingent was present and when missiles were returned from a section of the crowd in the direction of loyalist youths who had been throwing bricks and bottles over the perimeter walls, RUC officers in full riot gear seized the opportunity to charge, firing plastic bullets as they advanced. No one was killed on this occasion but the sense of fear amongst Cliftonville and Celtic supporters that day was palpable.[16]

A very different experience came when I went to Ibrox with my friend John Rooney for a Sunday evening Rangers-Celtic game on 3rd January 1999 which ended in a 2-2 draw thanks to an equaliser from Larsson. The highlight of the day, for me at least,

[15] Not The View (1988). No. 7, p. 5.

[16] See also Bairner, A. (2014). 'Emotional grounds: Stories of football, memories, and emotions', Emotion, Space and Society, 12, pp. 18-23.

came within minutes of boarding a Celtic supporters bus in west Belfast when the older men on board told some teenage girls to turn off the republican songs on their ghetto blaster and 'gie our heads peace'. I doubt that this was to spare the feelings of the Celtic-minded Par in their midst but almost certainly because they were nursing Sunday morning hangovers.

The real nadir as regards the previously harmonious relationship between Dunfermline Athletic and Celtic came shortly before I left Belfast when Chris Sutton accused the Dunfermline players of lying down to Rangers who had beaten them by six goals to one, thereby condemning Celtic to miss out on the 2003 Premier League title. Sutton later apologised for his remarks, with Celtic manager Martin O'Neill adding, 'In the cold light of day, Chris accepts that the motivation of those working and playing for Dunfermline should not be called into question'.[17] Those of us who had supported the Pars all our lives were well aware that our team was capable of losing heavily to both Rangers and Celtic even while playing to the best of its ability. It was primarily for that reason that Sutton's comments were particularly hurtful. NTV sided with Sutton, to some degree, questioning the approach to the Rangers game taken by Dunfermline manager, Jimmy Calderwood (he of the orange face and reputedly the Orange cultural persuasion). The fanzine's overall assessment, however, was close to the truth.

> Now some Celtic fans are suggesting that the reason we lost the league is because Dunfermline lay down to Rangers that fateful afternoon at Ibrox. But let's face it, leagues are not won or lost on one afternoon. Basically Dunfermline lost because they are shite.[18]

Preserve us in the future, however, from English players seeking to demonstrate their commitment to the cause whether by impugning the honesty of fellow professionals or, worse still, by mimicking the actions of a 'kick the Pope' bandsman. As NTV later asked about Sutton, 'is he just paranoid like the rest of us?'[19]

Both before and after the Sutton affair, there have been times when I have been annoyed hearing Celtic supporters bemoan the lean times, some of which might even have included at least

[17] The Scotsman (2003). 'Sutton's apology comes too late' http:// www.scotsman.com/ sport/football/ competitions/ premiership/sutton-s-apology-comes-too-late-1-649266 Accessed 23rd June 2017.

[18] Not The View (2003). No. 112, 2nd August, p. 9.

[19] Not The View (2003). No. 113, 27th August, p. 17.

one trophy win. Try supporting teams like Dunfermline or better still one of those clubs that have never won anything at all. But I can let this pass for the simple reason that it is in the DNA of all football fans to moan: indeed, it's possibly what we enjoy most about being fans. As for Chris Sutton, as the well-known dirge tells us, these days are past now and, in the past, they must remain: and so my Celtic-mindeness survives, watched over, I like to think, by the twin spirits of St. Margaret and Mr Stein and kept alive by memories of Tommy Callaghan and Jackie McNamara who went in one direction and Bent Martin, John Cushley (who starred in Dunfermline's Quizball triumph on BBC television in season 1971-2), David Moyes and, in particular, Joe McBride, who went in the other. I look forward to seeing the Pars back in the Premiership and having a team capable of beating Celtic but, in the meantime, I'll also be hoping for ten-in-a row.

Remaining faithful through and through: being Celtic Minded and acting to keep Celtic unique

Lorcan Gallagher

Claims are simply claims, unless there is substance. If there's no evidence to support the claim, no indications, no witnesses, then the declaration might become nothing more than words: wishful thinking even. Like many claims there will be truths as well as untruths, exaggerations, contestations, common sense views and God knows what else. In this vein, Celtic historians, writers and supporters see their club, their support, as different – different from much of what characterises many, most, or all other football clubs: certainly those in Scotland/Britain. Sure, Celtic shares many things with others, and especially with other big name football clubs: aspirations towards success on the field of play, communities of support, an origins narrative, good years and bad years, outstanding players, a social and cultural context, sometimes even a special history in relation to culture, politics, country, etc. Other contributors to Celtic Minded explore and express these stories. But there are some more, other aspects to our club and our support that also need to be mentioned.

In Scotland and beyond I've heard numerous football fans singing vile, inhuman even, songs and chants. In Scotland, 'The Famine's Over, Why Don't you go Home?', 'Paedo, Paedo, Paedo'.

In England songs against Jews, mocking the Manchester United air disaster, Hillsborough and Heysel: the racist monkey chants of the 70s, 80s and 90s. Even amidst great football rivalries such songs and chants can be beyond belief and comprehension. These kinds of chants and songs say more about groups of singers' bigotries, racist attitudes, socio-cultural identities, ignorance, prejudice and discriminatory tendencies. That these kinds of chants can be even worse in relation to the abuse and degradation some people suffer on social media says so much too about where society is going these days – a moral abyss?

Many football fans in Scotland, at all clubs, can be brutal, vulgar, crass and downright 'ugly' in terms of behaviour and attitudes: a very tiny minority are violent hooligans. Many, from all clubs, can be decent, faithful, a joy to be travelling with and sitting or standing with at games.

> Many football fans in Scotland, at all clubs, can be brutal, vulgar, crass and downright 'ugly'. . . Many, from all clubs, can be decent, faithful, a joy to be travelling with

Then, there's 'us': the lifeblood of Celtic Football Club, its historic support. For those that write for the Celtic Minded series, Celtic is about dignity, humility, charity, history, heritage, a club that welcomes all regardless of creed, class, colour, ethnicity and nationality, and, a club and a support that harbours respect for themselves and others. Historically, this has been the case for a massive majority of our support and our great institution itself. One of the great merits about the Celtic Minded series is that like no other collection of similar books, it has been the articulation of the meaningfulness of this unique football institution and the identities and experiences of its supporters. However, we might pause and reflect on whether our club, and its vast fanbase, appreciate, merit and mirror these credentials today? We're not perfect, though perfection is something we might find worthwhile aspiring to?

Of course, my own perspectives on Celtic and beyond are partly or greatly shaped by the various identities and relevant attitudes I carry: none of us is a blank slate even when we are born and we certainly aren't as we 'progress' through life. My own social and cultural identities primarily revolve around where I live in Scotland's west-central belt, my Irish ethnicity (with my previous family members fleeing to Scotland from Ireland during a period of about 70 years from around the Great Irish Hunger until 1920, from Galway, Donegal, Down and Monaghan), being brought up in a Labour minded, not well off, working class environment, having several sisters, a brother and plenty of cousins. I guess the most important part of my very being is my faith. I attended a Catholic primary and a Catholic high school – not doing particularly well academically. Ironically, I love reading now (unlike at school) and very much appreciate this opportunity to write for the first time ever: the Celtic Minded series of books (what else?) being my favourite sports volumes. But more importantly, my Catholic/Christian faith motivates me, provides me a rationale and comprises my very being. Sometimes, or maybe often, I'm not very good at being as I should be – but that's another subject. Along with several other sources, not least my parents, grandmother and listening, watching and learning, my Catholic school I believe was very good for me and many of those around me. It helped offer me a consciousness regarding other people, in and around the communities I was and am part of, and with regards the millions around the world that suffer at the hands of vast systems based on wealth, capital, greed, cruelty, exploitation, usury, and the rest. My Catholic schools complemented the family and community I was brought up in: and I'm thankful for that.

These are some of the most important reasons why Celtic FC and I have got together for all of my conscious life. I love Celtic. My parish priest once said that it isn't possible to 'love' Celtic. I know what he meant, 'I love New York', 'I love pizza' – yes, I know what he means, and those slogans and casual sayings do not represent what love means or is the same as St. Paul's letter to the Corinthians (1 Corinthians 13: 4-7). But he didn't quite understand or was able to articulate the nub of this in the Celtic context. I realise Celtic is a worldly matter and I can't take it with me when I leave this earth – even if I get buried in a Celtic top. I realise that it is not the same as my blood family or even any other human on this planet. I realise it's not my faith. But it's still possible to love this club, its history, its supporters, its meaning and, being faithful to it and all the best things it stands for. Archbishop Tartaglia got it right celebrating a Celtic remembrance Mass at St. Mary's in Calton a few years back when he said 'I love Celtic'. It is possible, for I know it is.

My first Celtic game was in the mid-1960s, my oldest cousin taking me along after a long time begging to be taken. My first European game, as a real young kid, versus Saint Etienne in the European Cup in September 1968. As the 1970s progressed into the 1980s and beyond I learned to go myself with friends. Home and away, cup finals and the 'very occasional' trip abroad (couldn't afford them – still can't). On the football park, I was at the Aberdeen Cup Final 1970, Leeds in the European Champions Cup semi-final in front of Europe's biggest ever crowd, against the rats of Athletico Madrid 1974, Rangers Cup Final 1977, the historic 4-2 game 1979, Charlie Nicholas at Ibrox 1983, the wonderful centenary year of 1987-88, the barren years thereafter, Tommy Burns winning the cup as manager in 1995, stopping the grand theft, deception and dishonesty of 10 in 1998, Seville 2003, fourteen titles since 1998, 'The Invincibles' of 2016-17 and a 'Double/Treble Treble' (still unknown at the time of going to press). And, so much more beyond the highs and lows of the football field itself; with relations, friends and across generations. Celtic is very much at the core of my life. My Catholic/Christian faith means infinitely more, but Celtic is not only at the core but is actually connected to my faith: in the way I view and connect to many other people and the world.

All of these things mean that when 'bad things' happen in and around Celtic it can pull the very life from within me. I'm a middle-aged, labouring man now, and am well used to all sorts of people. I judge none – I have no right. I'm too busy getting my own house in some kind of order and praying that my kids get it right too. However, I still recognise what I consider sometimes 'bad' and 'ugly' around the club I love. I mean within, and mainly in terms of the support of our great institution. I may not judge, but I still know right from wrong – my faith has taught me that.

Of course, there's always the perspective of age and experience. But age and experience aren't consumed and practised the same way by everyone and they can vary: and some youthful perspectives can be an improvement on some of those of the past: there's some right oul gits out there too. However, we absolutely require age and experience to have any kind of informed perspective on the subject of Celtic. We need to listen to the past, use it well for the present and take the good from it into the future. We shouldn't be arrogant enough to think we don't need to do this. As well as a rich source of memories, the past, as well as the present, can also be a warning that what we have is worthy of protecting – worthy of our love actually. Thus, Celtic is worthy of our love. So why worry? Well, sometimes we have to.

In recent years a number of supporters have asserted and articulated themselves in a way that has meant some of the ignorant and sometimes bigoted-sounding 'add-ons' to a few of our great anthems have been eradicated or marginalised. Apart from more often than not contributing hugely to a great atmosphere at Celtic games, the Green Brigade has been pretty good with respect to several songs and this has spread to the point that certain vulgar or abusive bits and pieces have gone or are almost gone amongst the wider support: but not entirely. Some members of the Green Brigade have not been quite as good on the pyrotechnics front of course, often giving the impression that they know best on this one, and 'stuff' the opinions of the rest of the support.

My heart sank at Tynecastle Christmas 2017 when Hearts ended our magnificent run of being undefeated domestically during the previous 18 months. No, it wasn't the defeat that hurt as much as my pre-match experience. In the toilets before the game I heard a 'Celtic supporter' sing a derogatory song about British soldier Lee Rigby who had been murdered by a violent human being acting in the name of Islam in 2013. Half a minute later I heard, possibly his friend, sing a ditty about Simon Weston, the British soldier horribly burned during the Falklands/Malvinas War of 1983. Few joined in and only some laughed – but it was there: it was horrible, and it ruined the match for me. For me the Brits should not have been in Iraq, Afghanistan, Ireland, the South Pacific and lots of other people's countries: but that has nothing to do with gloating over the death or serious injury of one of that Imperialist nation's armed representatives. I often oppose what British soldiers, under the command of their Government, have done and do in this world: but it is simply wrong to gloat over any of their deaths. Indeed, I frequently want the British Military to stop getting involved in wars in other

> the Green Brigade has been pretty good with respect to several songs and this has spread to the point that certain vulgar or abusive bits and pieces have gone or are almost gone amongst the wider support

people's countries, starting wars in other peoples' countries and for the British Government and media to stop being so militaristic – but I have no wish to see British military personnel dead. I might not buy or wear a Poppy for moral, cultural and political reasons, but I'm not for seeking their suffering. If they can't reciprocate, that's their issue, but it's not going to be mine.

That day in Edinburgh got me thinking more about some small elements of our 'support'. I remembered winning the league at Dundee United just after a 'real' role model, a real Celtic Minded person, Tommy Burns, had sadly passed away. Afterwards, in the 'carry-out' shop for a few tins to celebrate on the return journey in the mini-bus, some 'fellow supporter' in the shop was singing about Rangers player Charlie Adam's sister's pants – this after us winning the league at a close call and 'for' Tommy? Then there's that chant that has developed in recent years – 'Orange B......., Orange B....... Orange B.......' etc: it's embarrassing, and wrong, whether applied to Neil McCann, Walter Smith, Craig Levein or Kris Boyd. Sure, we have a decent knowledge of anti-Catholics, anti-Irish and anti-Celtic people in Scotland, some have given us cause for distaste, have been prejudiced against us in their actions and words. We have an understanding of their hostility to Celtic Mindedness. But still no, not that song: it just sounds like an ignorant bitter low-minded chant and one that our rivals would easily make up towards us – but it's not for us. Tit for tat: who's fans can chant the ugliest cannot be our way. Jimmy Bell and Nacho Novo: forget it – anyone that sings these kinds of chants are no better than the hate-filled thickos that would spit on a priest outside of a Catholic Church, or disrespect a Protestant Church too for that matter. It's definitely not for the Celtic Minded. We are different, but we need to draw in, marginalise the clowns that resemble 'them' more than 'us'. Surely, our moral codes, our moral compass, should guide us, even when the opposition might be full of everything that doesn't like us: hate us even? We still don't need to be the same as them: stooping down I think it's called?

I remember another Celtic fan (actually knew him), George, shouting at Manchester United players when they arrived at Celtic Park prior to us beating them in the Champions League in 2006.

He took great pleasure in giving them face-to-face personal invective as they stepped off their team bus for the short walk to the stadium: he called them for everything. Imagine coming from Manchester as one of the world's most famous clubs, amongst Europe's best players, playing a major European tie, to be faced with this torrent of ugly abuse on the part of someone that was saying in his own way, 'welcome to Celtic'? Most of the rest of us, including the many kids hanging around to get a glimpse of these same players, were embarrassed, baffled and ashamed: another couple of fans laughed of course too thinking this was 'funny': but not many. How tough? How cool George? Doesn't actually matter where else in the world such things happen at football: BUT not us, not at Celtic, not amongst the Celtic support! We've got to be different to maintain our uniqueness.

Our great club has amongst its roots Irish political affiliations. For six generations many of the club's supporters have 'softly' sang about their opposition to British imperialism in Ireland – it's a part of not only Celtic culture but a significant aspect of worldwide Irishness – of the diaspora: it is part of our history and is recognised all over the world where the Irish have settled. However, just as support for the historical Black freedom struggle in apartheid South Africa should not be simplistically equated with support for the military wing of the former ANC, just as contemporary support for the plight of the Palestinian people against the military might of the land-grabbing Israeli state certainly cannot be equated with support for militant Palestinians (or the Hamas authority), similarly, opposition towards British colonialism in Ireland should not be equated, always, with support for Irish nationalist militarism. Irish nationalism, the desire for Irish freedom from the historic British Empire (and contemporary imperialism) is a very broad church: our moral and political opponents wouldn't even want to recognise that even if they had the capacity.

If I sing a song which mentions the struggle, even the armed part of it, fighting back against the might of the British Empire, British Imperialism, a British war machine that has never rested for over three centuries, possibly sacrificing their own lives, it does not mean I support using a gun. The ignorant, or those

that support British imperialism of course, will say different –
but they're wrong. I'm certainly not like the 'Celtic fan' I witnessed
in Manchester a few years back, shouting into the faces of a
group of Man City fans, 'IRA', 'IRA', 'IRA'. Maybe that was all
right for his drunken (or coked-up) self, but not for me and not
for those around me. He was simply a yob that brought himself
down, our club, as well too as the many great men and women
that have opposed British militarism in Ireland. In that moment
he also brought down the names of Sean South, Fr. Murphy,
Robert Emmett and Raymond McCreesh too. His actions and
utterings were reminiscent of the yobs at Tynecastle, seemingly
celebrating the death and injuries to some British soldiers. I didn't
support what these soldiers were involved with but I don't
support someone apparently glorifying their deaths and injuries.
Tears are tears and pain is pain in the human game, no matter if
they are Irish, Scots, British, English, Catholic, Protestant, Muslim
or atheist. Common humanity is the name of the game: despite
the antagonism we may face.

I very much like Roll of Honour, Aidan McAnespie, Grace,
Sniper's Promise, Irish Soldier Laddie and many more – songs
that many if not most Celtic supporters sing at home, in pubs,
clubs and at various celebrations. But, I'm less comfortable with
those of our songs of liberation that only seem to emphasise
guns and more guns: and I hate that so-called version of 'Beautiful
Sunday' with it's silly and ignorant ending I I I I R A. I'm not sure
Padraic Pearse, Joseph Mary Plunkett, Francis Hughes or Joe
McCann would have been encouraged by that kind of chant.
Many great Irish 'rebel' songs (which can also be love, history,
emigration songs) like The Fields of Athenry, Let the People Sing,
Grace, The Wearing of the Green, Rock on Rockall, The One
Road, Joe McDonnell, Something inside so Strong and A Nation
once Again, etc, capture the essence of the Irish struggle for
liberation from British imperialism without 'always' directly
invoking militant republicanism.

People with a gun in their hands haven't been the only ones
that have struggled against our 'great' oppressor. Maybe even
our first Celtic FC Honorary Patron, Michael Davitt is a fine
example of how someone, a previous member of the militant
Fenians, and after a period of imprisonment, confined himself to

using education, knowledge, shame (the 'boycott'), morality and politics to expose the devilish tyrannical ways of Ireland's economic, cultural, political and military tormentor. Padraic Pearse never fired a shot in anger. Bobby Sands was certainly a soldier, but he 'gave' his life rather than take a life for Ireland. I believe we should try taking some guns out of our song-sheets.

In the wake of the media furore around a few unsavoury incidents when Celtic defeated Kilmarnock in the dying minutes of the critical league game there in February 2019, many of our antagonists had a go at us – as ever, they took the opportunity. Of course, a number of things occurred that day that simply shouldn't have, they were wrong, they shamed the support and club and the majority don't want these things to happen. However, as one Herald sports writer said when talking about these kinds of fans, 'it's all about them and they are never wrong; flares, a coin thrown at Kris Boyd, hostile chants directed towards him and of course Rangers' Jimmy Bell'. As that Herald reporter said, these people (Boyd, Bell, etc) are not the enemy. Just for the crime of being associated with another team, for being in another stadium, doesn't mean we need someone to break Kilmarnock seats (though a few were probably broken accidently and carelessly by boisterous behaviour), that we need 'young men in dark clothing act as if the law doesn't apply to them'. Then, this journalist added at last a bit of context with regards numerous – not just Celtic – football fans in Scotland:

> There is a breed of young football fan, from across all our clubs, who shame and embarrass their fellow supporter with what they say and do [and take]. Anything is fair game to have a song composed – Nacho Novo, the Lisbon Lions, Ian Durrant, the Ibrox disaster, child abuse victims, the guy who drives the Rangers bus and, worst of all, Jay Beattie, the young Celtic fan who has Down's Syndrome.
> (Herald Sport, Neil Cameron 20/2/19, p12)

I don't get to many away European ties but several friends of numerous ages in recent times have said they are reluctant to go back abroad with the club. Why? As a result of bad behaviour on the part of some Celtic fans – apparently Valencia was a big one? The most common complaints seem to revolve around absolute drunkenness, aggression and not respecting the people

I believe we should try taking some guns out of our song-sheets.

or cities we visit. Generally Celtic supporters have long had a wonderful reputation abroad. The majority shouldn't let the minority waste this for the rest of us, and the club's reputation into the bargain. No matter what other club's fans have done or do – we're different: let's keep it that way.

'Everyone keeps going on about the mindless minority but surely the mindful majority should police it better'?

So, we Celtic supporters can choose who we want to be like and what we want to be like. The vast majority of football supporters in Scotland are ok. A huge majority of Celtic supporters are the salt of the earth. However, if we truly are different, if we want to be better, if we want to keep and spread a faith in our club that is unrivalled across the globe, we need to be mindful of those that would blacken our name from within the club's support. In relation to that particular Kilmarnock v. Celtic game, Stevie Clarke the Killie manager said, 'Everyone keeps going on about the mindless minority but surely the mindful majority should police it better?' However much Stevie Clarke has contributed or will contribute towards football in Scotland, that statement might be viewed by some as one of his most significant utterings. For the majority of the Celtic support that are truly 'Celtic Minded' our love for our club is truly special, unique. However, we shouldn't take it for granted, it just doesn't happen by accident. It happens because our club IS special, unique, and the vast majority of people connected with our history, our culture, our morals, have been and are the ones that have made and do make it so. Hail Hail!!

Rolls of Honour: A Tale of Two Remembrances

John Kelly

In 2016 the Scottish Football Association (SFA) and Football Association (FA) became embroiled in a disagreement with FIFA over the British associations' insistence on their teams wearing the Earl Haig poppy (EHP)[1] on kits during the England v. Scotland World Cup qualifier match on November 11th, Armistice Day. This resulted in FIFA fining both assocations for breaching their rules. The implicit assumption was that FIFA had interpreted the EHP as representing a political symbol. Law 4.4 of the 'Laws of the Game' states, 'equipment must not have any political, religious or personal slogans, statements or images'.[2]

A number of British-based high profile commentators spoke out criticising FIFA and defending the British governing bodies, citing the central counter-argument that the EHP 'is non-political'. For example, Scottish Secretary David Mundell condemned FIFA's ruling as an 'inexplicable' decision before adding 'this isn't a political gesture; it's a gesture about paying respect'. British Prime, Minister Theresa May described the ruling as 'utterly outrageous'[3] and (through her official spokeswoman) expanded: 'We continue to believe that footballers and fans should be able very clearly to show their support for all that our armed forces do.'[4]

These rather representative quotes aptly illustrate the difficulty in judging the meanings and interpretations of such symbols. On the one hand, we are told the EHP is about 'paying respect' and on the other it is claimed to symbolise 'support for

[1] I use the Earl Haig poppy (EHP) as shorthand to describe the Royal British Legion poppy that was originally named after British military general Haig. This illustrates the original military-centred remembrance connection as well as distinguishing between alternative remembrance-related poppies such as the white, purple and black poppies which symbolise peace, animal victims, people of colour and conscientious objectors.

[2] International Football Association Board 2016

[3] Elgot J (2016) Theresa May attacks FIFA over 'utterly outrageous' poppy ban. The Guardian online. Available at: https://www.theguardian.com/uk-news/2016/nov/02/theresa-may-attacks-fifa-over-utterly-outrageous-poppy-ban-remembrance-day (accessed 2 May 2017).

all that our armed forces do'. Such interpretations require us to consider what words like 'respect' and 'support' actually mean in these contexts. Does support equate to support 'for the actions' of the British military forces? Considering the Prime Minister's spokesperson's quote, ('for all that our armed forces do') the answer must be 'yes'. Support for the actions of the British military forces – who act in accordance with the British government's foreign policy desires – are unavoidably political. In addition to contradicting those moral guardians who cling to the 'sport and politics doesn't (and shouldn't) mix' fantasy, this raises questions around the legitimacy and morality of sport being used to justify violence. Furthermore, by re-establishing the precedent that sport can be used for political purposes, this inevitably weakens the legitimacy future complaints about such use may have.

This recent FIFA and SFA/FA controversy has striking parallels with some of the key debates infusing the implementation of Scotland's SNP Government's Offensive Behaviour at Football and Communication Bill (OBFB). For instance, a key and unresolved issue around this bill – and the wider debates around football and ethno-religious bigotry ('sectarianism') – also relates to questions of representation and support.

Does singing Irish rebel songs equate to offering support for violent actions carried out in the name of Irish independence? When do such representations (of Irish independence) equal support for the alleged actions carried out in its name? Can symbols be displayed or songs sung (representation) without offering such support? If support is unquestionably evidenced, what does support actually mean? Does it mean support for the cause represented in the symbol or song? Does it mean support for the person or people (actor) closely connected to the alleged cause? Does this extend to include support for the violence (actions) carried out by the person or represented by the cause? If support for acts of violence can be attributed to the display of a symbol or person (even when the image is clearly not engaged in any violent action), does this apply equally to all displays? If displaying what appears to be an Irish republican military figure can be interpreted as supporting Irish republican military actions/ violence, does this mean that displays of other actors – such as

[4] News and Star (2016) FIFA condemned after UK national teams fined over poppy displays. 14 May 2016. Available at: http:// www.newsandstar.co.uk/ news/national/article/ Fifa-condemned- after-UK-national- teams-fined-over- poppy-displays- 182168a4-c64d- 4db5-b366- da4aa6ef6285-ds (Accessed 14 May 2017).

British military personnel – must also be assumed to offer support for British military violence including (as mere examples) British concentration camps in the Boer War (1899-1902) and Kenya[6] (1950s), or the killing of 14 civilians in Derry (1972)? Does the display of a symbol or person constitute support for historic actions that person (or her/his associates) may have carried out in the past and/or may carry out in the future? These (moral, political, historical, philosophical) questions are of central importance when considering what conflict-related remembrance means and represents, and they are at the heart of the controversy that surrounded the implementation of the deeply discredited OBFB and its consequences for some Celtic supporters (and other clubs' supporters).

This contribution to Celtic Minded discusses these issues by considering two contrasting examples of public acts of remembrance in Britain, some of which include remembrance of those who have been involved (personally or by group identity association) in conducting violence. It begins by outlining the most well-known and culturally embedded form of remembrance in Britain, Remembrance Sunday, enabling us to compare and contrast its meanings and representations with the second alternative form of remembrance outlined below – Celtic supporters singing 'Roll of Honour'.

This involves discussing what I term the Corporate Culpability Paradox (CCP) surrounding remembrance. The CCP reveals a central inconsistency in how remembrance is interpreted in Britain. Simply put, the CCP relates to treating remembrance differently depending on who is being remembered and whether or not the actions carried out by those remembered are supported by the British government and large sections of its corporate media. The ideological and political framings given to key elements of British remembrance such as the Earl Haig poppy (EHP) are illustrated. Furthermore, this reveals various ways in which sport is used for political and ideological purposes including supporting British military personnel and their actions. This groundwork clears the way for us to situate the discussion of the Roll of Honour song in this wider context of the meanings and interpretations of remembrance in Scotland and Britain.

[6] Harvard academic Caroline Elkins described the British concentration camps in Kenya as 'Britain's Gulag'. See: https://www.theguardian.com/books/2005/feb/05/featuresreviews.guardianreview6

Corporate culpability paradox and remembrance in Britain

The interpretations[7] of 'remembrance' in Britain are underpinned by a glaring inconsistency that not only treats British military-related violence as inherently justified, but when politically expedient, seeks to distinguish it from acts of British military-related remembrance and the political ideology infusing it. Conversely, the remembrance of others – such as Irish nationalists – is explicitly connected to violence (sometimes labeled 'terrorism') and its underpinning political ideology (Irish nationalism and/or republicanism). This forms part of what I call the Corporate Culpability Paradox (CCP). There is, of course, a wide spectrum of British military violence over many years and generations, just as there is a range of actions and contexts underpinning Irish nationalist violence. While politically motivated violence (carried out by the British state and Irish nationalists) has been contested morally, morality is of little consequence for this particular paradox and its significance in the wider debate[8]. The paradox is about how the relationships between four overlapping constitutive elements relating to politically motivated violence are treated differently depending on whether or not the violence was conducted by British military. These elements are:

> Ideological cause   Actor   Action   Outcome of action

When the ideological causes and/or[9] actors involve military violence that is supported by the British government, some of these four elements are sometimes considered separate and unrelated by the British government and the corporate media. For example, when British state violence occurs, British citizens are enabled and sometimes actively encouraged to 'support the troops' (actor) but 'not the war'. This unequivocally encourages the separation and compartmentalizing of these four constitutive elements relating to politically motivated violence. British military actors can, therefore, be publicly supported and 'remembered' yet simultaneously separated from the so-called 'war on terror' (ideological cause), violence (action) and destruction of other peoples' cities/towns and large-scale (civilian) death (outcome of action) that has been carried out by them[10].

[7] I purposely use the subjective and context-based 'interpretation/s' rather than 'meaning/s' to illustrate these are ideologically infused judgments rather than objective facts.

[8] Even if one argues it is a question of morality this simply reinforces my overarching argument that these debates are based on political and ideological judgments. For example, assumptions around the morality of violence and/or the rights of other humans to perform violence with in particular contexts differ according to a whole range of political and ideological standpoints.

[9] The actor (British soldier) is almost always universally supported by the British establishment, so this is usually a given. The ideological cause is usually supported too (whether it is labeled war or necessary self-defense) but the cause does not need to be supported for the claim to stand.

[10] This is not to deny there are also humanitarian actions carried out by British military actors too.

Crucially for this chapter, this means that British military personnel can be 'remembered' while separating such remembrance from their associated violent actions and outcomes. Yet when the ideological cause and/or actor are not supported by the British government and/or large sections of Britain's corporate media, these four elements are framed as inextricably connected. Indeed, when violence is considered by the British state to relate to 'terrorists' we are often told that they (actors) cannot be separated from the ideological cause, their actions and the outcomes of their actions. This exposes how the relationship between ideological cause, actor, action and outcome of action is judged differently depending on whether or not the violence carried out by those being 'remembered' is supported by key powerful opinion formers in Britain.

With regard to some Celtic supporters this results in acts of Irish nationalist remembrance (in Scotland) being treated differently from British military-related remembrance. Thus, the overarching paradox consists of British military violence (action) being (or encouraged to be) universally and dogmatically supported whilst claiming it is distinct from political ideology, the military actor and the outcome of military violence: yet violence conducted by others is denounced whilst claiming it is umbilically connected to these elements.

There is a further paradox that emerges from this overarching one. While the British government and a majority of Britain's corporate media often insist on British military violence being viewed as apolitical and separate from remembrance, their words and deeds sometimes − usually when propaganda activities are enacted − do the opposite; that is, they sometimes make the connection between the actor (British military), the political ideology ('war on terror' and/or 'protecting democracy'), action (shooting, bombing, 'service') and outcome of action (death, destruction or alleged 'freedom'). For example, despite previously defending British remembrance and the EHP as non-political, Prime Minister Theresa May described Remembrance Sunday 2016 in contrasting terms, commenting:

> The way of life we enjoy today depends upon the service offered by members of the armed forces and their families. Across

generations and in every corner of the UK, today we remember those who gave so much for our values, our democracy and our nation. At this time of reflection, we must not forget those members of the armed forces who are currently away from loved ones, whether taking the fight to Daesh, assisting UN peacekeeping efforts in Africa or fighting piracy on the high seas. As we are united in remembrance of those who have made sacrifices for our freedom, so we are united in our gratitude to those who continue to keep us safe.[11]

This example illustrates the contradiction in framing remembrance as non-political but then using it to represent the political[12]: and it also exposes how sorrowful remembrance elides into proud gratitude of past and current military action while re-presenting such action as necessary for the politically contested 'quest for freedom'. Way of life, values, democracy, sacrifice, freedom, safety, British unity and nation (state) are all invoked as integral to remembrance by May who even extends remembrance to include offering (and encouraging others to offer) gratitude to those who are 'away from loved ones' rather than dead or injured.

Similarly, whilst also ideologically representing British military action as virtuous, previous Prime Minister David Cameron incorporated British citizens into giving their support to soldiers, their actions and the ideological cause underpinning them when he promoted the newly invented Armed Forces Day:

These initiatives have the full support of the nation . . . [Armed Forces Day is] an opportunity for the nation to pay respect to those fighting for our freedom and way of life.

Despite the ubiquity of phrases such as 'support the troops not the war' being accepted as legitimate when applied to the British military, key opinion formers often contradict this in making ideologically contested connections explicit for their political ends when incorporating citizens by proxy into appreciating and supporting the 'initiatives' and 'sacrifices' of British military actors.

These common representations form part of the same discourse used to interpret the EHP. In the same year as the

[11] Sky News (2016) PM in Remembrance Day nod to today's troops. 13/11/16 Available at: http://news.sky.com/story/pm-in-remembrance-day-nod-to-todays-troops-10655753?dcmp=snt-sf-twitter (accessed 26 March 2017).

[12] Of course it is also revealing to note the ideologically virtuous examples of action May selects to highlight 'fighting terrorists' 'peacekeeping' and 'fighting pirates'.

latest FIFA and 'poppy' controversy occurred, the official 'poppy campaign' conducted by the Royal British Legion (RBL) presented the EHP not only as offering remembrance or sorrow but as supporting military personnel. Furthermore, leaving no room for doubt, the RBL explicitly re-appropriated 'support' to apply to current British military (as well as those who defeated Nazism). The official RBL branding, named 'Rethink Remembrance' stated:

> There's a new generation of veterans that need your support. This year, The Royal British Legion is asking the nation to Rethink Remembrance by recognizing the sacrifices made not just by the Armed Forces of the past, but by today's generation too. . . For many people, Remembrance is associated with the fallen of the First and Second World Wars. While we will always remember them, the Legion wants to raise awareness of a new generation of veterans and Service personnel that need our support.[14]

Thus, the shift in the EHP being a symbol of sorrowful remembrance of conscripted soldiers to symbolising awareness of current military volunteers has now been officially acknowledged and forms a central focus of the RBL's official branding strategy. Furthermore, this public relations exercise not only conflates sorrowful remembrance with awareness but also extends it to seeking recognition and support for the actions – linguistically sanitized as 'sacrifices' – of British military actors.

The calls for the British public to ideologically connect current troops to those who defeated Nazism have gained momentum in the last two decades with the development of an orchestrated multi-agency campaign to encourage British citizens to 'support the troops'. Beauty contests, prime time Saturday night television shows, military-related music albums, military branded food products, newly formed charities, recently invented traditions such as Armed Forces Day and homecoming parades have all combined to provide platforms for the hero-fication and celebritization of the British military[15] during periods of widespread public dissatisfaction with the invasions/liberations of Iraq, Afghanistan and other countries associated with the so-called 'war on terror'.

[14] (Rethink Remembrance this Poppy Appeal, British Legion 2016)

Sport being used for remembrance

A central aspect of these support the troops campaigns involves sport being used as patriotic platforms for the public to be incorporated by proxy into 'supporting' and 'thanking' national military actors.[16] Sport (and popular cultural activities more broadly) has been used where such practices infuse a sense of national identity (Scottishness & Britishness), and where they appeal to emotional and deeply embedded aspects of citizens' sense of self and patriotism.[17] And again, we witness the connections that expose the ideological interpretations and associations being made between British military personnel and the violence conducted by them. Lord Mawhinney, as chairman of the [English] Football League, incorporated football fans into supporting the actions of the British military and thanking them for such actions when discussing the Football League being sponsored by the newly invented military charity 'Help for Heroes'. Mawhinney stated:

> The contribution being made by our armed forces around the world is truly humbling. The football for heroes week will provide an excellent opportunity for supporters to show their appreciation for the outstanding work being done.[18]

These comments represent common discourses articulated about British military and its related actions and are unquestionably political. Despite the ontological detachment discussed earlier – 'Support the troops not the war' – these (and other) official pronouncements actually make the connections between supporting the troops and the war seamless and they unashamedly use sport as a platform to manufacture wider public support for British military violence and the ideological justifications used to legitimise it.

These paradoxes and controversies expose the limitations in permitting the state authority to define the meaning and interpretation of politically-charged terms such as remembrance, and these were exposed publicly in the treatment of Celtic supporters at the hands of the state's interpretation and application of the Offensive Behaviour at Football Bill (OBFB). Much of this controversy and disagreement has centred on Celtic supporters singing, for example, the Roll of Honour, and display-

[16] See Jansen, S.C. and Sabo, D. (1994) The sport/war metaphor: hegemonic masculinity, the Persian Gulf War, and the new world order. Sociology of Sport Journal, 11(1): 1–17; Silk, M. and Falcous, M. (2005) One day in September/A week in February: mobilizing American (sporting) nationalism.- Sociology of Sport Journal, 22: 447–71; Butterworth, M. (2017) (ed.) GlobalSport and Militarism. London: Routledge; Butterworth M (2005) Ritual in the 'Church of baseball': suppressing the discourse of democracy after 9/11. Communication and Critical/Cultural Studies, 2(2): 107–29; Butterworth M. (2008) Fox Sports, Super Bowl XLII, and the affirmation of American civil religion. Journal of Sport and Social Issues, 32(3): 318–23; Butterworth M. (2010) 'Major League Baseball Welcomes Back Veterans, and the Rhetoric of 'Support the Troops'. In R. Briley (ed.) The Politics of Baseball: Essays on the Pastime and Power at Home and Abroad.

ing banners that are alleged (by the state) to provide support for 'terrorism'. In one sense, it is unsurprising that Scottish/ British citizens and state actors (such as police, legal, political and media professionals) have sometimes interpreted aspects of Irish-British history and identity in Scotland in one-dimensional ways, viewing them essentially as, illicit. Potential ignorance is compounded in two related ways when Irish expression in Scotland – such as Irish nationalism – is viewed as culturally impermissible. These are captured in Bradley's observations:

> This overarching ideological production that obliterates knowledge and understanding of the conflict between and within these islands constitutes a master narrative that reflects an indolent representation of important strands of British/ Scottish-Irish relations. This can also function to 'forget' Scotland's significant contribution to military, political, cultural, religious and economic discord regarding its past imperialist activities and their deep and profound, often ongoing consequences.[19]

As Bradley further observes:

> . . . knowledge and understanding of Ireland. . . is virtually absent from the Scottish education system. It might be argued that the Irish have almost become invisible in most aspects of modern Scottish society.[20]

It may be the case that because of this alleged British master narrative – which caricatures and culturally reduces Irish identities, rendering some of them invisible while 'forgetting' key moments (and consequences) of British imperialism – that when Irish nationalist expressions are performed in Scotland, they appear magnified and assume heightened degrees of suspicion and hostility among the media, police and wider authorities.

If one soberly interprets the song 'Roll of Honour' it is clear that it remembers the ten Irish nationalist Hunger Strikers who died in 1981 protesting against the British state's treatment of prisoners whilst incarcerated in British prisons for activities deemed by the British State as 'terrorism'. At another level they were also protesting against historical British imperialism, including military violence, in their country. Two of the Hunger

Jefferson, NC: McFarland, pp. 226–40; Scherer, J. and Koch, J. (2010) Living with war: sport, citizenship and the cultural politics of post-9/11 Canadian identity. Sociology of Sport Journal, 27: 1–29; Kelly, J. (2013) Popular culture, sport and the hero-fication of British militarism. Sociology, 47(4): 722-738; Kelly J (2017) Western Militarism and the Political Utility of Sport. In Bairner A, Kelly J and Lee JW (eds) Routledge Handbook of Sport and Politics. London: Routledge, pp.277-291.

[17] Kelly, J. (2013) Popular culture, sport and the hero-fication of British militarism.Sociology, 47(4): 722-738; Kelly J (2017) Western Militarism and the Political Utility of Sport. In Bairner A, Kelly J and Lee JW (eds.) Routledge Handbook of Sport and Politics. London: Routledge, pp.277-291

[18] Sun Online, 'Footie Clubs Unite For Heroes', March 2, 2010, http:// www.thesun.co.uk/sol/ homepage/news/ campaigns/our_boys/ 2874672/Footie-clubs-unite-for-heroes.html

[19] Bradley, J.M. (2016) Who Fears to Speak? In Lusk and Maley (eds.) Scotland and the Easter Rising: Fresh Perspectives on 1916. Luath press. pp:49-55 (p.52).

[20] Ibid (p.52).

Strikers remembered in the song were democratically elected political representatives to both the British and Irish Parliaments whilst being held as prisoners of the British state. It is clearly a song of remembrance with a rather sad tone. It does not condone nor endorse any illegal acts. Its focus is on sacrifice and sorrow and may – by virtue of the subject matter – be interpreted as being linked to Irish Nationalism. Irish Nationalism, of course, is a broad ideological cause and as such, is not limited to one group or even type of group, and, as is historically evidenced, can both support or oppose the use of military actions which is in keeping with the song not mentioning any (proscribed or legal) organisation or military/violent action.

It is certainly true that Celtic supporters singing Roll of Honour are treated differently from other citizens in Britain who engage in acts of 'British military' remembrance. Furthermore, the basis on which value judgments are made and how they are made by applying the criteria differently is of central significance. When the remembrance is about those 'serving' Britain and is officially endorsed by powerful British opinion formers, it is deemed acceptable, nay desirable, and when remembrance focuses on those 'serving' alternative and oppositional groups, this remembrance is symbolically annihilated: in the case of Roll of Honour, the state's application of the Offensive Behaviour at Football Bill sought to criminalize those who sing it. The relationship between ideological cause, actor, action and outcome of action is judged to be intimately connected when it applies to Celtic supporters singing about Irish nationalist remembrance in contrast to how these four elements are often judged to be unconnected when they apply to officially acceptable remembrance in Britain. And this is despite the official interpretation (noted earlier) which sometimes make these connections explicit when seeking support for British militarism and its actions.

Of course, comparing British remembrance and the Roll of Honour song remembrance should not be mistaken for comparing British military actions with Irish nationalist actions. A greater depth of thought and understanding occurs by comparing the relationship between an act of remembrance and the ideological cause, actors, actions, outcomes of these actions to show that one example (British Remembrance) is presented as relationship neutral, in contrast to the other (Irish nationalist Roll of Honour) remembrance, presented as relationship active – supporting and endorsing the actors, actions and outcomes.

> Irrespective of who is doing the remembrance and what it claims to remember, it is inconsistent to claim that the relationship between the actors, actions and outcomes differs according to whose remembrance has the most supporters or whose is officially sanctioned by the state. In other words, given that discourses in Britain often stress British (military related) remembrance is not necessarily supporting the ideological cause, actors, acts or outcomes of such acts (illustrated by 'support the troops not the war'), then the remembrance behaviors of others must also be considered potentially non-supportive of the ideological cause, actors, actions, and outcomes. Indeed, to claim otherwise is to confirm that one's judgment is not based on logic but on (im)moral, political and subjective value judgments.[21]

The inconsistent and potentially prejudiced application of interpreting remembrance is exposed in these cases with Celtic fans singing Roll of Honour interpreted as supporting the IRA, the violence (actions) of the IRA and the death and destruction (outcomes of actions) of the IRA. Such interpretations are made despite the song not mentioning the IRA (or any paramilitary organisation) and despite three of the individuals named and remembered in the song not being members of the IRA. When seeking understanding on why this might be, one might consider how the so called 'Troubles' were typically represented in popular British discourses during the worst years of conflict from the late 1960s until the early 1990s. These interpretations of remembrance are in stark contrast to the ways remembrance for British military are framed and encouraged with Remembrance Sunday and the EHP being implicitly presented by the government and corporate media as not justifying or supporting any political ideology, military violence or death and destruction caused by it.

These protestations of political neutrality are at odds with the overwhelming representation of Remembrance Sunday which occurs with military uniforms, is performed in militaristic fashion and is wrapped in the paraphernalia of the British armed forces.

[21] Kelly (2017). The Paradox of Militaristic Remembrance in British Sport and Popular Culture in Butterworth, M. (ed.) Global Sport and Militarism. Routledge. pp149-162. (p.156).

Protesting political neutrality of 'the poppy' is also at odds with numerous propaganda statements made by government officials who themselves situate it in highly political contexts such as representing 'freedom', 'democracy', 'way of life' and 'anti-terror'.

Conclusion

National identity and ethnicity are often largely constituted through myth, heroes, remembrance and nostalgia and involve real and imagined communities and invented traditions which are often a mixture of the actual and mythical. Such features are not exclusive to Irishness of course. They are universal features of most (if not all) national or ethnic identities. Roll of Honour does not express hatred. Of course, the very fact that some individual/s claiming Irish ethnicity (and some who don't) choose to remember Irish republicans as major historical figures and/or national/political heroes will always, almost certainly, be offensive to some in Scotland/Britain. However, this illustrates the problem with implementing a bill based on offence. Like beauty, offence is in the eye of the beholder and making legal judgments based on it is highly subjective and often controversial.

It could be argued that criminalising Irish nationalist express-ions subjugates important strands of particular forms of Irish diasporic identity in Scotland. Criminalising these expressions along with the day-to-day ridiculing, mocking and questioning of their legitimacy and authenticity combine to deny individuals/groups their rights to perform (these elements of) their national identity/ethnicity: it may also be contradictory with regards democracy. Irish nationalism is a broad political and cultural ideology and it clearly represents part of some critical forms of Irish identity. If such expressions incite public disorder, then one is entitled to ask if the problem to be addressed is the intolerance shown by those who remain determined to deny an ethnic 'other' group its right to remember its historical and political figures. In fact, denying others these rights flirts perilously close to contravening some of the very laws that seek to protect people from prejudice/hatred based on national and ethnic identities.

The arguments set out here should not be misrepresented as either defending or denouncing the singing or chanting of 'IRA' in any context at football matches. However, as I have previously and unambiguously stated, although there might be debates, discussion, dissension, or even disapproval 'there should be no laws outlawing political expression at football matches'.[22] Acts of remembrance that relate to violence and political struggle are unquestionably political. The orchestrated act of footballers wearing the EHP accompanied by ubiquitous messages from various official sources that seek to frame this as fans expressing their support, appreciation and thanks for politically motivated military violence – sanitised as 'sacrifice' or 'outstanding work' – carried out by British military actors is undeniably political. The singing of the Roll of Honour is similarly, a political act.

[22] Ibid (p.220).

'This is our outlet, this is where we express ourselves': Celtic and Irishness

MAUREEN MCBRIDE

Introduction

In one chapter in the third in the series of Celtic Minded, Bradley et al explore the marginalisation of Irish identities in British society. They talk of Irish diasporic identities operating in a 'public sphere where their background culture is unrepresented or may be missing altogether'[1]. The relevant authors found that despite the 'denationalisation' over time of the Irish in Britain, the Irish cultural and national backgrounds of many British-born people of Irish descent is not an inevitable process and can be maintained and remain very powerful for them. There is, however, the important question over whether and how these cultural and national backgrounds are given an outlet in mainstream society. In Scotland, the authors argue that expressions of Irishness are primarily located in the realm of sport: 'the culture around Celtic is a site of struggle for ethnic and political identities that provides the Irish-descended in Scotland with a space to express their Irishness'[2].

There has been significant change over the past decade in relation to how Irish identities in Scotland are experienced and responded to. This might be seen, in one sense, by political shifts relating to a decline in support for Labour and a rise in support (a rise requiring much exploration and explanation) for Scottish

[1] Bradley et al 2009, p. 193

[2] Bradley et al 2009, p. 211

independence amongst those from Irish Catholic backgrounds: this for some people, indicating a more inclusive sense of 'Scottishness' than has been the case historically. On the other hand, changes are also evident in the context of football with the establishment and subsequent repeal (in March 2018) of the controversial Offensive Behaviour at Football and Threatening Communications (Scotland) Act 2012 (hereafter the OBTC Act), which I argue has particular implications for the Irish diaspora in (mostly) west-central Scotland. As such, the purpose here is to consider the question of Irish identities in the light of these recent changes. In doing so, I draw on my recently-completed PhD research entitled 'rethinking sectarianism', in which I sought to develop a deeper, empirically-informed understanding of sectarianism in contemporary Scotland and to critically explore the OBTC Act's impact on those football supporters who express certain national and political identities.

Of course, the Act's use was certainly not limited to the policing of Celtic fans or Irish identities: young, predominately working class male supporters across Scottish football have experienced higher levels of surveillance and police intimidation, in some cases resulting in questionable criminal convictions. However, the policing of Irish identities has been an important strand of the Act in practice: some might argue, the key strand. This chapter argues that the expression of such identities is often received negatively, and in the context of the OBTC legislation, sometimes criminalised. There is still a strong sense that Irish history, politics and nationalism have no place in Scottish football, indeed, Scottish society. The chapter looks briefly at the historical significance of Irish identities in Scottish football, reflects on the question of politics in football today, explores some contemporary examples of debates around commemorating aspects of Irish history to illustrate the 'cultural invisibility' and denial of difference and finally, reflects on the OBTC Act's significance in current debates on the expression of Irish identities in the context of football.

> a rise in support for Scottish independence amongst those from Irish Catholic backgrounds (for some people, indicates a more inclusive sense of 'Scottishness' than has been the case historically.

Scottish football and Irish identities

Although the centrality of Celtic as a 'space' for the expression of Irishness has been well-versed in these volumes and demonstrated in Bradley's academic work more broadly[3], it is useful to provide a brief summary here to contextualise this chapter's key arguments. In 1887/88, Celtic Football Club was established to raise money to help alleviate poverty for the Irish Catholic immigrant community living in Glasgow and the surrounding areas. The levels of poverty experienced by the Irish in nineteenth century Scotland was shaped and reinforced by the fact that the immigrants found themselves as 'outsiders' in Scotland, excluded on account of their perceived 'race', nationality and religion. Irish immigration to Scotland (and elsewhere in Britain) must be seen in the context of British colonialism, the racialisation of the Irish by British settlers in Ireland, and the British Government's critical role in the Great Irish Hunger which caused the deaths of over one milliion and mass displacement of millions of Irish people. Moreover, to be 'Scottish' or 'British' in the nineteenth century was to be Protestant[4]: and the Catholic religion of the majority of migrants further excluded them from these national identities. So, as well as the material purpose of Celtic's establishment as a means to support the Irish community, the club's establishment also facilitated the construction of an outlet for alternative identities to the dominant 'Scottish' and 'British' identities[5].

Yet Celtic's Irish identity was not positively received: as late as 1952, for example, sixty-four years after Celtic's first game, the Scottish Football Authorities threatened to expel the club if it refused to stop flying the Irish tricolour in the stadium: a threat which was only rescinded when it was established that the SFA had no legal basis for doing so. The Irish Catholic identity of Celtic was countered most significantly by the pro-Unionist, Protestant, and often overtly anti-Catholic identity of Rangers Football Club, which pursued an anti-Catholic policy until the 1989 signing of Maurice Johnston. It is notable that even as recently as this, the signing of Johnston resulted in some fans placing a wreath outside Ibrox stadium mourning the loss of '116 years of tradition'[6]. Scottish football has, therefore, been tied up in questions of ethnicity, competing nationalisms and religious identities since the outset, and, unsurprisingly, Irish-British history and politics have been an ever-present issue in football as elsewhere in society.

Clearly much has changed in the 130 years since Celtic's

[3] Bradley 1995, 2001

[4] Colley 1992, Virdee 2014

[5] Bradley 2006, p 1190

[6] Murray 1998, p. 44

inception, and indeed the last few decades have seen considerable progress in relation to the socio-economic position of Irish Catholics as well as experiences of anti-Catholicism and anti-Irishness. The Irish diaspora no longer occupy the same 'outsider' status in the Scottish nation, and the structural inequality that continued to exist in the twentieth century has diminished greatly, at least for younger generations of Catholics from Irish backgrounds. Political activity, such as the strong levels of support for Scottish independence amongst a significant proportion of Catholics in the 2014 referendum, illustrates for some that for the moment at least, a political 'Scottishness' as an identity, now more easily includes Catholics. A recent article by Michael Rosie and Tom Devine states that 'they would hardly have done so if they did not feel confident in their Scottish skins'[7]. However, this 'inclusive' conception of 'Scottishness' which undoubtedly emerged for many (but not all) in the independence campaign, may on closer analysis have resembled more of a social justice movement than a 'Scottish' nationalist one – and this might be seen as key as to how the change in Catholic voting patterns has emerged. If social justice is key we require to wait a long time before any such sociological conclusions can be made. We must also consider that when people vote for whatever they think is best for Scotland or Britain for that matter, doesn't necessarily make them any more Scottish or British in terms of their identities especially at the expense of their Irishness.

However, some assessments, academic and otherwise, of this sudden shift in an Irish and/or Catholic expression with regard to Scottish independence, might not solely be understood in language that talks of the Irish diaspora being in 'Scottish skins' and being more 'comfortable'. It certainly does not mean that people from Irish Catholic backgrounds have been 'assimilated' into Scottish society to the extent that their Irish identities are less important to them – and possibly even does not mean a rise in Scottishness amongst parts of the Irish diaspora. Leaving discussion of the differences between integration and assimilation aside for the moment, it likewise does not mean that the very recent memories of disadvantage or prejudice have simply disappeared because the material structures for sustaining the dominance of one social group (native Scots-British/Protestants)

this 'inclusive' conception of 'Scottishness' which undoubtedly emerged for many in the independence campaign, may on closer analysis have resembled more of a social justice movement than a 'Scottish' nationalist one

[7] Rosie and Devine, The Herald 1 April 2018

over another (Catholics of Irish extraction) are dismantled. Multi-generational Irishness in Scotland remains powerful, and for many, it is in the context of supporting Celtic that these identities find a 'home' – literally for many.

> football is in fact often a most appropriate cultural space for expressing political identities

Politics in football

Most of the participants in my PhD research argued that politics and football are not easily separable, and that football is in fact often a most appropriate cultural space for expressing their political identities. For many, family influences were important in this respect, as ethnic, national and political identities are passed down inter-generationally. This was not only the case for Irish politics: support for Scottish independence and protesting austerity were other political causes raised by participants. However, Irish-British history and politics was most frequently emphasised as central to fans' supporting identities. Interviewees talked about their attachment to particular Irish songs, flags or other symbols, and of activities such as writing for fanzines with an Irish Republican focus, or supporting campaigns in support of political prisoners, which were inextricably linked to the support of their team.

Patrick, for example, stated:

This is our outlet, this is where we express ourselves. . . Part of Celtic for me is Irish politics and Irish Republicanism. It has been since inception and it always will be for me. Take that away, it's taking part of Celtic away.

For Patrick, the club's historical link to Ireland was central to his supporting identity and experience, and there was a strong sense of concern from participants like Patrick that this connection was under threat by both the club, through the apparent playing down of certain aspects of Celtic's Irish roots, and the authorities' policing of Irish nationalist or political identities under the OBTC Act. Another participant, Peter, spoke about how he came to identify as an Irish Republican, despite most of his Irish family being more 'conservative'. He explained that one of his family members was a Republican and that he was influenced by their more 'radical' politics. Peter spoke about debates around the appropriateness of politics in football:

> There's obviously that argument, is there a space for politics in football. Well I'm a firm believer that obviously, there is, certainly the type of politics that we're seeing spoke about, republicanism, anti-fascism. . . we're marginalised politically so Celtic was a place to talk about these things.

As previously noted, it was clear that this was not limited to Irish-British history and politics but politics more broadly, including anti-racism and anti-fascism. One younger participant, Connor, expressed solidarity with different oppressed groups, including Palestinians, and commented:

> I don't think, without the politics, I don't think I'd feel as strong an affection for Celtic. You know, it's more than a game.

In my research, the range and depth of knowledge regarding particular politics challenges media representations of fans who embrace and publicly display Irish nationalist or political identities as young, uneducated men who don't know any better. Certain groups of football supporters – not only Celtic fans – are frequently portrayed as 'uncivilised' compared to 'normal' supporters. Supporters are vilified using emotionally charged language and imagery, and their identities equated with violence and sectarianism[8]. However, it was clear from discussions with research participants that such representations disregard the strength of political identities and the connection that football often facilitates between people and identities.

These examples are not intended to suggest that this is the case for all or indeed most Celtic supporters; some research participants felt quite strongly that politics – especially Irish-British politics – should be kept out of football. Other fans vary in opinions too: for some it's not quite so important, others might not think politically anyway. However, for some, this remains a powerful connection. Peter's point about Irish identities being 'marginalised politically' is important. To make sense of some of these stances on the question of politics in football, it is important to consider how these identities are expressed and responded to elsewhere in society. The next section explores how Irish identities are marginalised in mainstream British-Scottish cultures.

> Certain groups of football supporters – not only Celtic fans – are frequently portrayed as 'uncivilised' compared to 'normal' supporters.

[8] McBride 2011

Cultural invisibility

It was clear that Irish-British history and politics remain important for some Scottish-born (or in some cases English-born) people from Irish backgrounds. This is in spite of the fact that – as Mary Hickman has previously stated [9] – Ireland, and the so called 'Irish question', has historically been largely absent from the school curriculum in Britain. My own personal experience studying history and politics at school and at university in Glasgow very much echoed Hickman's point about a 'silence' regarding Irish-British histories and politics in Scotland, which I consider to be linked to the 'cultural invisibility' of the Irish in Scotland. One consequence of this cultural invisibility is that football – specifically Celtic – becomes a focal point for the expression of Irish identities.

> some who spoke of the importance of Celtic as an outlet for the expression of Irish identities emphasised the 'cultural invisibility' of Irishness in broader society

Indeed, some who spoke of the importance of Celtic as an outlet for the expression of Irish identities emphasised the 'cultural invisibility' of Irishness in broader society. One example of this in contemporary Scotland is that following requests to hold a St. Patrick's Day parade in Glasgow in 2015, leading politicians appeared to engage in a 'denial of difference'. Former Labour MP Jim Sheridan stated that the 'taxpayer' should not be responsible for funding events such as St. Patrick's Day parades: this despite the fact that other parades and demonstrations celebrating minority groups' ethnicity and heritage are frequently sanctioned. Official St. Patrick's Day parades are held all over the world in areas with a history of Irish migration, including in Boston, New York, Toronto, Sydney, Birmingham, Manchester and London, without controversy: but rarely if ever in Scotland.

The question of whether the Irish should be considered an ethnic minority with the right to publicly express this heritage is also crucial here. In a response to the question of 'labelling' the Irish as an ethnic minority, which emerged from the release of a report on the Irish in Scotland by the British/Irish Parliamentary Assembly in February 2015, former Conservative MSP Mary Scanlon claimed that:

> They are an integrated, fully respected and loved members of our community, they are not different. This to me, I am afraid, I think is a little bit divisive.

[9] Hickman 1996

As well as an indication that such public expressions of Irishness or an understanding of the Irish as an ethnic minority – regardless of how they self-define – could be considered–'divisive', this raises questions around what is meant by 'integration'. These comments could be interpreted (a cynic might say that the multi-generational Irish in Scotland simply misinterpret this 'love' they are faced with?) as an assertion that if sections of Irish Catholic society wish to hold onto that part of their identity, their status as Scots comes into question. Is it the case that being Irish and Scottish is somehow less compatible than Irish and English, or Irish and American?

The issue of public displays of Irishness and Irish-British history in Scotland also emerged in debates around a memorial to the Great Irish Hunger, which killed one million people and displaced one million others including, of course, many of the forebears of those who settled in Scotland. Despite being one of the major centres of Irish Famine migration, Glasgow has as yet to become home to one of the 142 famine memorials worldwide. After years of campaigning, Glasgow City Council were asked to provide an appropriate site to memorialise all victims of the Irish Famine (and as usually requires to be stressed in Scotland, including those from the Protestant faith). Yet those involved in the campaign were dissatisfied by the council's proposal to erect a so called 'joint' memorial for the Irish and Highland 'famines' (which were utterly different in roots and consequences), and eventually decided on a site dedicated to the Great Irish Hunger to be placed in St. Mary's Calton. The committee stated:

> It seemed to us that Glasgow City Council added on the Highland element because they knew, or believed, that there were forces in Glasgow even today who would not accept a memorial which involved the Irish alone.

This perception was shared by several of my research participants. Matthew, for example, expressed his frustration that 'the idea of a famine memorial becomes a sectarian issue' because it 'has' to emphasise that many Protestants were also killed or displaced by the Irish famine. He felt that this was an indication that 'expressions of Irishness' remain problematic in Scotland, as well as an attempt to play down the fact that the famine symbolised the 'ugly face' of British imperialism, the historic unequal power relations between Britain and Ireland and also that the vast majority (Kinealy estimates around 95%) of people killed were in fact, Catholics – as if that mattered.

Another example involves debates regarding the Fields of Athenry, an Irish folk ballad set during the Great Irish Hunger, which is of course frequently played and sung at Celtic matches. In the 2009 series of Celebrity Big Brother, former Scottish Socialist Party MSP Tommy Sheridan's singing of The Fields of Athenry was censored. Yet Reverend Stuart MacQuarrie, the University of Glasgow chaplain, appeared on a radio programme to criticise Sheridan for singing the song which he described as 'anti-British' and 'racist'. Similarly, in a 2011 Times column about a Celtic versus Rangers match, journalist Magnus Linklater appeared to equate the singing of the 'Famine Song' by sections of the Rangers support, which was declared racist in a court of law, to Celtic supporters singing the Fields of Athenry, which he described as 'the traditional Republican anthem'[11]. These claims ignore important historical power relations, including the racialisation of Irish people by the British colonial state, who subsequently experienced multiple exclusions on account of perceived racial and religious inferiority when arriving in Britain as immigrants[12]. That history is lost when a song about a Irishman arrested and sent to a British Australian penal colony for trying to steal corn to feed his starving family[13] is characterised as 'racist', or made equivalent to the overt xenophobic tone of 'the famine is over, why don't you go home'? The impact of neglecting these historical unequal power relationships also extended into the criminal justice sphere, as explored in the next section.

OBTC Act and criminalising Irishness

The problems outlined in the previous section stem from an understanding of sectarianism that pays insufficient attention to historic power relations between Britain and Ireland or the experiences of the Irish who settled in Scotland. Celtic Minded editor Dr. Joseph Bradley as well as contributor Dr. John Kelly have made this point in several international rated academic publications. As well as more general cultural marginalization,

[11] The Times 23 April 2011

[12] Bradley X, Garner X, McBride 2018

[13] Goodall et al 2015, p. 3

the absence of this historical context has, arguably, led to the criminalization of particular Irish identities in football. Resistance to public displays of Irish cultural, national and political identities has very much been played out in the context of the OBTC Act. The Act can be seen as an important tool in policing a general intolerance of supporters who use football as a forum to remember aspects of Irish-British history or politics – through songs or other symbols. Among its various functions was its use as an instrument through which to 'police values' through the de-legitimisation of expressions of certain identities and cultural practices.

In my PhD research, several participants spoke of being warned by police officers and stewards for carrying the Irish tricolor in or around football stadiums, echoing the example I mentioned earlier from 1952 when the SFA attempted to ban Celtic from flying the flag. In another example, a research participant was arrested for singing the Irish national anthem, which was deemed 'a sectarian song' by the arresting officer. The subjective nature of 'offensiveness', and the lack of clear guidance on what the legislation actually covered was a problem more broadly for the OBTC Act (and a reason why it was eventually the first piece of legislation passed by the Scottish Parliament to be repealed), but in this case it demonstrates that the Irish flag and national anthem can not only be considered offensive but sufficient reason for police attention and even arrest: this is both striking and revealing with regards 'modern' Scottish society.

Considered particularly 'unacceptable' appears to be anything involving specifically Republican elements of Irish history and politics. This was evident in the Act's frequent use to target Celtic supporters singing the Roll of Honour, a song commemorating the Republican Hunger Strikers who died in Long Kesh/Maze Prison in 1981. For many Celtic supporters who took part in my research, the song is an important part of Irish-British history and the struggle against the oppression of the British state. The meaning attached to the song itself, and the relatively recent historical context that it represents, was highlighted by Joe: 'Aye, it does mean a lot. Because essentially, it's about 10 men who had to starve themselves to death, so. . . it does, it sticks with a lot of people you know?' Another participant, Barry, discussed how he felt about singing the song in the presence of police with cameras at an away game the previous year: 'I knew when that song started if I start singing this here I could be in trouble. I don't know why, but I could be, so it impacted on me, kind of curtailing myself a wee bit, feeling a wee bit unsure of myself'. Barry described himself as 'very politically aware' and active in left-wing politics, and the Irish Republican songs associated with Celtic are something he feels very strongly about: 'they are just kind of political songs, expressions of freedom, and rights and stories, that's why I kind fell in love with the Irish music as well as becoming a Celtic fan, lyrically the songs are absolutely beautiful, they're amazing'. For Barry, it is impossible for Roll of Honour to be sectarian. He, like many other supporters, considers the song to be an example of anti-establishment sentiment – legitimate political expression – yet the threat of 'trouble' has caused him to curtail this.

Conclusion

This chapter has emphasised the multi-generational nature of Irish cultural and national identities in contemporary Scotland. For the individuals that took part in my PhD research, such identities were equally strong for younger third/fourth generation Irish diaspora as they were for older participants with a more 'recent' personal/family connection to Ireland. They were also strong for those people who believed passionately in Scottish independence, clearly indicating that more inclusive conceptualisations of 'Scottishness' does not entail the 'denationalisation' of Irishness. This poses a challenge to those who utilise an assimilatory framing in debates on the integration of people from Irish backgrounds in Scotland, as emphasised in the 'cultural invisibility' section of this chapter.

Celtic Football Club remains a key site for the expression of Irish identities, which do not easily find expression in other aspects of society. High levels of policing at football, especially in the context of the Offensive Behaviour at Football Act from 2012 until its repeal in 2018, shapes responses to displays of Irish identities. Many research participants strongly felt that Irish identities are 'policed' at football games, as though the history and politics that they are attached to are problematic and even criminal. This is not limited to specific expressions of support for Irish Republicanism, but also for symbolic gestures such as carrying an Irish tricolour or singing the Irish national anthem. The repeal of the OBTC Act may well signal a shift in this type of policing, but it appears that broader debates around the place of Irishness in Scottish society are as relevant as ever.

Celtic, Faith & Brother Walfrid

Emma O'Neil

There are numerous understandings of what constitutes faith and these never ring truer to me than when it comes to Celtic Football Club. It is really hard to pinpoint where my personal religious experiences with Celtic began but I can think all day long of encounters I have had with my faith and Celtic. I know I feel so thankful for my blessings, friends and family, and many other things that have restored my 'faith' over the years.

I suppose my own experience with faith and religion really came to fruition when in my teenage years I was diagnosed with Acute Anorexia Nervosa. Aged 15 I had a rapid decline in the depths of an eating disorder that would take away my whole adolescence. My parents were distraught throughout this period of pain shared by our family and it is during this time that I remember my mum being really called back to her faith. She invited religious messengers into the house to pray for me, share presentations, watch religious short stories and read from the bible. She took me back to Church and prayed for me openly. When I was later hospitalised for the eating disorder I think I felt I was truly praying for myself: how was I going to get through this?

I have in my possession a Peter Howson pastel, the first in my collection, called 'The Third Step'. It depicts a naked man lying in the dirt, dragging himself to the Saviour, with a church in the distance. While ill, this piece of art illustrated everything I was and what I was trying to do, and it hung, despite its worth, on my hospital room wall to inspire me. I had struck up a friendship with Peter Howson a few years after that and he used to come to visit me in hospital. Unfortunately, every relapse in my Anorexia I had was worse than the previous time. Ultimately reaching under 3 stones I was a complete shell of my former self: controlled by Anorexia. Peter would send me Christmas cards with religious figures and scriptures from the bible, each one giving me more faith to keep going. Subsequently I would go on to commission works by him that were drawn and painted from paragraphs I'd written about my illness and my idea of religion. Dark, dark paragraphs that only looking back can I now see how ill I was, though I was completely in denial at the time.

I've always had a connection with Celtic but this grew massively when I started exploring and researching the Club and its community's religious and faith origins. It might be worth noting at this stage that I am completely healthy and have been for around 8 years. I now have two children and work hard at my business. I have fought the monster that is my eating disorder whilst exploring the faith around Celtic Football Club. Much of this has come about from learning about, and learning from, Brother Walfrid's life, and, most importantly, his character of strength, kindness, gumption, and tenacity.

Throughout this time of exploring Brother Walfrid in the context of the Great Irish Hunger and in the famous depiction of Walfrid by Peter Howson, I have been healthy and thankful. This is not a coincidence. All the qualities of Brother Walfrid which I have come to learn about, have arisen essentially from this painting. Howson's painting of Walfrid inspires me immensely. I have never felt closer to my faith than when I have been drawn towards the Celtic Minded community by Brother Walfrid. Most of this had arisen when researching for the DVD documentary that would be sold as a part of the Peter Howson 'Brother Walfrid' limited edition print boxed set. Though the box set, of which there have been 1888 created, and, in the accompanying DVD, we explored a bit about Walfrid's life, the inspirations for Peter Howson, and a transparent look at him in this context, including exclusive interviews with Peter.

What actually happened was the full timeline of Walfrid being researched. This meant, filming in Glasgow Dumfries and Sligo, visiting St. Mary's Calton, Mount St. Michael cemetery, St. Joseph's, the national Famine memorial at Strokestown and Peter Howson's studio. It was directed by Bafta award-winner Paul Hineman: all original score music by Grammy award winner David Donaldson and narrated by Peter Mullen. To a large extent this all resulted from us being inspired by faith.

Surely art and Walfrid could inspire many others too? The spirit of Walfrid has the potential to change lives for the better. By exploring part of Walfrid's life through art, as we have in our commissioned portrait, we can show the despair, the torment, the isolation, the depression and starvation. However, amidst the torment, as a saviour and beacon of light, we can tell Walfrid's story: and, in turn, his own inspiration via his Christian faith. This through a single image.

It's a fact that if there was no Great Hunger there would be no Celtic: from evil can arise goodness, humility and kindness. This truism took on new meaning when I was starting the Peter Howson-Brother Walfrid Project. Similarly, you can't tell Walfrid's or Celtic story without taking into consideration the Irish immigrant community and its journey.

Faith is huge and immense when it comes to Celtic Football Club: that goes without saying. But what does this faith mean to so many people? For example, after some successful but not very inspiring seasons faith was restored to fans when Brendan Rodgers became the manager and created that invincible team of 2017-18. The faith that echoes and vibrates through the veins of every single fan as they stand in all weathers singing those epic songs. The faith the fans relived through the '67' celebrations: a passion reignited when seeing the footage of the Lisbon Lions.

The club was formed when a downtrodden community had a church as a place of refuge. The Celtic Park stadium was to be a cultural and spiritual extension of their faith and religion: 'Like moving from the graveyard to Paradise'. The nickname itself with such obvious religious overtones, especially in providing a vision of a journey and a better place to be, such a perfect name for a stadium that captures the supreme love that people have for the most successful underdog on a Scottish football field.

Several years ago I went to meet Fr. Tom White of St. Mary's Calton because we wanted to give something back to the parish, we wanted to give to the original site where these very first acts of charity were displayed, where faith in the community was the driving force for offering shelter, support and of course 'The Penny Dinners'. The church halls where the club was formed and where the community would gather for their meals no longer exists, so we wanted to explore the possibility of helping rebuild that. If we could support the physical re-establishment of the foundation hall for Celtic then that would be a great way of making the culture, the ethos, even more real and worthwhile. Hence, from the proceeds of the sale of Peter Howson's exact copy of his glorious work of art, we give 30% of proceedings to St.Mary's Calton, along with 10% to the Celtic FC Foundation: this arising from anything to do with the painting. Just like Walfrid, the passion of St. Mary's parish priest Canon Tom is inspiring, a true gentleman who speaks with such knowledge of the club's history. Every time I meet him I feel thankful for people like him: such a perfect parish priest for St. Mary's.

On one of the many meetings I had with Ronnie Convery, Director of Catholic Communications, we discussed St. Mary's, the Brother Walfrid art project and the future possibility of the canonisation of Walfrid. For any such occurrence we would firstly need to explore, to educate ourselves and others on the full story: a story where no stone was left unturned. For the reality was, what did we really know at this stage if such a prospect might ever arise? 'Now sponsoring a PhD on Brother Walfrid, that would be very interesting,' Ronnie suggested enthusiastically. That was the moment we, 'The Nine Muses' decided to sponsor the world's first PhD on Brother Walfrid. How might we find an academic supervisor and a student with enough passion and appreciation to engage in this enterprise?'

The faith didn't lie within these individuals. I'd worked with the editor of this collection of essays, Dr. Joe Bradley, on the first Brother Walfrid documentary and on later making the suggestion about a possible PhD, his reply was instant. 'I can't believe I didn't think of this myself.' Now for the student. After a couple of months of enquiries and searching, we came across Michael Connolly. I have to admit that at Michael's subsequent interview, even amongst the some-what interesting meetings I've had with the Archdiocese, Celtic FC, various famous artists, this was probably one of the most nerve-wracking experiences I have had. This in the intimate setting of three passionately-minded people, aware of the all-encompassing task possibly ahead. Dr Bradley and I had to choose someone we thought had all the credentials to fulfill a task that could stand the test of time.

By the end of 2019 Michael Connolly will be two years into his PhD. Already we have established a noteworthy and new contribution to understanding the life of Walfrid. A life that has lived in the shadow of the football club he made the most significant contribution to creating. One that will be explored and celebrated in its entirety in an emerging PhD.

By this point the The Nine Muses Art company had commissioned the 4x6 feet oil painting of Brother Walfrid that now resides on the altar of St.Mary's itself. We have the absolutely stunning limited edition prints of the painting (sold online and at the Celtic Superstore), all housed in the most ornate and beautiful presentation boxed set, certificate of authenticity and the exclusive 60 minute DVD documentary, 'The Founder'. Now, we also have a developing PhD. All of this, a journey over years, inspired by those very traits I'd learned from Walfrid himself.

So many modern and immensely important parallels can be drawn from the subject matter of this iconic painting and the time period between the Great Hunger and today. Poverty, homelessness, the crisis of immigration that is still so devastatingly present in many of today's nations: and of course 'famine', in times of plenty, and which, largely because of mans' inhumanity to man, continues to stalk the world. So this painting has evolved during a time of yet more need, a time where we might ask ourselves: 'what would Walfrid do to help those around us today?'

To ask this question is to be true to Walfrid and Celtic's roots. To reach out to help, support and change the lives of those negatively affected by ethnic and religious bigotry, prejudice and discrimination as well as economic, social and cultural marginal-isation: to provide the same answer as Walfrid and Celtic. This is legacy, this is uniqueness, meaningfulness, a moral journey: this makes us more than a football club.

To see and hear the response we have had from the campaign for Brother Walfrid has been wonderful. The Celtic Family? I completely understand that now. Football for Good, Art for Good, Walfrid's Way, Paradise, a Club for all. . . as corny as it sounds I know that with my faith in Brother Walfrid, I truly will Never Walk Alone.

Football Colours

Peter Kearney

A few years ago, when my eldest son was in Primary 7, one winter morning I told him to wear a scarf to school. He dually grabbed one as he rushed for the door, before heading off. When he came home that night he told me that as he was walking into the school, under the watchful eye of the headteacher, she stopped him and said: 'You better be careful with that scarf, you shouldn't be wearing it, take it off.'

The scarf was a Celtic one, bought for him by his uncle on the occasion of his first Celtic game. He liked it and wore it often. He had never associated it with division or discord or thought of it as in any way problematic. Now a doubt had been sown, a concern had been introduced into the impressionable mind of an idealistic 10-year-old. Had he caused offence? Had he done anything wrong? Should he stop wearing his scarf? His headteacher, a perceived fount of knowledge and authority, had pointed him out and warned him to 'be careful'. At the very least, he would, from that point on, be far more self-conscious about wearing what had been up till then an utterly innocent item.

Stories like this can be told about scarfs, shirts and shorts, in schools across Scotland, but especially in west-central Scotland. They give insight into a heightened sensitivity shown towards football allegiance. This hyper-sensitivity, forms a bizarre backdrop to football in Scotland, especially football in and around Glasgow and Lanarkshire where indigenous Scots, British, ethnic Irish, Protestant, Catholic and non-religious diversity is more evident.

For several decades, schools in west-central Scotland, denominational and non-denominational alike, have imposed a strict 'no football colours' rule on pupils. Why? What evidence exists to prove that this is either a worthwhile or sensible policy? What research or analysis has been done to justify its continued existence? As far as I can discover, the answer to these questions is none whatsoever.

More recently, in 2011, the worlds of Scottish politics, media and law enforcement competed to outdo one another in their denunciations and declarations of outrage following a Scottish Cup replay at Celtic Park between Celtic and Rangers.

According to one national broadsheet the relevant events triggered 'mayhem' (Guardian, 2/3/11). Three Rangers players were sent off and several yellow cards were issued during the game. Thirty-four people were arrested inside the stadium and at the end of the match both managers gestured angrily towards one another in a face to face tussle. BBC Scotland website reported that:

> The fallout from the game prompted Strathclyde Police Chief Constable Stephen House to call Mr Salmond [First Minister] and write to the Scottish government asking for a summit to address disorder issues surrounding the fixture. . . Mr Salmond said a summit would be held next week. . . He also told MSPs that he was prepared to meet with the other main party leaders to discuss the issues. . . The government will be happy to convene that summit to chart a way forward and to make sure that all parties involved – the government, the SFA and the clubs – are mindful of their obligations and wider role in Scottish society.

Despite such reporting, no one was killed, no one was injured, there were no pitch invasions, or flares or any of the seriously violent actions associated with football across Europe or the rest of the world. The relevant players received 'normal' punishments for on-field offences while Celtic manager Neill Lennon was the 'only' other person to suffer any 'beyond the norm punishment'? On the BBC website well-known football pundit, Chick Young, considered the game to be a 'crime scene'.

The 'top level summit' duly followed and in its wake the 'Offensive Behaviour and Threatening Communication (Scotland)

Bill' was fast tracked by the SNP majority Government into law, following a highly truncated period of consultation: thus creating legislation which, uniquely, demonised football and football fans. It allowed the actions, words, clothing and behaviour of supporters to be criminalised in the event that observers (almost always police members) of their behaviour or appearance felt offended.

As with the much older bans on football colours by schools such disproportionate action created or reinforced the perception that football in general, and Glasgow fixtures in particular, constitute explosive and intractable public order (frequently labelled 'sectarian') problems which must be rigorously controlled and managed. It is a perception, which is not substantiated by any empirical data. Yet it holds sway and shows no sign of fading. Why should this be so? Who benefits from the suggestion that Scottish football is a violently, aggressive and threatening business, a hotbed of hatred and a source of social disorder?

Surprisingly, some institutions may actually benefit from such a social and cultural construction. For the Police, the appearance of a serious public order problem can reinforce their oft-repeated call for more resources and funding to deal with what is portrayed as a significant issue. For politicians, being seen to deal firmly with a major social problem can enhance their reputation, even if the 'problem' is far from 'major'. While for the media, the old dictum that bad news sells will always hold true. With football being the most high-profile sporting activity in society anything which can be associated with it, especially suggestions of violence or intolerance, will sell newspapers.

In short, 'sectarianism' in football has become a proxy for discussing or avoiding discussion of religious intolerance in society. It is easier and certainly more comforting to indulge the myth of religious hatreds as being little more than, drink-fuelled, post-match, rivalry, than for a different action to take place. That is to open the can of worms that is Scotland's traumatic and intolerant religious history and examine it honestly.

So, the myth persists, in Government reports, in legislation, in education. A 2003 report into 'Sectarianism in Glasgow' prepared for the City Council found that 'Around half of the survey respondents agreed that sectarianism is almost entirely confined to football.' A Sense Over Sectarianism resource for schools offers a particular definition/construction of sectarianism then adds: 'This is often associated with football.' The same document suggests discussion points which might be used by teachers. Not surprisingly in such a context the first topic more than often suggested for discussion, in the context of 'sectarianism', is of course, 'football'.

Research, empirical analysis and hard data are nowhere to be seen in these publications or in countless others like them. But the facts are easy enough to find (if one wishes to), even if the public are kept in almost total ignorance of them. According to the Scottish Government's recent report on 'Religiously Aggravated Offending in Scotland 2016/17', religiously aggravated offences have increased by 14% since 2015/16. In fact religious hate crime in Scotland has been on the increase since 2013. Of the 673 charges with a religious aggravation reported in 2016/17, 72 (11%) were related to football. Put another way, 89% of religious hate crime in Scotland, has little or nothing to do with football. Yet the relentless focus on the game as the source of sometimes 'all' religious intolerance persists. Maybe a closer look at Scotland's anti-Catholic past and present would evoke a different critique?

Sadly, as far as children and school pupils are concerned, concerted efforts are made to distance and disconnect them from their family football identity (and for many people to disconnect them from a club that means so much in terms of culture, faith, ethnicity and heritage). While at the same time suggesting to them, that even having a football affiliation is of itself problematic. This is not only unjust but likely to be self-defeating. As opportunities to express football affiliations are curtailed, each generation becomes less and less acclimatised to encountering scarves, shirts or other items of clothing which indicate support for a particular team. The consequence of airbrushing such items from public view is to help create a response, a consequence, even to make reactions to them more marked, volatile and possibly inflamed. Attempts to play down any public friction associated with attachment to a team, ends up creating a more fractious public climate, where normalisation and acclimatisation would have been a far better approach.

It's difficult to imagine an approach similar to the one taken with my son, when he was asked to remove or hide his Celtic scarf, with any other aspect of a child's identity. Imagine a teacher in a Scottish school suggesting to a child, who'd just arrived from England that they'd be best to disguise or conceal their English accent, in case it attracted adverse attention or criticism (or hide their England soccer bag they bring along as a school satchel). The teacher may well think that a pupil with such an accent would be the butt of jokes or criticism in a Scottish playground, but in no imaginable circumstance would that lead them to suggest that the potential victim of such behaviour should be the one to change or conceal their identity. Instead, the other pupils would be told to be welcoming, open minded and tolerant, with plenty of warnings against intolerance and hostility. Quite rightly, intolerance would be criticised and the perpetrators of it warned to change. If only we could adopt the same approach in football matters, 10-year-old boys might not grow up looking over their shoulder and thinking twice before they pull on their Celtic scarf – in particular.

Football for Peace (F4P) is coming home: reflections on the ongoing contribution of sport to the peace process in the North of Ireland

John Sugden & Graham Spacey

This contribution to the Celtic Minded series draws on elements of the book, 'Sport and peace-building in divided societies: playing with enemies' (Sugden and Tomlinson, 2018). This account focusses mainly on the experiences of the Football 4 Peace (F4P) initiative within the north of Ireland. It features a critical narrative of the evolution of sport as a contributory tool to the ongoing peace process there and the adoption and adaption of the F4P values-based methodology and ethos within the youth strategies and peace and reconciliation programmes delivered by governing bodies of sport in the north of Ireland – namely the (GAA) Gaelic Athletic Association (in Ulster), Irish Football Association (IFA) and the Irish Rugby Football Union – Ulster branch, commonly known as Ulster Rugby.

The roots of Football 4 Peace International are buried deep in work undertaken in the 1980s and 1990s perhaps best represented in the work of Belfast United, possibly the world's first ever sport-based peace-building programme. F4P developed and matured through the initiation of the World Sports Peace Project in Israel in 2001 which brought Jewish and Arab communities together through football. The project was unique and innovative at the time and has endured to this date. Now called 'Sport for Life' this programme is run by teams of Arabs and Jews in conjunction with the Israel Sport Authority across Israel with a clear dominance in the northern Galilea region. As already mentioned, its roots, however, reach as far as the Emerald Isle and from the work of one the co-founders – John Sugden and his involvement with Belfast United

Belfast United (Sugden, 1991) was a cross community football team for university students at the then Ulster Polytechnic (now University) in the late 1980s and early 1990s. At this time, university was, for many, the first time numerous Catholics and Protestants came together. As a result of centuries of British colonialism and corresponding conflict and violence in Ireland, most social, cultural, economic and political facets of life on the island had been, or still were, 'divided'. Depending on which part of the island we were talking about, rugby was seen as a Protestant pastime and associated with Unionist ideals, given its roots to Britain and with the upper classes, and Catholics played traditional native Gaelic games such as Hurling/Camogie, Gaelic Football and Handball, which became closely linked to Irishness and nationalist identities. Football/soccer was played by both communities but as there were two countries on the island and therefore two governing bodies – the IFA in the North and the Football Association of Ireland (FAI) for the Republic, the IFA were often seen as linked to the unionist cause. Sport was highly politicised and to use it to bring conflicting identities together through football was considered radical and risky (Sugden and Bairner, 1995).

Belfast United developed and grew throughout the 'Troubles' with a 50/50 split in participants from both communities. Coaching staff were dedicated to bringing students from different/opposing communities together and making their interactions more meaningful. On several occasions the team was taken to the USA where they shared a room with the so-called 'other' in a host family. Being in a new culture, overseas and far from home, the players soon found that there they had more in common with their teammate than they were often led to believe and it led to friendships that lasted lifetimes – and engendered a desire for peaceful co-existence.

In 2004, the World Sports Peace Programme became the in-house NGO of the University of Brighton in England and was renamed 'Football 4 Peace International' (F4P). The experience and associated research of F4P in Israel and from work conducted in the North and from Belfast United showed that simply bringing people together was not enough. The interactions needed meaning and purpose in order for participants to create significant relationships with each other and to engender a desire and commitment to peaceful co-existence. A values-based method-ology was created by the F4P team led by Gary Stidder and John Lambert which focused on the values of respect, trust, responsibility, equity and inclusion. Activities, drill and games were conditioned to promote the positive behaviours associated with each value and which also create 'teachable moments', where the negative behaviours can be tackled and spoken about in a safe space.

Michael Boyd, a former student at Ulster University with a great passion for football and a fresh role working for the Irish Football Association (IFA), joined the F4P team working in Israel. Through him, the F4P team were contacted by Damien McColgan who had set up a cross border project called 'Grassroots Soccer' in the Derry/Donegal border region. Its premise was along similar lines as Belfast United but with a desire to scale up. Funded by the International Fund for Ireland and led by the Inishowen Development Partnership, it was to provide opportunities for schools and clubs along the Derry/Donegal border to come together and play soccer to harbour peace. Damien and his team didn't believe their programme would work if they simply took the approach of using football as a hook to draw people into the project. They didn't see how simply playing football would solve any of the issues related to centuries of conflict.

Through working together in Israel and on the island of Ireland, training was developed for the Gateway coaches in Buncrana in Donegal and coaches from both the IFA and FAI. It was the first time the two 'rival' governing bodies of football on the island had come together to work on a project and the coaching kit reflected this. Shortly afterwards, the project decided to rename itself 'Football 4 Peace Ireland' and the IFA, FAI and F4P logos were stitched side by side on coaches and players chests.

In March 2013, F4P Ireland secured funding from the International Fund for Ireland and the 'Derry/Londonderry' City of Culture to host the annual F4P international training camp. The annual camp had been hosted in England and Germany before and brought coaches from around the world to learn the F4P values-based methodology of teaching values and life skills through physical activity. Coaches were sent from governing bodies including Boxing, Hockey, Football, Rugby and GAA codes as well as a number of NGOs and teachers. In all, 116 were trained and given the skills to incorporate the methodology and adapt the curriculla to their own sport and work (University of Ulster, 2013).

The Anglo-Irish Agreement of April 1998 confirmed the shared political and institutional structures through which, with the British military withdrawn to barracks, the Loyalist and Nationalist communities in the North could come together to jointly and peacefully govern the area, formally ending more than four decades of war. But bringing political society together and decommissioning military and paramilitary hardware is one thing. Without corresponding shifts in civil society arrangements, it is unlikely that any peace process will succeed in its goals. In other words, peace processes need to have strong educational and cultural dimensions and the fact that the city with two names – Derry/Londonderry – is at the vanguard of this peaceful Cultural Revolution is hugely symbolic.

With Derry/Londonderry acting as the United Kingdom's City of Culture, in March 2013 the annual F4P international training camp was located at the city's St. Columb's Park House: a residential centre for conferences and activities promoting peace and reconciliation. This is also next to the old British Military Ebrington Barracks along the River Foyle with the newly constructed pedestrian Peace Bridge uniting Derry's predominantly Catholic City-side with the traditionally more Protestant Waterside neighbourhoods.

The schedule for the St. Columb's F4P training event involved a mixture of theoretical explanation, contextual discussion, and practical tuition and learning. It was mainly targeted towards local governing body coaches and community and youth professionals and volunteers working with sport on each side of the border. It also attracted a healthy number of people working in similar contexts in other parts of the world including a group from South Africa. While the main focus of the practical element had traditionally been a combination of football and off-pitch adventure activities, latterly there had been a gradual shift to a more multi-sport approach whereby in addition to soccer, other games, such as rugby, netball, basketball and cricket were used to identify and amplify the core values at the heart of F4P's coaching curriculum.

By coincidence, the F4P camp was not the only sporting event planned that week as part of the City of Culture programme. The city was also host to the Gaelic Athletic Association's World Congress. Given the historical role played by the GAA in the wider struggle against British imperialism in Ireland, and its subsequent nationalist positioning during the 'Troubles' (mainly in the north), the GAA's decision to host this event only for the third time in its 130-year history in the North of Ireland and for the first time in Derry/Londonderry was of itself a significant gesture towards reconciliation. Quite deliberately, the President of Ireland, Michael D Higgins, was on a state visit to the city to honour its designation as the UK's City of Culture and to open the congress. During his address, whilst honouring the GAA's historic role in the service of Irish nationalism, he also praised the organisation's contemporary commitment to peace and reconciliation, quoting the organisation's current mission statement which reads, 'we welcome people of all nationalities, religions, ages and abilities into our association and we make it easy for everyone to take part' (Higgins 2013). He continued by giving particular praise to local GAA-led peace building initiatives, saying, 'I greatly welcome and commend the various initiatives that the GAA has taken – especially the Ulster Council – in promoting reconciliation on this island and in extending the hand of welcome and friendship to communities in the North who traditionally did not participate in Gaelic games'.

Not all in the city embraced the celebrations or held out their hand. Flag protests – pro-unionists waving the Union Jack and showing support for retaining ties with Great Britain and disgust at what they perceived as a pro-nationalist event – were strategically placed around key locations during the state visit. Thus, F4P coaches from around the world experienced hostility first hand as they drove to the camp in hired cars with Irish number plates. They witnessed a glimpse of the anger some individuals harbour for 'the other side' in the form of hand gestures, unwelcoming shouts and the surrounding of the cars in order to intimidate. The incident only proved that even 15 years after the Good Friday agreement, sport could still provoke political desires, peace was still fragile and civil action was an ongoing necessity to maintain peace and promote further co-existence and reconciliation.

Despite this, the IFA has also changed beyond recognition. The end of the training camp saw international participants travel to Belfast to a snow-bound Windsor Park to see the Northern Ireland versus Israel international Football World Cup qualifier (Tuesday, March 23, 2013). On this bitterly cold late March evening it was clear how the National Stadium had changed spiritually if not physically since peace was struck. The experience of decades was of sounds and symbols of anti-Catholic and anti-Irish hatred which cast a dark shadow over any proceedings on the field. It made Windsor Park an extremely inhospitable place for visiting fans as well as any local Catholics who might dare to come to support the Northern Ireland 'national' team in the bastion of Ulster loyalism that is south Belfast.

It was even worse for the players who, if they happened to be Catholic, would be abused by spectators regardless of their skill. Even during the height of the recent conflict, while Catholic spectators may have stayed away, the Northern Ireland team always had a good proportion of Catholic players. Those few whose professional careers had taken them across the Irish Sea to play for Scotland's emblematic Irish diaspora club Celtic, were the objects of bile from the hard-core, Union Jack-waving loyalists massed on the towering Spion Kop end of the ground.

Windsor Park is also the home of Irish League team, Linfield

FC – a club that for years was infamous for its policy of not signing Catholics as players, and it was from the Kop end that vile and vicious bigoted chanting routinely roared out on match days, particularly when local rivals Cliftonville, a team with a largely Catholic following, were visiting. During their careers Catholic players like Anton Rogan and Neil Lennon received death threats both on and off the field. When the latter went on to manage Celtic this abuse continued with him even being sent a letter bomb to his home in 2011.

On that bitterly cold late March evening, there was little or no evidence of this. With the exception of a tiny group of Israeli fans, the supporters were adorned uniformly in the green and white livery of the Northern Ireland team. There was no racist or political chanting directed towards any players. With just fifteen minutes to go, Celtic's Paddy McCourt was asked to warm up on the touch line by Northern Ireland's Catholic manager, Michael O'Neill. This was met by loud cheers and praiseworthy chanting led by the raucous chorus massed behind the goal in the Kop end of the ground.

Sadly, these signs of progress in Northern Ireland football's cross-community profile were not matched by the composition of the team they were facing. More than twenty per cent of Israel's population are Arab and football is the number one sport in Arab communities there. In the squad of 22 named for the NI match, one might reasonably expect around five players to be Arab. As it turned out, only one Arab player, the Maccabi Tel Aviv striker, Maharan Radi, started for Israel and he was taken off after sixty minutes, making the Arab representation less than two per cent. As already pointed out, the combination of institutional anti-Arab bias, overt racism, and internal Arab community resistance to playing the game under the Israeli flag, means that few Arabs make their way onto the national team. Those that do are often the subject to torrents abuse from some Jewish fans when they play home games in Israel.

In 2017, the IFA department working at community level became the newly formed IFA Foundation – the charitable arm of the body with the remit to 'to help promote, foster and develop football for all in Northern Ireland' and to deliver the 'Let Them

Play' youth strategy. Linked to their strategy, the foundation continues to take a prime position within promoting 'good relations' in the realm of sport by working closely with both the GAA and Ulster Rugby – blending the F4P values methodology via their everyday coaching practices in schools, communities and clubs.

Peace processes are messy affairs: hugely complex enterprises that move forwards or backwards according to conditions prevalent in the transcending social and political order. Usually they are driven by activities and actors in political society. However, if there are major social and cultural impediments, 'road maps to peace' that take account of the political sphere alone they are doomed to failure. Changes of heart and mind do not ordinarily take place because of political initiatives. Peace is only possible when significant proportions of ordinary people are ready for and open to conflict resolution. This comes gradually through social and cultural engagement in everyday life. The challenge for peace activists is to discover ways to join up specific grass-roots, civil society, interventions with more broadly influential policy communities and those elements of political society that hold the keys to peace.

Sport offers one cultural forum amongst many wherein the ideas for change can be formulated. In this regard we find it useful to think of peace processes in general as massive, multi-dimensional jigsaw puzzles that have to be solved without the benefit of having a picture on the box. There are political pieces, economic pieces, military pieces and cultural pieces including sport. Some are violent while others are passive. Some are sky blue and others are covered red with blood. For the picture to be imagined and completed all of these pieces will have a part to play and while some, for instance the political and economic corner pieces and straight edges, may have more significance than others, all the pieces will be necessary for the picture of peace to fully emerge. Those of us who choose to try to use sport as a creative forum through which to influence broader political agendas do so in the belief that when peace does come to societies currently in conflict, and we look back at the events that contributed to that peace, we will be able to identify the positive role played by the 'piece' that is sport.

photo by Donal Cassidy

The inspirational Hands Across the Divide statue seen daily by those international sports coaches attending the 2013 annual Football 4 Peace training camp in Derry

Whilst Football 4 Peace Ireland faded away in 2014 as a stand-alone programme of work for schools and clubs, its legacy can be found overtly in the three sporting codes of football, rugby and Gaelic games. Whilst working together and while continuing to run their own community and school programmes with good relations at the core of their approach, the IFA, GAA and Ulster Rugby continue to adopt and adapt the F4P values methodology and associated curriculla and contribute to the ongoing peace process. Leaving us to conclude that Football for peace (F4P) has indeed come home!

References:

Colgan, P, 2014 'The PEACE Programmes Ireland – Shared Future: Building and Sustaining Peace – the Northern Ireland Case Study. https://www.osce.org/cio/90147?download=true

GAA, 2018 http://hoganstand.com/Cavan/Article/Index/282901

Higgins, M.D. (2013) Transcription of speech to St. Columbs Park House City of Culture Event

IFA, 2018 https://www.irishfa.com/foundation/community-volunteering/sport-uniting-communities

Spacey, G.B. (2017) 'Learning and Teaching Values Through Physical Education' in Stidder, G and Hayes, S 'The Really Useful Physical Education Book' (2nd Ed) p201-213

Sugden, J (1991) 'Belfast United: encouraging cross-community relations through sport in Northern Ireland', in The Journal of Sport and Social Issues, volume 15, number 1, pps. 59-80

Sugden, J. and Bairner, A. (1995) Sport and Sectarianism in a Divided Ireland, Leicester, Leicester University Press.

Sugden and Tomlinson, 2017 'Sport and Peace-Building in Divided Societies: Playing with Enemies'

Ulster Rugby, 2013 http://www.ulsterrugby.com/news/9012.php#.WuaXJOSWzIU

Ulster Rugby, 2016 http://www.ulsterrugby.com/news/15446.php#.Wu6x5OSWzIU

Ulster Rugby, 2018 http://ulsterrugby.com/news/16944.php#.WuaXJOSWzIU

University of Ulster (2013), Football 4 Peace Ireland: A Review of tutor training and programme delivery in Ireland https://cpb-eu-w2.wpmucdn.com/blogs.brighton.ac.uk/dist/a/1098/files/2016/03/Football4Peace-tutor-training-evaluation-Ulster-2013-13x345c.pdf

MOJO RISIN':
Rangers' signing of Maurice Johnston was a missed opportunity in any fight against ethnic and religious prejudice in Scottish football

STEPHEN O'DONNELL

It's nearly thirty years now since Graeme Souness' Rangers rocked the world of Scottish football by signing striker Maurice Johnston from under the noses of rivals Celtic. Johnston had previously spent three seasons with the green part of Glasgow, scoring fifty goals in a hundred appearances for his boyhood idols. However, he had passed the last two years in relative anonymity with the French club Nantes, where he had fled in 1987 to escape the press intrusion and anti-Catholic abuse which he had been subjected to after a number of high profile incidents during his playing days at Parkhead.

On 10 July 1989 however, the Scottish game collectively fell off its chair in astonishment, as a sheepish looking Johnston, flanked by his new manager, was ushered into the Blue Room at Ibrox Park and presented to the media as free-spending Rangers' latest acquisition. The signing was remarkable because Johnston came from a 'mixed' religious marriage (Catholic & Protestant) and, ever since the days of the Edwardian era at the turn of the

This article is an edited extract from 'Tangled up in Blue, The Rise and Fall of Rangers FC' by Stephen O'Donnell, published by Pitch in the summer of 2019.

nineteenth century, Rangers had been operating an exclusionary and discriminatory employment policy whereby they refused to sign players from the Catholic minority in the Scottish population.

For the most, Rangers' policy went largely uncommented upon in polite society. For many of the victims of this prejudice what was going on at Rangers was simply a high profile version of what was going on elsewhere in terms of anti-Catholic and anti-Irish discrimination.

One or two individuals did manage to slip through the net. In the 1950s South African striker Don Kichenbrand had a short, largely unproductive spell at Ibrox. Known as 'the Rhino' and lambasted for a series of outrageous misses in front of goal, Kichenbrand went to extraordinary lengths to disguise his Catholic upbringing and fit in with his new team, even confirming his induction into the Ibrox faction by joining a Lanarkshire Masonic lodge. His secret remained safe until the day after Johnston's transfer to Rangers more than thirty years later, when the Daily Record, having missed out on the scoop of the century after Souness confirmed the story of the signing to his favourite newspaper the Sun, carried an interview with Kichenbrand. In the article, the former striker admitted: 'My teammates and bosses at the club just assumed that I had been vetted before I was signed. Every player was.' In fact Rangers' South African scout, Charlie Watkins,. had forgotten to look into the player's background and only remembered to ask the pertinent question as the pair were waiting at the airport before boarding the flight from Johannesburg, as Kichenbrand remembered: 'Charlie Watkins, the man who had convinced Glasgow Rangers that they should sign me, suddenly said, "By the way, you're not Catholic, are you?" When I told him "Yes" he nearly collapsed. Then he growled, "Do not mention that again – to anyone!" I never did.'

Other than the odd aberration, Rangers blazed a trail as the unblemished bastion of Protestant supremacy in Scotland. Revelling in their role as the establishment club and the foremost British-Scottish-Protestant sporting institution in the land, with only a few intermissions Rangers ruled the roost in Scottish football for decades, dominating the domestic game under managers William Wilton (1899–1920), Bill Struth (1920–1954) and Scot Symon (1954–1967). By the late 1960s/early 1970s, very isolated murmurings of disapproval and occasionally even criticism of Rangers' stance appeared in the popular press and elsewhere, usually in association with rioting fans in Birmingham, Newcastle, Barcelona and various other locations. After the club's defeat to Newcastle United in the semi-final of the Inter Cities Fairs Cup in 1969, former player Willie Waddell, then working as a journalist with the Scottish Daily Express, condemned the scenes of violence at St. James' Park after Rangers fans invaded the field when the Tynesiders scored a second, decisive goal in the tie. 'I felt like crawling stealthily back over the border under cover of darkness, stunned and shocked that I had been connected with this club and its fans for more than thirty years,' Waddell lamented. Curiously, however, once he was installed as Rangers manager later in the year, and subsequently as general manager in 1972, Waddell instead took the view that the club's internal affairs were its own business and nobody else's, and he refused to make any correlation between the issues blighting Rangers at the time, namely hooliganism and bigotry.

Some others disagreed. After rioting in Newcastle, veteran tabloid journalist Alex Cameron, writing in the Daily Record, called for: 'A vigorous clean-out of inbred bigotry which coincidence no longer begins to explain or excuse,' while a few years later decorated journalist Ian Archer, a Scot who had grown up in England and therefore perhaps had a less indulgent attitude towards the whole Rangers phenomenon in Scotland, appeared to arrive at the apex of media criticism towards the Ibrox club when, in response to further rioting by Rangers fans after a friendly in Birmingham against Aston Villa, he wrote in the Herald: 'As a Scottish football club, they are a permanent embarrassment and an occasional disgrace. This country would be a better place if Rangers did not exist.' Such public comments about Scotland's establishment club were almost unique.

Eventually, in response to a UK-wide wave of indignation in the 1970s over hooliganism, and Rangers' no-Catholics stance, general manager Waddell announced in 1976, 'We are determined to end Rangers' image as a sectarian club. . . no religious barriers will be put up by this club regarding the signing of players.' It was one of the first public references to a so-called 'sectarian' (which should have been properly designated as anti-Irish and anti-Catholic) agenda at Ibrox, and there was some joy and hope amongst elements of the wider community that Rangers might eventually, in the not too distant future, sign a Catholic football player. But as the years went by and no Catholic player appeared in the light blue, these were dashed.

In his book Glasgow's Giants, Murray observed of Rangers' habitually empty promises: 'To the media and the public at large these statements were taken with large spoonfuls of scepticism. They had heard it all before: they were a necessary disclaimer to keep any investigators from FIFA at bay. A sop to the media and a wink to their fans who knew that everything would continue to be as it should be at Ibrox.'

During the 1980s, tales continued to abound about players at Ibrox even being ushered towards the exit door if they happened to fall in love with and marry Catholic girls. One such was forward Graham Fyfe, who claimed that, despite his wife effectively renouncing her Catholic faith and their marriage taking place in the Church of Scotland, he nevertheless felt the need to leave Ibrox in 1980, after being questioned by the club's manage-ment about his wedding arrangements and his private life in general. Fyfe's allegation was contested by other players at the time who had also married 'Catholic' women (or maybe women who were once Catholic or who gave it up once they realised the difficulties involved if married to a Rangers player), such as Bobby Russell and Derek Johnstone, both of whom remained at the club into the new decade. By 1982, striker Gordon Dalziel felt comfortable enough to announce publicly his engagement to a Catholic girl, telling the press, 'I have already had the all-clear at Ibrox. It will not make any difference. I'm not going to get married in the chapel or anything like that.' Manager John Greig added to the general tone of reassurance, informing the media, 'It doesn't matter who he is marrying. It doesn't matter to me and it doesn't matter to Rangers. Bobby Russell's been married to a Catholic for years. Gordon Dalziel has a right to marry who he wants.'

Despite these occasional calls from the Church and elsewhere however, when Jock Wallace was reappointed Rangers manager in November 1983, he seemed less than taken with the occasional and ambivalent promises to end the club's discriminatory practices. On the day of his appointment, Wallace emerged from the stadium onto Copland Road and told the waiting media, 'I have been told by the board that I have complete control over who I select, and I will sign players on ability. Religion will not come into it.' He then turned on his heels and departed without taking further questions. A few days later, when he was asked explicitly about the signing policy, Wallace replied:

> To listen to some people you'd think all the problems of Rangers could be solved at a stroke – by signing a player who is Catholic. But for me, that's not a priority. . . I have signed many Roman Catholics – and released a few. When I was with Leicester I also signed several coloured players – and freed some of them too. It's ironic that in my last spell with Rangers, when we were winning the occasional Treble the subject of signing Catholics seldom came up, but now that the club is going through a difficult spell, everyone is jumping on that particular bandwagon. It has been turned into a campaign and exploited by people who should know better.

Maybe Jock Wallace and Rangers were radicals after all: signing Catholics AND 'coloured' players!

Wallace, it seemed, having returned to his 'dream job', was still living out his schoolboy fantasy as manager of his favourite team. 'I've always been a Rangers fan,' he announced after the first game of his second spell in charge at Ibrox, a 3–0 defeat to Aberdeen at Pittodrie, 'ever since I was a lad of nine and they came through to play near my home on the east coast. The team that made me a Rangers fan for life still trips off the tongue; Brown, Young, Shaw, McColl, Woodburn, Cox, Waddell, Gillick, Thornton, Duncanson and Caskie.' He rattled off Bill Struth's team from the immediate post-war period.

On that first trip up to Pittodrie, Wallace invited his agent Bill McMurdo, whom he had dubbed 'Agent Orange' because of his Rangers allegiances and his political views, onto the team bus. A founder member of the Scottish Unionist Party and a proud Orangeman and Freemason, McMurdo had turned his Uddingston home into a Rangers shrine, naming it 'Ibrox' and decking it out in the club's colours of red, white and blue. On the journey north, McMurdo provided Wallace with a cassette so that he could play Rangers songs over the speaker system and the manager encouraged his players to join in the singing of 'No Surrender'. McMurdo later confided: 'Jock acted as compere and. . . those who didn't know the words were urged to learn them for the next away game. [Ulsterman] Jimmy Nicholl knew the words inside out and Jock said to him, 'Brilliant Jimmy, you know all the words, you're the captain today'! It's an apocryphal story. Nicholl had only just arrived at the club, having been signed by John Greig in his final days in charge at Ibrox, and the player from the North of Ireland didn't in fact captain the side that day. But nevertheless, it's easy to see how a Catholic player – or even one that married a Catholic of sorts – might have struggled to flourish in such an environment.

Wallace's replacement as team manager in 1986, in the wake of a boardroom coup at Ibrox which had cleared out a cabal of old guard custodian-directors, was the former Liverpool and Scotland midfielder Graeme Souness. Immediately on his appointment, Souness was quizzed about the signing policy: 'I was asked the question the very first day I went to Rangers, would you sign a Catholic?' he later recalled. 'And my answer then was quite simple. I said, look, my wife is a Catholic, I've got two kids who've been christened Catholic, so you're saying to me I can't come to work with a Catholic, but I can go home to a Catholic? I said of course I would sign a Catholic.'

Souness seemed determined to end the policy and privately, behind the scenes, he was making enquiries about the potential impact of such a signing, almost from the moment he arrived. The sheer iconoclasm of the idea appealed to Souness' maverick personality and, as well as the backing of the new Rangers board, Souness also found that there was tentative support from others in the wider community for the potentially seminal change, with one young Rangers supporting journalist telling the new manager that he thought such a signing would be accepted 'as long as it wasn't Peter Grant or Maurice Johnston'.

Publicly however, as time went on, the old issue reappeared from time to time, with the situation not helped by the fact that Souness was a provocatively confrontational figure, who seemed to be always looking for an enemy, and who now found himself at the centre of one of the most heated and intense rivalries anywhere in world football.

Johnston made headlines during his career. As early as November 1986, the player, then turning out for Celtic, was involved in a particularly notorious incident at the end of the Skol (League) Cup Final against Rangers at Hampden, which would turn out to be Souness' first trophy as Ibrox manager. In the wake of numerous perceived biased refereeing decisions – seen by the Celtic support and indeed management, as prejudicing and materially affecting Celtic's ability to win the Cup – and after being sent off late in the game, in the face of gleeful abuse from the Rangers supporters, Johnston blessed himself as he left the field. For Rangers this was considered highly provocative in light of their anti-Catholicism. Ironically however, although he was brought up in the faith, Johnston was not, unlike many of his Celtic teammates, a practising Catholic, and it was later pointed out by an indignant press that the striker was the only member of Celtic's large Catholic player contingent who had not attended Mass on the morning of the game. In addition, the custom of making the sign of the cross, common amongst football players around the globe, was unofficially 'outlawed' in Scotland at the time.

Johnston's actions subsequently became the precursor to a controversial series of incidents in Scottish football involving the sign of the cross, or blessing oneself. In December 1994, Rangers chairman David Murray had warned his newest signing, the French defender Basile Boli, not to make the sign of the cross publicly in case it 'infuriated Rangers fans'. Such fury was evident in February 1996, when Partick Thistle's Rod MacDonald blessed himself after scoring an equalising goal against Rangers. This provoked a number of the Ibrox club's fans to complain to the police. Match referee Jim McGilvray subsequently called the player into his office at half-time and issued him with a yellow card. McDonald was later sent off in the second half following a second yellow. Thistle chairman Jim Oliver hinted at the reason behind the apparent taboo: 'because we have the Rangers situation here, it seems a different set of rules are invoked', while manager Murdo MacLeod reflected: 'As far as Rod is concerned, it is normal practice for him. It's at times like this you know which city you are in.' As further incidents over the likes of Artur Boruc and Mark Viduka attest, it would be some time later before it became apparent to the Scottish football authorities that players being cautioned for blessing themselves was not something which was likely to go unnoticed in the global village of world football. Indeed, akin to Rangers policy regarding Catholics, such prejudices in Scotland could now more easily be exposed for what they were as technological change, not so much a change of heart and mind, began to have an influence in ethnic and religious equalities across the globe.

As the Sunday Mail lamented in June 2006, in the wake of an 'Artur Boruc blessing himself again' incident: 'Each time the story is retold, it is explained how sectarian hatred is a scar on Scottish society. The image of Scotland being beamed around the world is not one we can take any pride in.' Regarding the Boruc episode, the finger of blame seemed to be pointed more at Boruc himself, rather than those who were apparently upset by his religious gesture. The player's actions were denounced as a provocative, 'sectarian' act, with the Scotsman reporting: 'Last night a Rangers fan spokesman accused the Celtic goalkeeper of trying to incite the crowd by blessing himself during yesterday's game.' The same paper, an allegedly respectable Edinburgh-based broadsheet, was later the subject of a complaint from the Catholic Church in Scotland after it featured an image of Boruc blessing himself on its front page, with a tagline which noted: 'For the second time in a year during yesterday's Old Firm match, the Celtic goalkeeper Artur Boruc provoked Rangers fans by making the sign of the cross.' Unsurprisingly, when Boruc departed Scotland to play in several other countries his habitual religious practice was never again brought into question.

Back in 1986, Johnston's actions sparked outrage. The idea that he might one day sign for Rangers seemed utterly unthinkable. Yet a little over two and a half years later that's exactly what happened. The striker had apparently grown restless with the slow pace of life and the relatively low profile of football in France during the period of his sabbatical from the Scottish game. After initially vowing that he would never return to Scotland as a result of the scrutiny and abuse which he was subjected to following the Skol Cup final incident, Johnston announced publicly, in May 1989, that he was indeed on the verge of returning to his boyhood heroes Celtic. The Parkhead side were then managed by club legend Billy McNeill, who had been made aware of the player's willingness to return home by his captain Roy Aitken, whom Johnston had been entreating while the pair were together on international duty with Scotland. Johnston was subsequently paraded at a press conference wearing a Celtic shirt, where he professed, amidst a lengthy roll call of footballing platitudes and truisms, his undying love for the club.

With the benefit of hindsight, some of Johnston's quotes from this period expose just how meaningless and trite the kind of carefully contrived soundbites we're typically used to hearing from footballers on these set-piece occasions really are. It's difficult to think of a better example of a footballer talking in carefully coached media-speak and telling people what he thinks they want to hear, which in this instance was particularly egregious, given the complete volte-face that Johnston was about to perform. 'When I joined Celtic in 1984 it was like an answer to prayers, and I don't say that lightly,' the striker assured readers of the Celtic View. 'At that time I fully intended to see out my career at Celtic, if the club would have me,' he continued. I never fell out of love with Celtic... when I joined Nantes it had always been my intention to return to Celtic one day. No one can accuse me of being two-faced. . . I didn't intend to leave Celtic then and I don't intend to now,' Johnston maintained, while rumours of a desire to join Manchester United were fabricated, chiefly because: 'there is no other British club I could play for apart from Celtic.'

The son of a Protestant father and Catholic mother, Johnston attended St. Roch's secondary school in the Royston area of Glasgow and supported Celtic as a boy. He played for Partick Thistle, then Watford, before Parkhead manager Davie Hay signed him as an intended replacement for Charlie Nicholas, who had left Celtic for Arsenal the previous year. He went on to form a prolific partnership with the intelligent Brian McClair, scoring 52 goals in 100 appearances for the Parkhead side.

Even at this time, though, Johnston already had something of a history of hyperbolic statement when it came to his feelings for Celtic. Back in 1984, he told Radio Clyde that he would walk from Watford to Glasgow in order to play for the club he loved, while earlier in the same year, after he had appeared for Graham Taylor's team in the FA Cup final and suffered the disappointment of a 2–0 defeat to Everton, Johnston later declared that he was equally upset over Celtic's loss to Aberdeen on the same day, 2–1 after extra time, in the Scottish Cup Final. 'I suppose it was round about then that I was reminded of where my heart really lay,' he later wrote. After handing in a transfer request, as rumours of Celtic's interest grew, he finally signed for the Parkhead side in October 1984, with the club spending £400,000 on the player, a record Scottish fee at the time. Hay's previous six signings had cost a combined total of £375,000, so this was a considerable outlay from a parsimonious Celtic board and evidence of their commitment and belief in the striker, who was still only 21 years old at the time. A few years later in his autobiography, Johnston spoke of the reception he received from the fans on his debut against Hibs: 'I'll never forget that ovation until I breathe my last. It was so emotional I just couldn't speak.'

After Johnston's infamous Celtic press conference in May 1989, the player travelled with his proposed new colleagues on the team bus to the club's final league fixture of the season against St. Mirren in Paisley, where winger Joe Miller scored the only goal of the match to give Celtic a 1–0 win. The following week, Miller repeated the feat, lighting up the showpiece Scottish Cup Final with the game's solitary strike against Rangers, leaving Souness furious at being denied a potential Treble. The Rangers manager is reported to have told his players in the dressing room after the defeat that he had something up his sleeve which would rock Celtic, and that the Parkhead club had a shock coming. Something had evidently changed during the week between Miller's two winning goals and over the summer rumours continued to circulate that the proposed deal on Johnston's return to Celtic might not be as cut-and-dried as everyone assumed.

For many Celtic supporters, the fly in the ointment was the player's agent Bill McMurdo, 'Agent Orange' himself: the same man who had represented Jock Wallace and whose Rangers allegiances and political views were a matter of public record. McNeill had informed Johnston that he would not deal with

McMurdo and the striker appeared to accept this condition when he signed a 'letter of agreement' to join Celtic, which, although not a contract, was later ratified by FIFA as being legally binding, the equivalent of a modern-day pre-contract agreement. It was on this basis that Celtic decided to go ahead with the May press briefing and photo shoot, but the jilted McMurdo sent a letter to the club informing them that it was his company, rather than Nantes, who owned the player's registration and that the agent could not therefore be bypassed in any transaction. While Celtic were pondering the implications of all this, McMurdo was offering the player to Souness on the other side of the city.

The Rangers manager soon became aware of the contractual difficulties over Johnston's proposed move to Celtic, and he immediately expressed an interest in the striker. Souness admired the player and he persuaded the club's new owner, David Murray, that with one swoop they could secure the services of a talented forward who had apparently been destined for Celtic, deprive Celtic of a good player, and at the same time end their exclusionary signing policy, which with every passing year was becoming more of a black mark on the club's reputation. At the time FIFA were investigating racist and religious prejudice in the game and Rangers' unspoken policy was sure to come under the microscope at some point, with the world governing body holding the power to impose the ultimate sanction of withdrawing licences and shutting errant football clubs down. Johnston and McMurdo subsequently met Souness at the manager's Edinburgh home, where a deal to bring the player to Rangers was agreed in principle.

Meanwhile Celtic, who had been unable to contact Johnston over the close season, were becoming increasingly aware that their putative deal for the striker was unlikely ever to be completed. Souness and McMurdo had turned the player's (possibly not very bright) head and it wasn't long before Johnston was privately threatening to quit football altogether if he was compelled to honour the recent agreement with his former team. Despite the FIFA-endorsed letter, and with Nantes waiting expectantly for receipt of the £800,000 balance which would conclude the transfer, the Parkhead club, faced with the prospect of having an unhappy player on their hands, announced publicly that they were pulling out of the deal. At the time McNeill was still on holiday in Florida and he received his employers' statement down the telephone, read out to him by a journalist. Had Celtic dug their heels in, they could have controlled Johnston's future – even if he would never go on to play for the Parkhead club, they could have had a hand in his ultimate destination.

As late as July 2nd, Bill McMurdo was still describing the rumours of a link with Rangers to the Sunday Mail as: 'a complete fabrication – you can run that story for ten years and it still wouldn't be true'. When the paper's chief sports writer Don Morrison called Ibrox to try and get to the bottom of the matter, he was told by assistant manager Walter Smith: 'Remember the traditions of this club and, if we were going to break them, it wouldn't be for that c..t.' But with Celtic now officially out of the way, things moved forward quickly and the deal to bring Johnston to Rangers was finally concluded in a Paris café.

It seemed inevitable that news would leak, despite all the mendacity and espionage, and by July 9th the Scottish edition of the Sun appeared to have the story, thanks to a 16 year old trainee reporter who had noticed that Johnston's name had mysteriously appeared on Rangers' insurance documents, which were being handled by his girlfriend's father. The young lad, having apparently unearthed the biggest story in the history of Scottish football, presumably with the help of his intended father-in-law, dutifully conveyed his information to the paper's editor, Jack Irvine, who had just stepped off a plane after holidaying with Souness in Majorca. 'Print it,' the Rangers manager eventually confirmed the story to Irvine, who went ahead and devoted sixteen pages of Monday's paper to their scoop. Still nobody could quite believe it, with the other papers, clearly paralysed with incredulity, refusing to run the story, even after early editions of the Sun hit the stands.

It wasn't until Johnston was unveiled at the press conference on the morning of Monday, July 10th that the rumours were finally confirmed. The striker was ushered into the Blue Room alongside Souness and McMurdo, where he spoke, in more guarded terms this time, to his astonished audience of his 'huge admiration' for the Ibrox club: something which, in amongst all the Celtic-loving hyperbole, he'd clearly managed to keep to himself up to that point.

After Johnston's signing some Rangers fans burned scarves, cancelled season tickets, and even laid wreathes at the gates of Ibrox, while others who had perhaps seen a move of this nature coming for some time were heard to observe: 'It's not that I object to us signing Catholics, I just didn't want us signing that Catholic.' Fans spokesman David Miller summed up the general mood when he told the Herald:

> It's a sad day for Rangers. There will be a lot of people handing in their season tickets. I don't want to see a Roman Catholic at Ibrox. It really sticks in my throat.

Miller then went on to claim that signing a Catholic from the continent would have been easier to stomach. Within the club itself, opinion on Johnston's arrival was divided. The English contingent at Ibrox, including Terry Butcher, Chris Woods and Ray Wilkins seemed largely bewildered by all the fuss and agreed to attend a press conference, welcoming the new player to the club. Their Scottish counterparts declined the same request and refused to be photographed with Johnston, while Ibrox kit-man and bus driver, Jimmy Bell, snubbed the club's new acquisition, preferring not to provide him with his playing gear and drearily even withholding chocolate bars from the striker.

Over on the other side of the city, Celtic fans reacted to Johnston's perceived treachery with predictable fury. They might not have believed every word of the striker's regurgitated platitudes anyway (such was his track-record when it came to matters of 'trust'), but the last thing they could have expected was that he was about to join their greatest rivals. The Celtic fanzine Not the View, perhaps reflecting Johnston's penchant for overstatement, captured the widespread sense of revulsion when they described the player as: 'the human incarnation of the contents of Beelzebub's dustbin'. Others dubbed their former idol 'Judas', 'le petit merde' and during Old Firm games sang songs aimed at the forward, such as 'Who's the Catholic in the Blue?' and 'What's it like to sign a Tim?' At least they did for most of the game, until in November 1989, Johnston scored an injury time winner at Ibrox against his former club, silencing the Hoops faithful and precipitating something of a turning point in his acceptance – partial and otherwise – at Ibrox.

In the aftermath of the signing, the press lavished Murray and Souness with praise for finally allowing Rangers to employ a prominent Catholic footballer, often with far greater enthusiasm than they had criticised the club's now former, unofficial policy: which, given that it had just been so spectacularly done away with, was now able to be openly acknowledged.

However, in retrospect, the signing of Maurice Johnston has to be seen as something of a missed opportunity in the fight against religious bigotry in Scottish football. In the years following the signing, there appeared to ensue a period of equivocation, appeasement and 'whataboutery', where Rangers fans and their supporters and apologists in the press seemed more inclined to try to deflect the problem onto other clubs, rather than acknow-ledge or attempt to deal with the ongoing issue at Ibrox. Some even claimed that Rangers now occupied the moral high ground, and the label of 'sectarianism' could no longer be applied to the club's cultural environment. What was lacking from Rangers was some sort of admission of previous wrongdoing, or even a degree of humility or contrition after the Johnston signing. Instead, it was almost as if a switch had been flicked: the club weren't employing Catholics before, but now they've bought one and they did it while managing to stick two fingers up at their rivals at the same time. David Murray's motivations and role in all of this are as yet publicly unrecorded.

In May 1999, after victory over Celtic in the Scottish Cup Final handed Rangers a rare Treble, the club's then vice-chairman, Donald Findlay, was caught on camera going through the club's perceived anti-Catholic and anti-Irish repertoire, singing songs including 'The Billy Boys' and the Loyalist battle anthem 'The Sash' at the Rangers Social Club later that evening. Findlay, an advocate known for his distinctive appearance – mutton-chop sideburns, pocket watch and pipe, like something out of a Sherlock Holmes novel – was forced to resign his directorship at Ibrox, after footage of the ten minute impromptu karaoke session was obtained by the Daily Record. Under the headline 'Findlay's songs of hate', the paper subsequently reported:

> Donald Findlay was secretly filmed bellowing songs full of
> bigotry and hate at the weekend. . . Flushed and sweating, the
> QC grabbed the microphone to launch into a poisonous musical
> medley. . . Findlay is seen punching the air as he sings and struts
> in front of hundreds of cheering supporters.

Findlay, who the paper alleged (maybe rather comically) does not celebrate his birthday because it falls on St. Patrick's Day, subsequently had to face up to the loss of his position as Lord Rector of St. Andrews University and he was also fined £3,000 by the Faculty of Advocates in the wake of his indiscretion. Later the same year, this was one of the things that prompted the composer (and Celtic Minded contributor) Sir James MacMillan to observe in a famous speech to the Edinburgh festival on anti-Catholicism in Scotland:

> The sanctimonious Scottish myth that all bigots are uneducated
> loutish morons from the lowest level of society was undermined
> at a stroke.

Findlay later admitted that he felt so ashamed of his actions that he contemplated suicide, telling BBC Scotland's Kirsty Wark Show:

> I'll never be free of it because the one thing that I know is that,
> come the day when somebody writes my obituary, it will be
> there somewhere, large or small, and that is an appalling
> thought.

'Right-minded' individuals will understand Findlay's sense of regret (and should not wish him harm), and it is only right that Celtic supporters 'forgive' such discriminatory and prejudicial indiscretions: especially if they are to rise above, and differentiate themselves from, the very bigotry they often oppose. Nevertheless, it might be those of a more Catholic/Christian perspective who will note that although in this statement Findlay expresses 'regret', he does not explain why he was wrong or who he wronged: or, that such attitudes, labelling and proclamations can not only express racism and religious prejudice, but can also justify, validate and incite others to think and act similarly. Much the pity for Donald that in this instance he didn't 'achieve' this.

From the boardroom down to the fans, any notion that the signing of Maurice Johnston, and Rangers' subsequent recruitment of other Catholic players and even coaches, might have brought about an end to the wider problems associated with the club has proved to be misguided. Rangers supporters in recent years have continued to sing anti-Catholic and anti-Irish songs from the stands at Ibrox: even inventing new ones, such as 'The Famine Song', which was first aired in 2008 and has been subsequently proscribed, and the particularly unpleasant chant 'Big Jock Knew', a reference to a child abuse case at Celtic Boys Club in the 1960-70s, which was weaponised by Rangers fans and used as a stick to beat the Parkhead club and its supporters. As journalist Graham Spiers noted in the Times when the slogan was first heard at Ibrox:

> I have to admit I never thought I'd ever see the day when Scottish football supporters sang a song about a child sex abuse case, yet Rangers have duly delivered. Even more amazing is Rangers FC's ongoing silence on the matter, as this cretinous chant builds up its head of steam among supporters.

Spiers was correct about the increasingly frequent usage of the slogan and 'Big Jock Knew' or 'BJK' later migrated from the Ibrox stands to become a ubiquitous acronym graffitied around Glasgow as well as a salutation used by Rangers fans when they greeted one another in the street. Some other fans in Scotland have also glorified in this chant while several clubs' fans show a kinship with Rangers as well as their anti-Celtic (Catholic and Irish) identities singing similar songs and ditties towards Celtic supporters in terms of former British TV, radio and pop music celebrity and abuser Jimmy Saville. That his mother was Catholic (a mother that he later admitted never trusted him) seems to be enough for some fans in Scotland to abuse and slander the critical Catholic/Christian aspects of Celtic Football Club and its support.

In the end, rather than any domestic authority, it was the European governing body UEFA who took exception to Rangers' sectarian songbook and sanctioned the club after a number of high profile cases in the 2000s, including, in May 2006, a fine accompanied by a warning over any future misconduct, after incidents of hooliganism and bigotry surrounding the club's Champions League tie earlier in the year with Villarreal. Privately, UEFA were disturbed and appalled when they uncovered what was still going on at Ibrox in the twenty first century, with one official telling Spiers:

> Yes we have racism today in football and many other problems. But it still shocking to us that, in the year 2006, we still have supporters in Glasgow shouting 'Fuck the Pope' and such things. We thought the world had moved on from this.

The signing of Maurice Johnston may not have been the seminal moment that many were hoping for in regards to the wider problem of anti-Catholicism at Ibrox and in the wider culture, but over the ensuing years, once Rangers had officially abandoned its dogmatic, discriminatory policies, it was as if the floodgates had been opened and numerous Catholic players eventually arrived at the club. The majority of these were non-Irish and non-Scottish-born Catholics, at a time when British football was opening up its doors to the world. Rangers have now been captained by a Catholic, and managed by a Catholic, an unqualifiedly welcome development for those who seek equality and justice in a society.

Despite what some consider 'progress', a glaring lack of contrition or humility, and a corresponding attitude of natural superiority, might suggest the changes at the club have been largely cosmetic and have been adopted chiefly for reasons of expediency. Regardless, what can be said with some certainty about the club is that Rangers were finally exposed – to a degree – on a higher stage. Rangers, Scottish football and society experienced something new when Mo Johnston signed. We may need to wait a few decades more to see if it might help make any positive difference.

Níos Mó na Cumann

NIALL MURPHY

I regret to commence my thoughts, with a declaration, indeed, a confession, 'of sorts'. I am a Gael living in Belfast and my first and primary sporting, cultural and community allegiance is to the GAA: especially my club and county. The Gaelic Athletic Association has wrapped me in its warm embrace since my infant years and I am proud to state that all of my fondest memories and all of my longest and best enduring friendships, have been forged through the GAA. The GAA exists primarily as a sporting organisation, administering the affairs of Gaelic Football, Hurling (the greatest game on earth) and Handball, but it is so much more than that. It is where communities gather for pints after a funeral, it provides a focal point for rural communities forgotten by government to perform and take glory on a national stage and, it is where the Irish emigrant can find refuge when seeking to forge a new life in foreign lands. The GAA is Ireland and Ireland is the GAA.

Ironically, it is on that basis that I recognise and appreciate Celtic FC. I recognise precisely the same qualities and integrity that Celtic FC present as a social hub and institution for the Irish in Scotland, as that which I cherish and love about the GAA in Ireland and beyond in the diaspora. As is the motto of another patriotic sporting institution, Barcelona FC, we are part of a movement which is more than a club, 'Mes Que un Club'.

I have often spent time in the company of Donegal men living in Glasgow in the Tolbooth, conversing 'as Gaeilge', watching club county finals or National League games on GAA Beo on

TG4, before or after games at Celtic Park, with the conversation exchanging as fluently from Irish to English from the affairs of Celtic to those of the GAA. I have exchanged tickets for Croke Park for European games and Cup finals and truly understand the unique iconic role that Celtic play for the Irish-born and descended community in Scotland, not to mention the burgeoning role in career opportunities for Gaels from the north! Recent manager Brendan Rodgers played Gaelic Football and hurling for years before soccer[1], while the GAA credentials of other Celtic illuminati are glowing in their exceptionality. Former manager Martin O'Neill is on record as describing his greatest sporting defeat, as not being the UEFA Cup Final of 2003 but rather the Hogan Cup final defeat in 1970[2] whilst playing for St. Malachy's College against Coláiste Chríost Rí of Cork.

> That defeat in the Hogan final was a massive disappointment and a game we should never have lost. Coláiste Chríost Rí scored a goal in the last minute – devastating. I'd put it on a par with losing the Championship with Celtic on the final day of the season in 2005. You can say: 'Well, who'd worry about a college game?' Well, I do – all the time!

> Martin O'Neill to Paul Kimmage, Sunday Independent, June 2016[3]

Indeed Martin O'Neill comes from a home of impeccable GAA stock. His father was a founding member of Kilrea Pearses in 1956, while his older brother Leo, played in the 1958 All Ireland final for Derry against Dublin. Another brother Gerry, managed Armagh to the All-Ireland final in 1977 also against Dublin.

Neil Lennon of course played for Armagh minors in the 1989 Ulster final against Derry losing on a scoreline of 2.15 – 2.03. However, all of these achievements pale into insignificance when one considers the stellar GAA career of Jim McGuinness, All Ireland champion as a player with Donegal in 1992 and as an epoch-defining manager in 2012, also with Donegal. It was the national prominence that his achievements as Donegal manager that brought him to Celtic's attention. That's why he was recruited as the club's first performance consultant, with special focus on the club's academy structure at Lennoxtown. His managerial insight and gifted sports science saw McGuinness

[1] Liverpool's would-be manager is a GAA man to the core https://www.joe.ie/uncategorized/liverpools-would-be-manager-is-a-gaa-man-to-the-core-36606

[2] Martin O'Neill & The Team That Came From Heaven https://www.cumminssports.ie/photos/martin-oneill-team-came-heaven/

[3] http://www.independent.ie/sport/soccer/euro-2016/battles-with-the-media-ringing-phonein-shows-and-getting-beat-up-during-a-gaa-game-paul-kimmage-meets-martin-oneill-34792710.html

recruited by Paul McGinley for the 2014 Ryder Cup. In 2017 Jim became the short-lived assistant manager to Roger Schmidt at Chinese SuperLeague club Beijing Sinobo Guoan, having met and mesmerised Schmidt on a chance meeting at Dublin airport!

The Celtic-Gaelic Sport connection is extensive. Sean Fallon, Charlie Tully, Packie Bonner, Anton Rogan, Niall McGinn, Liam Miller, Roy Keane, Cillian Sheridan: to name but a few GAA players to have played for Celtic FC. Even through the work of the editor of this book Scots-born players like Tony Watt and Stephen Welsh (currently in the reserves at Celtic) played 'GA' at school, as have several of those that have been recent and current members of Celtic's Ladies side.

Whereas those reflections are macro overviews, well known to many who have an interest, the micro experiences of our shared experience conjoin for the purposes of this recollection. I did not have to reflect long to highlight a tragic example.

Fifteen years ago, on 22nd July 2002 (Celtic was at that point in time playing a series of pre-season friendlies and this event was jammed between games against Werder Bremen and Ajax), an 18 year old boy who played midfield for my club St. Enda's GAC in Glengormley, on the threshold of his life, was shot dead. His 'crime' was that on his way home from the pub, he was wearing a Celtic jersey.[4]

I would like to outline the events of that day.

On Sunday 21st July 2002, Gerard Lawlor arrived at St. Enda's GAC at 1:15pm for a senior football match against Sarsfields, due to throw in at 2pm. St. Enda's had been relegated from division one the previous year, and were rebuilding for the future. The 2002 season was not going any better than the previous, and despite winning the first game in division 2, the team had lost the last four, and were in danger of a second straight relegation.

The senior team was in the process of being remoulded with the intention to rebuild around young players like Gerard. Gerard had been selected to play in the crucial position of midfield that day, such was his physical strength and work ethic around the park. As St. Enda's took the field awaiting the arrival of Sarsfields,

4 https://www.theguardian.com/uk/2002/jul/28/northernireland.henrymcdonald

the referee appeared, but with no sign of the opposition, the home side were awarded the precious league points in the absence of a team to play. Without a league match to play, the management ensured that the opportunity for a hard training session in the July heat, was not lost and a lung bursting hour of running and tackling drills exhausted the players, many of whom, especially the younger players, were lamenting their enforced and now unrequired abstinence on the Saturday night. Kevin McKeown recalls ribbing Gerard for his missed pints.

The opportunity to rehydrate presented itself when the seniors came into the club house after training. A double bill of round 4 qualifiers from Croke Park was on RTE's 'Sunday Game' with Donegal defeating Meath by two points before the shock of Sligo beating Tyrone, on a comfortable score line of 1.14 to 0.12. Conversation also turned to the breaking news that Rio Ferdinand had just joined Manchester United for a record transfer fee of £30 million. All was well in the world of the young sportsmen, who played, trained and socialised together. Midway through the first half of the Tyrone game, the Sarsfields team began to arrive – it transpired that they had been mistaken with regards to the throw in time. After some gentle aggravating, with Gerard prime among their tormentors about their lost league points, Sarsfields joined the St. Enda's team for a few pints before returning, no doubt to criticise their club secretary for their erroneous information.

Unbeknownst to the team, north Belfast erupted that night. There were four separate attempted murders which culminated in the killing of Gerard as he walked home from the Bellevue Arms. Notwithstanding the overwhelming evidence that armed loyalists were known to be intent on murdering a Catholic that night, no police checkpoints were erected at strategic stress areas. One such defined area was the junction at the top of the Whitewell Road and the Antrim Road. The allocation of one police car, with two police officers, less than half a mile from Glengormley police station, would have saved Gerard's life, as he was murdered just yards from the junction.

It is through this kind of intersection of a shared experience, that the hypothesis that ours was 'more than a club' and that the GAA and indeed Celtic FC represent the best traditions of the concept of community becomes evidenced. Our community through our club, monitored the police response to the murder very carefully. Albeit that such care and attention need not required to have been exhaustive, as no one was ever charged, no one was ever prosecuted and no inquest has, to this day 17 years on, ever been convened. Gerard's faithful and devoted family complained to the Police Ombudsman as to the lack of investigative diligence by the police, and still, 13 years on from the lodgement of that complaint, no report has yet been published.

Whereas the world has looked away from the murder of our friend and midfielder Gerard, the last Catholic shot dead by loyalists in Ireland during our so-called recent 'Troubles', our club and community stood up. We engaged a panel of highly respected human rights law practitioners and academics and convened a Community Inquiry. In circumstances where the State had failed the family and our friend, our club would not. The Community Inquiry report[5] was published and the independent panel's conclusion that collusion was a feature in Gerard's murder was reported widely in the media. The report has been submitted to the Coroners Service for Northern Ireland and will form the basis of the family's submission at the Inquest if and when this is ever convened.

For many people, it is that same robust sense of commonality of spirit that exists in the Celtic family and community. Whereas many aspects of the Irish Catholic experience in Scotland is recognised and identified by many of its victims as Scotland's Shame, Celtic has stood out in the sporting and cultural field as a relatively safe haven for the Scottish-born Irish to gather to spectate, sing and celebrate the virtues of their heroes on the football pitch but also of the virtues of their country of origin, their community's will to survive, of which Celtic is an institutional embodiment.

[5] Gerard Lawlor Community Inquiry Report and Recommendations http://krw-law.ie/wp-content/uploads/2013/10/Gerard-Lawlor-Community-Inquiry-Report-and-Recommendations.pdf

CONTRIBUTORS

Professor Alan Bairner was born in Kirkcaldy and grew up in Dunfermline. He attended Dunfermline High School, the University of Edinburgh and the University of Hull. He lived for 25 years in Belfast while working at the University of Ulster at Jordanstown. He is currently Professor of Sport and Social Theory at Loughborough University. The most memorable Celtic match he has attended was on 27th January 1968 when Dunfermline Athletic beat the European champions 2-0 at Celtic Park in the 1st round of the Scottish Cup. Favourite Celtic Minded songs; The Unfinished Revolution (Christy Moore) and Phil Coulter's The Town I Loved So Well (Kevin Rowland).

Martin Beatty is from Lurgan, Co Armagh and is a lifelong Celtic supporter. While still living in Lurgan he has commuted for the last 30 years Monday to Friday to London with work. He is married to Aine for 25yrs and has a daughter Olivia 21 and is the father of Jay Beatty. Favourite Celtic minded songs: Isle of Innisfree and Slievenamon.

Dr Joseph M Bradley is editor of the collection of 'Celtic Minded' essays. He is also the author of Ethnic and Religious Identity in Modern Scotland (Avebury 1995), The Gaelic Athletic Association and Irishness in Scotland (Argyll, 2007) and joint author of Sport Worlds: a sociological perspective (Human Kinetics

2002). The latter book was translated for China in 2009. Dr Bradley has published in edited books, journals and newspapers on sporting matters in relation to religion, ethnicity, diaspora and politics. His publications in journals in Britain, USA, France and Ireland include works on Orangeism in Scotland, Scotland's international support, politics in Scottish football and the Irish diaspora in Scotland. He is senior lecturer in Sports Studies at the University of Stirling.

Dr Roisín Coll is Director of the St. Andrew's Foundation for Catholic Teacher Education at the University of Glasgow. The Foundation is responsible for providing Catholic teachers for Catholic schools across Scotland. She is married and mother of two girls. She enjoys traditional Irish music and relaxes by playing with her children, attending Celtic matches with her father and spending holidays in Donegal. One of her most memorable matches was the one against Barcelona in Camp Nou in March 2004 when Celtic knocked the Catalonian giants out of the Uefa Cup. Favourite Celtic Minded songs: Boolavogue, Four Green Fields, Down by the Glenside and The Town I Love So Well.

Jim Craig was born in Drumoyne, Glasgow in April 1943, attended St. Anthony's Primary School in Govan and St. Gerard's Senior Secondary, three years behind Joe McBride but with Billy Connelly in the same year. Dad from Leith, and a Hibbie, but took a young Jim to first Celtic match v. Aberdeen in the St. Mungo Cup Final at Hampden in 1951: a trophy, still in the boardroom at Celtic Park. Spent season 1961/62 at Parkhead as an amateur, playing mainly for the 3rd team, then signed pro forms in January 1965, made the first team in October 1965, qualified as a dentist in October 1966 and over the following 7 years won 7 League Championship medals, 4 Scottish Cup medals, 3 for the League Cup, one for the Glasgow Cup and, the European Cup medal in Lisbon on 25th May 1967. Written articles on sport and religion for various publications and had spells as a broadcaster with Radio Clyde, BBC Scotland and Celtic TV. 50 years married to Elizabeth whom he first met at Celtic Park the night the team returned from Lisbon with the European Cup. Five children and 9 grand-children. Favourite Celtic Minded song; When Irish Eyes are Smiling.

Denis Canavan is a former Labour MP and Independent MSP, who came out of retirement to chair the Yes Scotland Campaign 2012-2014. Born and brought up in a Fife mining community, he has never forgotten his roots and is now a trustee of the National Mining Museum of Scotland. His autobiography, 'Let the People Decide', was first published by Birlinn in 2009. His most memorable Celtic match was at Hampden in 1970, when he saw the Hoops beating Leeds United 2-1 in the semi-final of European Cup. Favourite Celtic Minded song: Belfast Child (Simple Minds).

Michael Connolly is based at the University of Stirling in the second year of a PhD-level research project titled 'Searching for Brother Walfrid: Faith, Community and Football'. Previously graduated with an MA Hons in economic and social history from the University of Glasgow. Michael's earliest Celtic memory was going with his Dad and wee brother to see the 'Three Amigos' side train at the old Barrowfield training ground off London Road. He treasures pictures with big Pierre, Tommy Burns and 'The Maestro' Paul McStay.

Bob Davis is Professor of Religious and Cultural Education in the School of Education in the University of Glasgow. He also coordinates an important Social Research Hub for the university out of the Olympia Building at Bridgeton Cross and is widely involved in research and teaching across the work of the university. He enjoys good music, the outdoors and lots of books on lots of topics. He dreams still of being an ornithologist. One of his most memorable matches was the 4-2 victory over Rangers, and winning the league, in May 1979. A true triumph. Favourite Celtic Minded song: Fields of Athenry.

Dr Aidan Donaldson is an associate consultant in ethos and Catholic schools for the Diocese of Down and Connor and a member of the Diocesan Missionary Council. He is former Chaplain at St. Mary's Christian Brothers' Grammar School, Belfast, and works on a range of projects which advocate for the marginalised and dispossessed in both Ireland and Zambia. His recent works include 'Playing for the Hoops: the George McCluskey Story' and 'The Beatitudes of Pope Francis: A Manifesto for the Modern Christian'. Dr Donaldson is a member of An Bráthair Bhálfrid CSC. Favourite Celtic Minded songs: Óró, sé do bheatha 'bhaile and Grace (Wolfe Tones).

Lorcan Gallagher lives in Lanarkshire. He has 5 children and currently has one grandchild. He was educated at two local state Catholic schools. He has been attending Celtic matches for 50 years. He left school at 16 to begin an apprenticeship but failed to complete this. He has worked all his life in labouring roles in factories and building sites. He was also unemployed for several months in the early 1980s. Favourite Celtic Minded songs; Our Lady of Knock & Oró, Sé Do Bheatha 'Bhaile

George Galloway was born in 1954 in the Irish quarter of Dundee. Known as Tipperary, the area of Lochee was the site of a large cluster of jute and flax mills and heavily populated by Irish immigrants. Born to a family of Scottish trades union activists and Irish republic-ans Galloway grew up mindful of Irish traditions. Annual family holidays were mainly spent in Ireland. Galloway left school at 17 to work in Michelin Tyres, joined the Transport and General Workers Union and became Chairman of the Scottish Labour Party aged 26. He defeated Roy Jenkins in Glasgow Hillhead in 1987 making Glasgow an 'all-Labour' city for the first time. In 2003 he was expelled from the Labour Party by Tony Blair over the Iraq War and his constituency was abolished. He was thereafter elected in Bethnal Green and Bow in East London in 2005 and Bradford West in 2012. He has been elected to Parliament six times. He is now a film-maker, broadcaster and writer. First Celtic game v. Dundee United 1962/63 when 8 years old.

Tony Hamilton celebrates 25 years at Celtic in 2019. Having made the tea for the guy who makes the coffee, through to leading the Multi Media team, he now heads up the club's charitable arm – Celtic FC Foundation – as its chief executive, after gaining an MBA from

the University of Strathclyde. Tony's Celtic collaborations include the publication of the Celtic Opus, and he co-produced and wrote a series of Celtic films including The Official History of Celtic Football Club, as well as film biographies of Jimmy Johnstone, Henrik Larsson, Tommy Burns and Billy McNeill, among others. His most memorable match was his first: an abandoned, foggy affair against Hibernian at Paradise in October 1975. That's where the love affair began, and it's all thanks to his big brother, Michael. Tony was born and raised in the east end of Glasgow and still resides five miles from Paradise. Happily married with six children. Favourite Celtic Minded songs: Samhradh, Samhradh (The Gloaming) and Fields of Athenry (Paddy Reilly).

Peter Kearney was born in Paisley and attended St. Modan's High School in Stirling. He graduated with an MA (Hons) degree in Politics and Economics from the University of Glasgow. He is the Director of the Catholic Media Office and spokesperson for the Catholic Church in Scotland. He has written for most Scottish and UK newspapers on a range of social, moral and ethical issues and has a particular interest in the Scottish Reformation and its connection to contemporary anti-Catholicism. He is married and has five children. His ethnic and national roots lie in Scotland's western isles and County Armagh in Ireland. Favourite Celtic Minded song: The Green Fields of France (Fureys and Davey Arthur).

Dr John Kelly graduated with a doctorate in the sociology of sport from Loughborough University in 2007. Currently based at the University of Edinburgh, he has published a range of sport, politics and identity articles and books including 'Bigotry, Football and Scotland' (2013). His first match v. Partick Thistle was in 1977. Favourite Celtic Minded songs: James Connolly and Grace.

Matt Lynch was born in Govan and raised in the Ibrox area. He attended Our Lady of Lourdes Secondary School before joining the Daily Record at the age of sixteen where he started his journalist career as a features sub editor. Eight years later he joined the Daily Express where he became the paper's youngest ever chief sub editor. His first editorship was with the Paisley Daily Express and then with the Ayrshire Post. In 1979 he co-founded the Free Press Group of newspapers in Ayrshire which had a combined weekly circulation of 100,000. Eight years later he was appointed production editor of he Sunday Times in Scotland. After a two-years spell as associate editor of The Peninsula, Qatar, he returned to Scotland, and bought the Govan Press title which he sold two years later. His most memorable Celtic game was watching his brother Andy score the winning goal in the 1977 Scottish Cup final against Rangers. Favourite Celtic Minded songs: Lady of Knock (Dana) and The Rose of Tralee (Christy Moore).

Dr Maureen McBride is from Glasgow and a lifelong Celtic supporter having been taken to her first game at the age of two. She attended Lourdes Secondary School and in 2002 became the first member of her family to go to university, studying History and Politics at the University of Glasgow. In 2018 she returned to Glasgow University after several years away from academia and completed her ESRC-funded PhD, entitled 'Rethinking Sectarianism in Scotland'. She currently works as a Research Associate in the School of Education on the Children's Neighbourhoods Scotland project in Glasgow. Her research interests include poverty, class inequalities, racialisation and racism, religion and nationalism. In 2018 she co-edited and contributed to 'No Problem Here: Understanding Racism in Scotland' by Luath Press. Her most memorable Celtic game was the 6-2 victory over Rangers in 2000, when she vividly remembers sitting a few rows in front of Noel Gallagher as 'Roll With It' came on over the PA. Favourite Celtic Minded songs: James Connolly and No Time for Love (Christy Moore).

Brendan McCarron born and bred in Coatbridge. Attended and loved his schooling at St. Monica's and Columba High Schools. Attended Glasgow University studying medicine and graduated in 1985. Married Karen, a member of the Celtic supporting Ferns family and has 4 intermittently well-behaved children. Works as an Infectious Diseases Specialist in England. Attended first game, as a 7 year old, against Motherwell with his father James and friends Arthur Craig and Father James McNaughton. Best Celtic day was in May 1998 beating St. Johnstone 2-0 to 'stop the ten'. Favourite Celtic Minded songs: The John Thompson Song and The West Awake.

Alan Milton was born and bred in Clondalkin, Dublin where he still lives. After studying at UCD and DCU he was a print journalist for 10 years and is now Director of Communications for the Gaelic Athletic Association, based at Croke Park in Dublin. His first visit to Celtic Park was for a home league win over Hearts in 1996 (Craig Burley winner in a 1-0 win) and amongst the most memorable games he attended was the Champions League home win over AC Milan in 2007. Favourite Celtic

Minded songs: Grace & The Lonesome Boatman.

Niall Murphy is a partner at KRW Law LLP, a leading human rights practice, based in Belfast. The practice is instructed by a significant number of clients engaged in legacy litigation relating to conflict-related deaths and injuries, appearing for those bereaved as a result of atrocities such as Loughinisland, Claudy, Clonoe, Kingsmill, the Dublin-Monaghan and McGurks Bar bombings, the Glenanne Gang series of killings, Ormeau Road Bookmakers, the 1974 Birmingham Pub Bombing amongst others. He is instructed on behalf of several families to act at the reopening of the 'John Stalker/Shoot to Kill' Inquests, relating to the murders of 6 unarmed men in 1982 by the RUC. Niall is a Director of Belfast-based NGO, Relatives for Justice and has made representations at the European Parliament in Brussels, to the EU Human Rights Commissioner in Strasbourg and also to the UN Human Rights Committee in Geneva as well as having presented lectures to universities in Washington, Pittsburgh, Jersey City, Fordham University New York and Harvard. Director of Brassneck Theatre Company, a Panel Member of the Human Rights Fund, an Honorary Chair of the Belfast International Homecoming, sits on the Antrim GAA Human Resources Board and is vice chairman of St. Enda's GAC and a founder and Governor of Gaelscoil Éanna. Favourite Celtic Minded songs: Samhradh, Samhradh (The Gloaming) and Grace.

Stephen O'Donnell is a freelance writer of football-themed fiction and non-fiction, who was born and lives in Glasgow. His novels 'Paradise Road' (2012) and

'Scotball' (2014) were published by Ringwood to critical acclaim and his articles have appeared in The Blizzard and Nutmeg magazines. His new book 'Tangled up in Blue, The Rise and Fall of Rangers FC' is published by Pitch in 2019. He was first taken to see Celtic play Juventus in 1981 when he stood in the Jungle and couldn't understand why the Celtic fans were all cheering the opponents' man, Liam Brady. He was too young to appreciate it was because he was from Ireland. Favourite Celtic Minded songs: You're in my Heart (Rod Stewart) and The Inter Milan Song (Charlie and the Bhoys).

Emma O'Neil is Managing Director of The 9 Muses (www.the9muses.co.uk), the original fine art company wholly responsible for the commission of the iconic 'Walfrid' the 5x4 feet original oil painting by Peter Howson and the launch of the World's first PhD on Brother Walfrid. Favourite Celtic Minded song: You'll never walk alone.

Joe O'Rourke was born in and has lived all his life in Port Glasgow. Attended St. John's Primary and St. Columba's Senior Secondary in Greenock. First Celtic game was against Clyde at Celtic Park in the mid-1950s. His favourite game would be the 1965 Cup Final victory against Dunfermline and favourite player Jimmy Johnstone, closely followed by Bobby Murdoch. Attends every game home and away. Favourite Celtic Minded songs: I just can't get enough (Celtic Support) and The Town I Love So Well (Kathleen Largey).

Paul Quigley was brought up in Cumbernauld and attended St. Maurice's High School. His first games were with his dad and uncle. His earliest hero was Paul McStay, and he was lucky enough to meet the Maestro at a young age. Paul attends university in Glasgow as a post-graduate student. He was involved in the Fans Against Criminalisation campaign which helped to force the repeal of the Offensive Behaviour at Football Act. His favourite moment following Celtic was Rogic's last minute winner at Hampden to clinch the invincible treble in 2017. Favourite Celtic Minded songs: Raglan Road & The Lonesome Boatman.

Professor Graham Spacey is the Head of Operations at Football 4 Peace International, based at the University of Brighton. He is also a PhD candidate at the University of Johannesburg. Whilst a trained Physical Education Teacher and working for an organisation with football in its name, he has never claimed to be a footballer. His highlight was scoring the winning goal in a 4th form match against a rival school – which turned out to be a home goal whilst in defence. Graham followed Wimbledon FC when they beat Liverpool FC in the 1988 FA Cup and then lost interest when the team moved to Milton Keynes in 2001 – where, ironically, he lived at the time. Despite this, it was the grassroots of football and sport in general that inspired Graham and set him on his career of utilising the beautiful game to motivate and bring people, families and communities together in peace.

Professor John Sugden is Emeritus Professor of the Sociology of Sport at the University of Brighton. He is also co-founder and honorary life President of the University's in-house non-governmental organisation, the celebrated sport-based co-existence and conflict resolution programme, Football 4 Peace International. Professor Sugden is an honorary life member of the International Sociology of Sport Association (ISSA) and a Research Fellow of the North American Society for the Sociology of Sport (NASSS). Professor Sugden is also well known for his work on the sociology of boxing; and with his colleague Alan Tomlinson for their tireless investigative and transformative work into malpractice in world football's governing body FIFA, an extensive corpus of work which has made a significant contribution to the downfall of disgraced former FIFA President Sepp Blatter and FIFA's house of corruption. This ongoing saga is covered extensively in their latest book, 'Football, Corruption and Lies: Revisiting Badfellas', the book FIFA tried to ban. Sugden and Tomlinson (2017). Favourite Celtic Minded songs: Ballad of James Connelly and Streets of New York (both by The Wolfe Tones).

Brendan Sweeney was born and bred in Clydebank to Donegal parents and is a lifetime Celtic supporter. Favourite ever Celtic match was the 6-2 victory over Rangers in 2000 at Paradise. Was a founder member of the Celts For Change group who helped oust the old board in 1994 and has been active in a number of Celtic supporter groups since 1997, including the Celtic Supporters Association Executive Committee, the Jungle Bhoys and currently the Celtic Graves Society, where he was also a founder member. Author of Celtic: The Early Years and currently writing the follow up, Celtic: The Battle For the Club's Soul. Favourite Celtic Minded songs: You'll Never Walk Alone & The Fields of Athenry.

John Paul Taylor was born in Robroyston, Glasgow and grew up in Millerston/Stepps attending school at St. Joseph's Cardowan and on to St. Patrick's Coatbridge until 1981. He attended his first Celtic match in 1972 against Ujpest Dozsa and been a regular ever since. Idolised Kenny Dalglish as a kid. His greatest Celtic moment was the 4-2 victory against Rangers to win the league in 1979. First employed by Celtic FC in October 1993, had a brief career change in 2008 and re-joined in 2013 as SLO. Favourite Celtic Minded songs: Teenage Kicks (The Undertones) and Zombie (The Cranberries).

Canon Tom White hails from Carmyle in the east end of Glasgow. He went to school at St. Joachim's, Carmyle and Holy Cross in Hamilton. He attended the Pontifical Scots College in Rome at the young age of 17, where he began his degrees in Philosophy, Theology and later specialising in Canon Law. Ordained St. Joachim's, Carmyle in 1999, on the feast of St. Thomas. He is proud of the fact that Cardinal Winning ordained him, and it was a Thomas, ordaining a Thomas on the feast of Thomas in 1999. He served as Assistant priest in St. Maria Goretti's, Cranhill, and as Chaplain to Our Lady's High, Cumbernauld. Served on the Scottish Ecclesiastical Tribunal as an Advocate and Judge. In 2003 appointed Vice-Chancellor of the Archdiocese and later Chancellor, until the retirement of Archbishop Conti in 2012. Currently Executive Chair of St Margaret's Adoption Society. Appointed to serve as assistant priest at St. Mary's Calton in 2003 and remains there as Parish Priest. Also Dean of the City East Deanery and Canon De Numero of the Cathedral Chapter. Favourite Celtic Minded songs: Four Leaved Clover & Over and Over.